Overseas Operations

The Lost Soldier

Rich Jones

Copyright © Rich Jones

Visit the author's website at: IamRichJones.co.uk

First Edition: 20 Nov 2023

Ebook ISBN: 978-1-916826-03-8

Paperback ISBN: 978-1-916826-01-4

This is a work of biographical fiction.

Cover Design: Yon Alexanders

Editor: Julian Moseley, JulianMoseley.com

Book formatting: Liz Raguindin, LizRaguindin.com

Book and Publishing Consultant: Rob Culpepper, MrBookCoach.com

Proofreader: Elaine Smith (me mum❣)

Publisher: StoryUp Media, StoryUpMedia.com

StoryUp Media

"Another gripping book by Rich Jones, hooked from the first sentence, yet again I didn't want to put this book down. Phenomenal."

Simon Adams

"A gripping insight into the dangerous world of drug trafficking, just like the first book I couldn't put it down. Thrilling from the first word to the last."

Stewart Spensley

"Overseas Operations takes you on a nerve-wracking rollercoaster of emotions, the perfect mix of fear, excitement, anxiety and humour. A fascinating insight into the darkest of worlds"

Adam Price

"Wow!... Rich Jones has pulled out another belter and a superb addition to the TLS series! Rich's way of pulling you into the book and making you feel the adrenaline and suspense is second to none!

A perfect five-star read for anyone who loves True Crime."

Benedict Deans

"The feeling you get of the mindset and thoughts of the author is captivating. The narrative is hard-hitting and has a flair that makes you want to continue reading. A good insight into the underworld of narcotics and distribution"

Dave Long

"An avid read with a dusting of army humour. I could feel the anxiety causing hypervigilance jumping out at me. This is good in a criminal way!"

C. Ollis

As a book consultant and publisher, I've had the privilege of a front-row seat to the writing of this book. When Rich asked me to publish his second book (and publish the second edition of his first book, Charlie Four Kilo), I was beyond honoured. Overseas Operations is a nail-biting, sweat-inducing story of drug dealing, cartels and twisted and dysfunctional relationships. Buckle up as Rich, the Lost Soldier, travels through England, France and Spain to settle his debt. Does he get it sorted? I'm not telling. Pick up OvOps today and block off your weekend because you won't be able to put it down!

Rob Culpepper
Book and Publishing Consultant,
MrBookCoach.com

Thank you to everyone listed below for your pre-orders and for helping me to fund the publishing process

A Special 'Thank You' to Michael Lawless for purchasing the **Golden Top Tier!**

Michael will be the character "Lawless"

Tier 1

Jonathan Green is "Blob", as that's his old nickname. In tribute to his mate, Simon Adams has sponsored the character "Hassan"

Stephen Wood is sponsoring the character "Barry" in honour of his fiancée's father who recently passed away.

Tier 2

Claire Weide * Amber Critchley * Nathan Hill
Benedict Deans * Steve Davies * Donna Cooper
Blake Evans * Jason Duckworth
Jamie Cox * Dave Nicholls * Kieron Murphy
Nick Duckworth F.N M.I.B

If you want to purchase a tier and be in my next book:

Part IV "END-EX END-EX END-EX"

Please contact me via:
www.iamrichjones.co.uk
or email: info@iamrichjones.co.uk

Dedication:

I would like to dedicate this book to my father Rob Jones who recently passed away.

You were more than just a Dad you were a friend and an inspiration.

Gone but never forgotten.

Robin Jones

27th December 1948

31st January 2023

Table of Contents

Chapter 1 BACK FROM THE BRINK 1

Chapter 2 WHITE CHRISTMAS.................................. 6

Chapter 3 THE END OF A SHITTY YEAR 24

Chapter 4 A NEW YEAR BRINGS A NEW ADVENTURE... 39

Chapter 5 BUREAUX DE CHANGE 53

Chapter 6 EUROPEAN ROAD TRIP 61

Chapter 7 HURRY UP AND WAIT 80

Chapter 8 YOUNG GUNS AND COCAINE............ 89

Chapter 9 HOMEWARD BOUND 100

Chapter 10 REBUILDING THE BUSINESS - A 2nd TIME.. 124

Chapter 11 PREPPING FOR ANOTHER RUN 138

Chapter 12 ANOTHER EUROPEAN ROAD TRIP 156

Chapter 13 OVERSEAS OPERATIONS-1........................... 169

Chapter 14 OVERSEAS OPERATIONS-2........................... 183

Chapter 15 OVERSEAS OPERATIONS-3........................... 183

Chapter 16 ZOLTAN THE ….................................. 221

Chapter 17 THE MONEY 228

Chapter 18 PSYCHO BITCHES 239

Chapter 19 CHANNEL HOPPING 265

Chapter 20 DON'T FUCK WITH THE CARTELS 290

GLOSSARY 301

RICH JONES
OVERSEAS OPERATIONS

Chapter 1

BACK FROM THE BRINK

These pills are fucking nuts—I've done a lot of pills and these boys have got to be the best yet. To think less than a week ago I was ready to open up my wrists and redecorate the interior of my car in a beautiful shade of red, and now I feel almost normal—whatever normal is, anyway. Twenty milligrams of Fluoxetine, that's it—one a day every morning and I've got my life back. I should have gotten onto these fuckers years ago, then maybe my head wouldn't be so written off and I might not have even ventured into this messed-up world of drugs.

They have this strange effect of making me feel as if I should run or jump. I'm not kidding; I'll be walking out of a shop or going to my car and I get the sudden urge to have a little skip—fuck knows why but that's how they make me feel. Plus, I'm sleeping again and more importantly, I'm getting up at a respectable time without that sense of impending doom. Up until recently during the evening I'd have necked a few beers and stressed about the phone ringing, but now I just neck the beers and go to bed. Mornings used to bring huge anxiety, especially when I knew I had to look at the phone, but now, it doesn't feel like it matters—it does matter but I'm all out of fucks to give. I've inherited an almost flippant attitude towards everything. It's a refreshing break, as I've always been so serious and tried my best to not let anyone down.

It's all well and good having this casual approach to everything, but that puts me in a potentially dangerous place. I'm treading a precarious path; the variables and risks have been significantly increased, or at least they will be very soon, and if I'm too chilled that can be dangerous. I've lasted this long because I've always remained sharp and vigilant. I cannot afford to allow my senses to be numbed or altered, but what the fuck can I do? These happy pills have saved my life and they're helping me to get through this shit, but they won't be forever. I know for a fact that once Cliff has all of his money I'll be out of this game. I'm not going to risk this happening again—not a fucking chance.

Happy pills aside, it doesn't change the fact that I still owe 27 bags to Cliff, who incidentally has calmed the fuck down and is kind of off my case, but then he would be if I'm stepping into the breach to bring it over for him. To be fair, I didn't think that through, and he did ask me when I was in a bit of a predicament and somewhat vulnerable. He could have asked for anything, and I'd have probably said "Fuck it why not?". I'm quite glad though he didn't ask for a mouth wank. Nonetheless, I'm not gonna change my mind, because right now I feel ok. I've got my mental strength back and it's enough to rethink my business plans with the whole coke thing. The car parts stand has been jogged on, so I have as little stress as possible. Stress was my downfall; furthermore, Lance and Carl were fucking useless at it. So, we shook hands and went our separate ways—not forever, I just said I needed to focus on sorting my life out, plus Lance does like to talk, and you know what they say about loose lips. Carl and I swapped vehicles, so I'm gonna get rid of the van ASAP; that'll free up some much-needed dough to buy a nice blender, which is a must if I'm going to be running drugs everywhere.

The other advantage of losing my shit is I can now go on the sick with the Jobcentre. This means getting some free money and the rent paid; the downside is I have to now convince the missus we have to move. I'm pretty sure she'll be ok with it, but it will mean we have to downgrade to a house that the benefits will cover. The luxury four-bed we are currently in will become a less luxurious three-bed. The added result of this is that I will have a clean slate with a new address. Fuck the electoral roll, and don't tell any fucker where I've moved to. I'll certainly sleep a little bit better, knowing that nobody knows where I am. It's the same feeling of dropping a burner and getting a new number, with the added value of my family being safe.

Re-gathering my thoughts and motivation has been relatively easy. Trade is slowly ticking over and strangely, it almost feels secondary to the job I'm gonna be doing for Cliff. Any money earnt at the moment is keeping the household bills covered and allowing me to catch up with some arrears. Christmas is knocking on the door and Cliff's given me an indication that his thing won't be happening until after the holidays, so in true drug dealer style, I prep for a potentially busy festive season. The plan is for Cliff to load me up and I'll get everyone sorted well before the festivities begin, so I can shut down and for once focus on my family. Well that's the plan, but you know what it's like—anything can go wrong. It only takes one idiot to drop the ball—look at what happened to Alfie a few months ago, a total catastrophe that damn near killed me.

Talking of Alfie and poor old Jeff, they should be getting sentenced soon. I've had very little contact with anyone associated with them as I just didn't see the point. Kate is doing her best to support Alfie, but apparently Milly has turned into a right fucking scrounger and is doing Kate's head in. I haven't even bothered to reach out to Spice or Red because they're so unreliable and as for The Boy, I hear he's getting his shit back together and is still waiting for his charges of possession to be handed out by the courts. It's a straight-cut case. He was banged to rights and caught with it, but if he chucks a guilty in, he might avoid a bit of time in the jug. I like The Boy and I still think there's hope for him as a runner. Either way, they are all way too fucking hot for me to contend with, and right now not one of them can help me with what I have to do, so they'll all have to crack on until I'm in a position to let them back into my circle.

My loyal customers are hanging in there and this is great for business as it's putting me in a much stronger position with trade. The more I shift, the more Cliff gets off my back. Despite everything going tits up, I'm still his biggest customer, and he knows I've got the potential to grow. He now knows that I'm prepared to end it all, which makes me very unpredictable and potentially dangerous. I think he's beginning to understand that applying unnecessary pressure puts my whole business at risk. If he screams at me, I scream at my customers, and they ultimately bail out. If he chills the fuck out and lets me do my thing, I can begin to trade under better conditions, without the need to panic buy or sell anything for silly money. The less profit I make, the less money he gets back—it's not fucking rocket science, is it?

A few weeks back the concern of me getting nicked was overshadowed by my buildup towards my mental breakdown. I was running on empty—autopilot—and I was so fucking stressed that I couldn't think straight. If I'm to be brutally honest, an arrest wouldn't have bothered me at all, as I wanted everything to stop. Not now though, fuck that, I'm about to embark on some kind of adventure. I'm not exactly sure what or who this so-called adventure is going to involve, but I do love a good road trip—just ask Murray.

Chapter 2

WHITE CHRISTMAS

C hristmas is just over two weeks away and they all want to double up on the coke orders, so a couple of nines each, which is fucking great news. Billy wants a box, as does Thornton who jumped back on board last week because his other supplier became a tad unreliable. Thornton is a fucking good customer; everything's on tick mind, but he's never late and always on point. He's guaranteed to take half a box at a standard price, plus he's a big, hard, nasty-looking fucker, so nobody dares to fuck with him. We met by chance when he was looking for a pill supplier back in the late 90's and the thing that sealed it was the guy that was running for him was ex-forces, so we hit it off immediately. I went for it and fortunately it's been good business from the start.

Miles has decided to fuck off abroad and by the looks of it, it's a permanent move. It's a bit of a shame as I liked him, however he's taken on a guy called Wedge to run his thing. The bonus is I know Wedge as he used to do a bit of running for Mick, who incidentally is no longer a valued customer of mine. The coke scene finished him off and he went back to doing just pot, which I wasn't interested in as the profits didn't make it worthwhile. Also dealing with him was a nightmare because he was so fucking unreliable. Out in these rural areas it's a bit cutthroat, as they all know each other and they're constantly fighting for one another's customers, more so than in the city. It became quite obvious that Mick couldn't handle the coke market, and I'm pretty sure Miles did a bit of an aggressive takeover. Something along the lines of "Mick, you're a useless melt, so I'm taking your customers, now fuck off". Naturally this suits me fine as Miles was always spot on and Mick was a complete helmet. Wedge is a good lad; he's a bit fucking scatty but a good runner, and if he can carry on Miles's style of business then it ought to work really well for all of us.

Boe wants a nine but fuck me he's becoming almost impossible to work with. Now I don't know whether he's overcharging his customers saying he's got some proper coke, or just being cheeky and trying it on. It's more than likely a bit of both, and it doesn't matter because whatever he does it will not work, as he doesn't have the room or margins to make it viable. I can almost guarantee that as a result of his excessive greed, he'll always bring at least half of it back. I keep saying to him, "It's fucking pub grub, sell it as it is, cheap and cheerful", and seeing as this stuff is coming from Cliff I know for a fact it's smashed to fuck. It's not even worth testing, as I know it'll be a two or three out of ten, so there's no fucking way that you can mark it up as anything but "cheap and cheerful".

What I find interesting is that now I've got my faculties back, and I'm not stressing out about money as most of the customers that jumped ship have returned, along with a couple of new ones salvaged from Alfie's circles. The new ones are yet to be battle-proven and only want pills, so I have to take them at face value for now, but the likelihood is that I'll not bother with them. The main issue I'm facing currently is that after I'd sacked off the new firm that was set after everything went tits up, I was having to do all of the work. The only way I could keep the wheel spinning fast enough to keep the pennies rolling in was to drop the prices to certain people. Now this has come back and bitten me on the arse, as these people are prone to taking the piss, as at the time they could sense my desperation—something I tried so hard to conceal, but when you start applying pressure and dropping prices, they soon cotton on. Consequently, this means I'm making next to fuck all on some of the kit, resulting in a lack of collateral to afford a decent runner. Then again, as far as I can tell I'm the best runner I know, so for now I'll keep a hands-on approach.

Not all is lost though, as on average I'm still making about a monkey on each corner that goes out. That gives me two bags on each box, and I reckon that if everyone takes on and more importantly sells and pays for what they want, then I could bring in a good seven or eight grand. This makes me a happy man. Well, it will do as long as everything goes to plan. I don't even have to remind myself because the whole Alfie saga is so fresh in my head it's made me very pessimistic, and no amount of happy pills will save me if it goes Pete Tong again. The numbers alone this Christmas are beginning to scare me. The last time I took on a load like this I didn't even get to see it, and I ended up with a bill that wiped me out. Now I'm back here again looking to take on three or four boxes. I'm gonna have another 60 or so bags on my bill, and that makes me very fucking nervous. I've got nothing left to cover it with and if I lose this load I'm done for—fucked—the kind of fucked where either I'd have to disappear or Cliff would, and that's a very worrying position to be in.

I desperately want to look forward to a busy and prosperous Christmas. I also want to do my best to enjoy it with my wife and kids, but I have this mountain in front of me—moving house is a total fucking ballache. I've already broken a cardinal rule—I've had to reveal my new address to someone in order to get a cheap removal deal. Jay from down the road has recently set up a small firm and says he'll do it for a drink. Maybe I'm being a little unfair to him, as he isn't the sort that will broadcast my whereabouts, because he's not from the area and besides he's a customer, so I'll never be in the situation where I owe him money. The hardest part is ensuring that he doesn't let it slip about how we know each other in front of my family. He won't, but it's always a concern, as he is a bit of a cokehead at times. Actually I'm being generous; he's flat out on the nosebag. The chances are that he'll be paying his workers in kind and probably in advance, so they'll work hard and fast, to get the job done in good time. They'll be sniffing and suffering from the Colombian flu mind—but as long as nobody notices any white residue around their hooters, then we should be all good.

We've found the perfect house with a doable price and in a perfect location; the only problem is that the move day is scheduled for next week, the week before Christmas, the same week I'm due to load up. I'm fucking praying that the kit lands soon and I get it gone way before the move date is here. This won't affect Jay, as he won't be having any of my shit since he's strictly a minimum seven out of ten, but he will be wanting some gurners. As it happens the gurners are good at the moment and Terry as usual is ready at the drop of a hat. On paper, all of this looks good, but it's flawed; flawed with the reality that I lack a safe house for the storage of my goods. Whatever I take on needs to go out immediately; I do have a short-term stash place to bring a short respite while offloading, but this is at my current address and not the new one. So basically, I'm counting on everything turning up in the next two or three days—certainly by Friday, because then I can mag to grid the fucking lot and then focus on the move. Maybe round up some dosh if it's about and give Cliff some as a sweetener, but all the drugs need to be gone.

It's Wednesday and Shriek is due to call; this brings me a huge sense of relief as the kit has landed well early; by almost a whole week. Shriek is Cliff's new runner; Cliff still has Flash and Skimmer but they're seemingly busy with other things, so Shriek is my first port of call. He's actually all right and doesn't appear to carry the inherited attitude that some of Cliff's lads have; i.e., he doesn't scream and shout like the Duke from Layer Cake, and as a direct result of this decent behaviour it makes business quite agreeable. Mind you I still can't stand working with this firm, but if I must then let's at least make it a professional set-up, as opposed to the noisy, shouty get-up that seems to appear by default from some of Cliff's runners.

Terry is on standby with 5,000 pills. I normally take 10,000, but the market is fucked and even though they are good pills, there's no money in them. They are literally covering a few costs. The only reason they make sense is thanks to the ones that Jay takes, which he pays for in cash, but even that's fuck all as they are literally pence. Jay wants £3k and I'm making twenty pence on each one, so £600. Shite considering I used to make at least a pound on each one. It just isn't worth the risk anymore, but the pill market is where it all started, and out of some ridiculous sense of loyalty I can't or won't shake it loose.

The game plan is to grab the pills during the move day and load Jay up straight away. I've got the move date confirmed— it's on Wednesday next week. Terry has been given the heads up and is ready for me to grab them during the transit between the old and the new house. Thornton wants 500 and Wedge wants 1,000; that'll piss Mick off no end. Boe says he might want a few, but you can almost guarantee he'll end up dicking me around. The tempting thing is to offer them up at a slightly over-inflated price, allowing for the pending problems, and possibly try for a cash-only deal. I'm gonna hang back and tell him to let me know what he wants by Monday next week, and if he doesn't know by then, then he can do one. Wedge will come to me, and I've suggested he do two runs; one for the pills and the other for the coke. Again, the plan is to see him during the move day—my only problem is that the pills will come in bags of a thousand, or at least they usually do. On a rare occasion they've been in bags of 5,000, but that's only if I've bought directly from someone who deals in the hundreds of thousands or millions, and I'm pretty sure Terry isn't doing those kinds of numbers.

So, presuming they come in bags of 1,000 then I'll need to plot up somewhere and count them out. The only option I have is to pull a fast one at what will be the old house. I'll get the van loaded up with Jay and his boys and send them on their way to the new address, where he can meet the missus who can direct the unload. While they're all busy doing that, I'll go collect the pills. Once collected I'll shoot back to the old address and quickly count them out; shouldn't take long as I'll only have to split the one bag, plus the house isn't being handed over until the next day. So, I'll stash the leftovers there until then. I can then quickly see Wedge and Thornton en route to my new address where I'll load up Jay—payment in kind for Jay so he'll get about 500 as payment for the move. Then all I have left is the last 500, which Boe may or may not take. If he doesn't I'll try and dish them out to Alfie's contacts. One way or another those gurners will be gone by the close of play on Thursday next week, and I'll have a bit of cash back from Jay. Terry won't want anything until after the new year, so it may come in handy to have a bit of cash knocking around.

Whilst on these pills, all this planning is making me feel like the old me. I don't feel the stress. I feel somewhat excited and I can sense the adrenaline wanting to kick in. I can almost feel the high I used to get after a successful drop. I'm actually wanting the phone to ring; I'm almost tempted to call Shriek and chase him up. It's mid-afternoon and this call needs to be soon—any later and I won't have time to offload. I'm still debating whether to go for three or four boxes; three won't be enough and historically four kilos of Charlie makes me very nervous, but four will be too much. Maybe three and a half; Thornton and Billy want one a piece, Wedge and Boe want half a box each, and Victor wants a nine. That's three and a quarter—fuck it, I'll be sensible and get three and a half.

Cliff is doing them for 16 bags each, hence the pub grub pricing, so I'll be back in the hole for another 56 grand, plus the three grand for the pills. Almost 60 grand, not forgetting the old debt of 27 grand, although that's not really part of it anymore—that's just there to fucking annoy me or for Cliff to remind me that he still owns me. The worst thing is that when

Cliff isn't being a dick, he's alright. We both share a common interest in cars and are both more than likely to plough unrealistic amounts into them, causing no end of drama. The difference between Cliff and me is that I try my best to be discreet and he doesn't. I guess people like Cliff make life interesting.

Finally the phone rings and it's Shriek. I pick it up and say, "I was literally seconds from calling you, how are we looking?". Shriek replies, "Yep all sorted, what numbers are you looking at?". The thing with Cliff's firm is they don't care about coding or being careful. They talk in clear—they always have done, and I doubt they're gonna change anytime soon. So, I reluctantly reply, saying, "I need three and a half". Shriek immediately says "Can you take four?". Maybe some of Cliff's methods have rubbed off the pushy fucker; I promptly shut him down with, "No mate, I'm not taking any more on than I need". To that he accepts it and says, "I'll be ready in an hour, see you at the big Tesco's". The words "Big Tesco" bring me up in hives—the fucking place brings back memories of meeting the lads and breaking the news of the seizure, but I reluctantly agree as it is local and convenient. "Ok mate, give me the usual heads up". Shriek agrees and cuts off; I'm guessing he's gonna be flat out, as it's a lot of work for one man to do. Cliff definitely gets his money's worth out of these boys.

Time for me to get on it and plan my run. This is going to be a heavy one. First is to get Wedge on his way up here; he can meet me towards Billy's place. Thornton is who I'll see first, then Victor, as he needs to come over the Bridge, and then finally pop down to see Boe—that's if he sorts his shit out. I'll have to get home and prep up first; this is high risk as the missus will be in. Either way I'll be in the garage, but as usual I'll lay down some smoke and say not to come in as I'm wrapping presents for Christmas. This is absolutely true because that's the beauty of trading this time of year; everything gets wrapped up in Christmas paper, providing the perfect cover for delivering coke. Even when it's not Christmas I always like to wrap it up as birthday gifts, write a nice fucking message on it and sling it on the seat. The package sizes are easy to tell apart and the quality is the same throughout, so no one gets the wrong one. Get ready lads, Santa is a-coming.

The lads have been fully briefed, and apart from Boe who says he's not about until later, everyone is chomping at the bit. The obvious ballache for me is that the two biggest customers live at opposite ends of the city, so no matter how I do it, I'll be transiting at least a whole box across town. Boe's will be left in the safe place for him to come collect when he's ready, and he'll be getting a dead letter drop. I have a few of these and they are handy for drop-offs that I would prefer not to be at; I'll be fucking watching mind, just not doing a direct handover.

Shriek drop calls my phone and I head towards the dreaded big Tesco's; it's not dark yet but another hour or so and it will be. I drive in, carefully scanning my arcs as I approach, and as far as I can see everything looks good. I de-bus, with a Tesco carrier bag in my pocket. It's cold and cloudy but not raining. I head towards the main entrance of the building and clock Shriek in his car; again I scan the area around him. I approach and get in.

He's looking quite stressed, so I calmly ask, "You ok?". "Yeah" he replies, "I've got a lot on board, here's yours," he says gesturing towards the back seat. I reach back and grab the bag, saying "Three and a half yeah?", Shriek simply nods in agreement. I place the bag, which happens to be way too bright, into my slightly less conspicuous Tesco's bag; I then ask him to drive around the car park and drop me back at the entrance. We move off and again I'm scanning everything. I can tell Shriek is a bit bewildered by my actions, but fuck it he's new at this; either he'll learn or get caught. We approach the entrance, he pulls up and I get out. "Cheers", I say as I close the car door. Once again Shriek just nods with a slight smile; I can sense his relief as he's now a little bit lighter, with a part of his responsibility now passed on to me; it's like passing a baton of stress to one another.

Carrying this newly-acquired baton of stress I casually head back to my van. The goods I have are double-bagged and in a bag that matches the surroundings, but I'm still conscious of what I'm carrying. I've not touched weight like this for a while, maybe even years, as I've had runners on tap; Little Man, Tops, Tucks, Fairy, Robsy, The Russian and Alfie's old firm. These boys have done so much for me—don't get me wrong, they've all been paid but between them, they've shifted so much. Now it's all down to me, back to the shop floor and carrying the lot. I guess what I'm saying is, I wish I didn't have to do this but who else is there? Who can I currently trust? Nobody, because I'm on my own.

The journey home is relatively quick; thankfully my timings are looking pretty good as I'm aiming to transit across town during the rush hour. During the short trip home I've contacted everyone, and they're all getting ready to link up over the next couple of hours. Boe is the only one who'll be dealt with differently as he's probably still sorting his shit out. The burner is disconnected as I approach home, the missus and kids are home, so I pull up and quickly pop in. I immediately lay down the smoke screen needed to get this job done—gotta love Christmas, haven't you? I head back out to the van and grab the bag, then dive straight into the garage, securing all the doors behind me. I'm locked in and feeling relatively safe. The garage is fairly empty, with a few removal boxes, the rest is the landlord's stuff.

I grab the Christmas paper and Sellotape, find a space on the floor and for the first time take a look at what I have. The good start is that it smells good—quite strong in fact, which will at least offer up a placebo effect, much needed for the likes of Boe and those inclined to try and pass it off as quality gear. The numbers are also good; I don't have any James whales but a nine is a nine, and if done properly, it will have at least 252 grams of weight. That way everyone who wants their ounce gets the full 28 grams. We must keep the front-line troops happy; those two grams mean a lot when they run out. To my relief, there are three and a half; in the past Cliff's been inclined to push a little bit extra, but I feel that the way things have developed between us, he might just need me more than the money I owe him.

Wrapping the coke up as gifts is a quick process and I'm not putting too much effort into it—I simply want it covered and to look the part. One box each for Thornton and Billy, half each for Boe and Wedge, then Victor and his corner. This gives me two large, two medium and a small, that's four drops and a dead letter. I'm gonna do two runs, Thornton and Victor first, then fly back to reload and do Billy's and Wedge's—job done.

I listen carefully at the garage door, which seems to be quiet. I crack the door and drop the bag of pressies onto the passenger seat of the van. I pop my head into the house and shout, "Quickly popping to the shops, do we need anything?", I get a muffled reply saying, "No, we're fine". I close the door and get off to see Thornton, who is about 20 minutes away; darkness is closing in, and it's not yet five, but the traffic is building up nicely. I call Vic to let him know I'll be there in about 30 minutes. Vic's another one that I find highly reliable; always on time, and has his own business so he usually rocks up in a work van.

Driving into Thornton's neck of the woods isn't a problem. It's a small town just outside of mine and has very little police activity, it's a nice area as well. It just goes to show though, that you can never predict an area is nice because of its looks; these slightly richer areas are a harbour for activity because a lot of these professionals like a bit of bag on the weekends. Although he can drive, Thornton is usually on foot. He knows his area well so can easily disappear into the estate and ditch any evidence in the process. I'm fucking hoping this doesn't happen, as asking him to pay could be problematic since nobody likes to pay for stuff they haven't had. Trust me I know, and if Thornton says, "Go fuck yourself", there's usually only one way to deal with these things.

Drop calls and very few words are needed when you've been working together for so long. I let his phone ring once when I'm two minutes out and no sooner than I pull up, a large ominous figure emerges from the shadows and climbs into the van. The exchange is quick and easy. It's done as I pull away and drive 100 metres or so down the road, where I pull over and Thornton exits the van, again he melts into the shadows as he heads off down a small lane. One down, three to go; time to see Vic.

He's already called me so I know he's close. I call back and he promptly answers, "Hello bud" in a slightly Welsh accent. I reply, "Hello bud, are you local?", to which he responds saying "Yes, fairly". We agree on a suitable place and both zero in on it. It's easy to keep meeting in the same place for convenience but it's just as convenient to set up a new one. I approach slowly; it's now dark and I can make his vehicle out—he gets out and climbs into mine as I pull up. We shake hands and talk polite shit for a bit; he's glad that I'm ok and getting back on top of things. He grabs his Christmas present and smiles. It's the sort of smile that says, "Thanks mate, the little effort you've made has just made my life a lot easier". Vic bails out and gets on his way.

Back home now to reload, and this is where it gets tricky. Heading out to the shops once is a plausible reason to go out, but trying to find a second and potentially third one gets progressively harder. I pull onto the drive, pop into the house and explain that I have to go out and help Lance clear some space down at the yard. She doesn't know we're not currently talking and doesn't have his details to check, So, I can blag that the old stock from the car parts sales is getting in the way of some of his stuff. This particular brand of bullshit can only buy me two or three hours, so I'd best make haste.

The final load is on—I've wrapped up Boe's and done my best to waterproof it with a black bin liner. Despite what he does it's getting stashed at the dead letter, which is two minutes away. I head back onto the road and head for the dead letter location. It's an old phone box, which has been slightly overgrown by brambles. It's still serviceable, so offers a plausible reason to be in there. I drive right up next to it and park the van, blocking the view of the phone box to any passers-by. If anyone sees me offload here, it could spell disaster and will require a fuck load of wasted energy trying to blag it, so due diligence is best. I grab Boe's pressie and, forcing the door open I step inside, looking up and down the road, checking all is clear before stashing the coke. I bend down and reach around and under the back of the box, effectively stashing the coke behind the phone box and in amongst the brambles. I slowly stand up and check the coast is clear before exiting the box and getting back in my van.

Driving off I check my wing mirrors to see if there's any movement. There's a mini roundabout at the end of the road so I do a 180 and drive back, just to give me that extra piece of mind. Everything looks clear and I'm as happy as I can be— right, onto the next one. A good 40-minute drive across town to Bill's and seeing Wedge en route. The intention is to get Wedge to come towards me—I'm not meeting him anywhere near Bill's as the area is way too fucking hot. Calling Wedge cracks me up because of his scattiness. I dial him in and make the call. He answers with a loud "Hello, can you hear me?", I answer "Yes mate, how are you getting on?", he repeats "Hello, can you hear me?". For fuck's sake! I say "Yes mate", and he replies with, "Eh?". I hang up. I know where he is, it's a black spot for signals and the timings indicate that he's about 20 minutes from the edge of town. He'll call back when his signal improves. I know the area he's in because it's the exact same road where I initially lost my shit, turned around and nutted myself off.

One and a half boxes on board, I'm sitting in traffic and occasionally look at the bag of gifts on my seat. I ask myself "How plausible is it, that if I do get pulled for something random, they'll think to search the bag? Or will they let it go?". I'm always asking myself these kinds of questions. I can quite easily put myself in the position of a police officer and if I saw myself driving past, my suspicious mind would at least say "What's in the bag, mate?". The phone rings—it's Wedge, and presumably with a better signal. I answer the phone and say nothing, giving him the opportunity to start the convo. "Hello, can you hear me?", says Wedge; you can tell he's used to living in the middle of fucking nowhere, if that's how you start your call. I reply "Yes mate, loud and clear". Wedge says "I'm almost there, where do you want to meet up?". Roughly knowing where he is, I suggest a spot that is approximately halfway between the two of us. If my memory serves me correctly, his sense of direction is atrocious, so I do my best to keep it simple.

I've had to opt for a meeting place near the main train station—what is it with these places today? First big Tesco, now the very station where Alfie got us all in the shit. Either way, outside of the station there are plenty of safe and discreet places to catch up; some would call them clandestine locations, and they'd be correct. As to the meeting, this will be a quick one. It'll be a lean "through the window, asking for directions" kind of drop. I've got another box to offload and the clock is against me. I've also got to dial in time for a cup of coffee at Bill's, who's expecting me in about 15 minutes.

This is a busy area with inner-city rush hour traffic, and this is precisely why I chose this route at this time; the cover of people, cars and darkness. I approach the meeting spot. It's on one of the main routes out of town next to an old Kwik Fit garage, with no cameras and free parking just off the main road. I pull in, do the standard scanning drills, park up and get out with Wedge's gift in hand. As I close the van door, he pulls into the car park and waves with a big smile. Fucking hell, now I have to be polite as he's happy to see me, so instead of the planned quick drop, I reluctantly get into his car. We have a chat for a few minutes, catch up and slag off Mick, who I quickly learn has now ended up with no customers at all, courtesy of Miles and Wedge—naughty bastards. We shake hands and I quickly bail out.

Almost there, the final drop. I can feel the stress easing off a bit, but I've still got the biggest one to go yet, and Bill's area is a fucker, but yet again this is why I choose this time of day. I re-join the flow of traffic and head for Bill's. It's slow but as safe as can be. I don't need to call as he's expecting me. I successfully get into the estate—no police presence, and coming out I'll be clean, unless Bill has any dosh, which I'm not expecting. Every time I close in on a deal done in a house, I get very nervous. The area is rough but usually no police activity, but house deals are just an uncomfortable affair. I can see my destination, and as suspected my anxiety does spike a bit as I approach Bill's house, once again checking the area for anything suss.

I park up nearby and walk the last few feet to his house, which is flooded with Christmas lights. I knock on the door and predictably Clive answers with a can of cider in his hand. I smile and say, "Very festive mate"; Clive smiles and rolls his eyes, gesturing me in. He says, "Bill's had to shoot off but you can leave it with me". I reply, "That's a shame, is everything ok?", but secretly I'm somewhat relieved as I can get on my way sharpish. Clive says, "He's fine, just busy, he did say to ask if you were gonna get any pills in". Perfect. I quickly say, "Yes mate, I'll have 500 spare". Clive juts his bottom jaw out and nods; that's his way of saying "sounds good", or at least I think it does. I say, "They'll be in next Wednesday, so if you can let me know by Monday as I have another guy interested, but he's a bit unreliable". Again, Clive nods; he's a man of few words, and this being the case he won't mind if I make my excuses and get the fuck on my way. Which I do and make a hasty exit. Walking back to the van is nice; I now have this feeling of liberation—carrying lumps of coke across town is fucking stressful.

I enter my van and head back down the road I came in on, this time noticing all the Christmas lights outside the houses. Funny how none of that even registers when working. This just goes to show how tuned in my mind is for certain things. As I approach the end of the road I see blue lights, and my adrenaline spikes as I continue along the road, but the blue lights fly past in the form of an ambulance. I take a deep breath, compose myself and stick the radio on. It's time to go home, so I just hope that Boe is ready to go soon. Fuck it I'm calling him. The first attempt rings off, and a few moments later, the second attempt also rings off. I'm not a fan of calling people more than once, but there are some people who choose to not answer their phones or can't hear it ringing because of a house full of stoners—the latter is usually Boe's case.

The drive home was pleasant enough and I'm almost there. The timings are good as well; I've been gone for just over two hours. My issue is that if Boe doesn't pick up soon, my burner will be off and he won't be able to arrange the collection. He fucking knows this as well and although the dead letter is good for a deal, it's not a stash place. I can feel the frustration building up inside me, as I know he'll be sitting there fucking stoned looking at his phone ringing. I'm trying one more time—no answer. I'm now forced to text; he does know where the dead letter is, so I text "I'm offline now, DL1, I'll call you tomorrow". Sent. Prick.

Last leg; I dismantle the burner and start to shut things down for the night. I can't completely relax though as there's half a key under a bush and a quarter in the garage. I just hope dickhead collects it and is honest about it. I reverse onto the drive, putting the dismantled phone under my seat. It's time to continue the charade of being happy and unstressed; it's better than it was but far from ideal. Still, I'm here and that's a lot more than I could have been a few weeks back.

Chapter 3

THE END OF A SHITTY YEAR

Thankfully Boe's dead letter drop went well and he was honest enough to drop a text saying "sorted". I'm still harbouring a nine in the garage, which is basically spare. Christmas being what it is, I have no doubt that it'll go out in the next few days and thankfully Bill has been in touch and wants the 500 pills. Right now though, none of that is relevant because today is move day. The wife is dropping the kids off at school and Jay is on his way here. Terry is still on standby. Initially I've suggested about midday as Jay is due here at 09:00, giving three hours to load up. I hope he can squeeze it all into his van. I won't tell him he's moving a quarter of a key for me, that shit costs money to get done.

I'm dreading Jay coming here. He's very good at business but operates in his own unique way. I find it hard to understand how someone can be both discreet and obvious, yet Jay is capable of effortlessly achieving both. Of course, the unknown thing at the moment is who he is bringing with him. Do they know the score or not? I can almost guarantee that they will be customers of Jay's, and I do know that Jay will keep a lot from them, but how much is what I'll need to ascertain. I'll pull him when he gets here and get all the details sorted. I need to speak to him about the plans for the pills, anyway.

It's approaching 09:00, and I'm standing here fucking pacing. It's not stress about the move or even the drugs, it's more associated with timekeeping. I'm always on time—that usually means five minutes before the agreed time and it baffles me why people are late. I know the wife will be here shortly—she was just gonna get some brew kit and snacks for the lads. I tried to talk her out of it because she'll neglect to realise that any food will be pointless if the lads are coked up, even a brew won't really be appreciated. A crate definitely, and even if a crate is on the cards, it doesn't look good if your removal guys are hammered while driving between locations and carrying drugs; drugs they don't realise they are carrying. Probably best to stick to tea, coffee and biscuits for now.

It's just after 09:00 and I can hear a van approaching. I look down the road and see a white Luton van heading my way, I can see Jay sitting next to another lad in the passenger seat. They all look hanging and a bit worse for wear; it's removals though, what am I supposed to expect? I've intentionally left the driveway clear for them to reverse onto. As they approach I stand in a position to guide them onto the drive, which they totally ignore and pull up onto the pavement blocking the drive—fucking genius. Jay gets out and walks towards me. "Morning mate, shall I show you around?", I say, hoping to grab a quiet few seconds with him. Surprisingly Jay appears to pick up on this immediately and asks the lads to sort the van while he recces the house.

We walk into the house and out of earshot, Jay says "We're all good, I've got the money for the pills. The lads don't know the score with you, so we'll keep it discreet if that's ok". He hands me an envelope, which I take and confirm saying, "Two grand yeah?", Jay replies, "Yes mate". Music to my ears, that's why I love Jay, no matter what my reservations are, he's one of the best I know for cash deals. With a sense of relief, I reply, "Thank you mate, I'm picking them up once we leave, how long do you think it'll take to load up?". Jay looks around the house and says, "We should be on the road in about two or three hours", which is exactly what I was hoping for. I say, "Spot on, that's perfect, the missus is due back soon with the brew kit, so once we head off I'll get on and sort the pills out".

We head out of the house to see the van doors fly open and the lads beginning to get busy. I ask Jay if he needs any help and he says, "No bud, these boys are here for a reason". Cool as fuck, this means I can focus on what I need to do. I'm half tempted to grab the pills now, come home, offload some and sort out the other lads while the move is being done. I'll wait for the missus to return then I'll let her know that I'm going to sort the keys for the new house, with a sneaky little meeting with Terry. The lads are flying—hard workers for scruffy bastards, even Jay is putting a shift in. I can't stand watching and every time I'm tempted to pick up a box they immediately grab it off me, so I accept that I'm surplus to requirement.

Another half hour passes and she's back with a bag full of food and drink, which is certainly appreciated, as the lads don't appear to be under the influence of anything, but then again it's not even 10:00 yet. She goes in to pop the kettle on, which is one of the few things we've not packed, along with a few cups. I pop in and let her know that I'm off to the estate agent's to sort the keys out and will be back as soon as possible. She's more than happy and in a relatively good mood. This move is gonna do us all a lot of good. It's been tough covering the bills this year, and she's done so well holding us all together after I lost my shit. She manages things so much better than I do. I know she's in the dark about everything but that makes her so much better, as she's willing to keep our family together despite my failings.

I let Jay know that I'll be back soon. He simply nods, as his hands are full carrying a poorly packed box; that'll be one of mine no doubt. I get in my van and drive off, assembling the phone as I do. I'm not expecting anything to come through, but this doesn't prevent a little anxiety troubling me, which is short-lived as the phone fires up and gives me no notifications. Firstly I call Terry and let him know I'm aiming for him soon, which is all good. Then a pre-arranged trip to the estate agent's where I need to sort out the transfer of funds and keys. This isn't as easy as it sounds. I'm on benefits and it took a while to find a private landlord to convince that it would be a good idea to take on a person who's recently lost the plot, but we did and thankfully they have been really helpful. My appointment is at 10:00 and it's fast approaching that time. I pull into the car park and go in, just hoping everything goes smoothly.

One hour later and a quick run through the inventory. I'm now the key holder to a considerably smaller house, but that really doesn't matter because the old house brings nothing but bad memories. Since moving there, I've had nothing but bad fucking luck. The Russian fucking off, Murray causing all the shit and then the loss of four kilos landed me with an £80,000 debt, none of which the missus is aware of, so moving out of there has lifted a huge weight off my shoulders. Now for the real stress to start. Terry won't travel far, which is fair enough as he's laid back and doesn't bring any drama. He's about half an hour from the estate agent's and only requires a few minutes' notice, which again isn't a problem—it is what it is.

I call Terry and give him the heads up. He's ready and waiting. The only issue I have is Terry can be a creature of habit and tends to go to the same place to meet. I guess this is ok as long as we aren't being watched. A few minutes out I call him to let him know I'm close by, and no sooner than making that call the meeting is done and I'm heading home. It's like doing it on autopilot. No words, not even a hello; I parked up, walked over to the car, was handed a bag and left—job done.

As I head home, I'm hoping I can find a place to sort the pills. The best option I can come up with is to hand the new keys to the missus and see if she fancies heading on over to check it all out, while I oversee the move here. I use this drive productively by contacting Thornton, Wedge and Bill, letting them know I'll be ready soon, and the general consensus is a good one. I take a sneaky look into the bag, sincerely hoping the pills are bagged up into thousands. As I peer inside I'm hit with a strong smell of aniseed; this brings me joy as it's a good sign. You can't pick up on this smell when in small batches, but when presented with a big bag full, it really hits you. More to the point, the pills are in five separate bags—thank fuck for that.

The timings are set; all I need to do is separate the last bag into two batches of 500. Wedge will drive to me, but I don't want Jay to see him because they live in the same area and that will be a conflict of interest. No matter what I'll be lighter by three thou, straight away. Wedge next, then Thornton. I'll take a trip over to Bill's later, once again using the rush hour for cover. I dismantled my burner; these are SOPs for me now and thankfully don't require much thought. I'm half hoping to see the van full up and done when I get back, or at least close.

The van is still being loaded and judging by the look of it they've made good progress. Jay alluded to the fact that they could get it done in one load, plus I have my van on standby if need be. The van that I need to get rid of, I wonder. I call out to Jay, "Mate, do you need a second van for your firm?", he says "Possibly", as I look at mine and say, "This one's up for grabs". He looks at me, smiles and says, "It's not ideal, what are you asking?". He's interested, and I wonder if I can get a grand out of him. "I'm looking for about a grand", as I try to maintain a serious face. Jay has a look over it and checks the mileage; there's no damage apart from a few dents inside from when Si and Murray were launching everything into the back, aiming for me, but successfully missing. This is it, everything I currently own. It reminds me of stress and bad times—so much shit has gone wrong this year. I need to cleanse myself of everything and have a fresh start.

Jay looks at me, his lads beavering away in the background, and says "Ok I'll take it, but can't pay you yet because I need the cash for the other thing". Feeling somewhat relieved I say, "That's fine mate as I need to get another motor sorted, how about after Christmas?". Jay agrees and we shake on it. "Also mate, I've got your Christmas present here, I just need to wrap it for you". Jay grins and says, "Thanks bud". I head into the house and see how it's looking. Pretty fucking empty as it stands. I see the missus is cleaning around, the rooms are looking quite empty and a slight echo forms as we speak. I suggested that maybe she could head over to the new address and prepare for the van while I wrap things up here. I know she's gagging to see the new house and as soon as I produce the keys she's gone in a puff of smoke.

I need to find a place to sort these pills. I head upstairs to see how it's looking. Seeing as the lads are emptying the lounge, I have to presume the bedrooms are empty. I get to the landing and see empty space everywhere, result. I run back down, see Jay and let him know that I'm gonna clean the bedrooms so they're off limits, as is the upstairs bathroom. If the lads need a shit they can use the downstairs bog. Jay acknowledges this, as I head into the garage and remind the lads of what's mine and what's to stay. I locate and grab the wrapping paper and Sellotape, then head to the van and grab the pills, hastily run upstairs and lock myself into the bathroom.

Feeling a temporary sense of refuge, I lay everything out and look at what I have to work with. Back in the day, I'd have counted every fucking pill into bags of 100 and pocketed the extras. Now I can't be arsed, I simply want the job done. I take the first three bags, put them together and wrap the fuckers up; it's a bit messy but it'll have to do. I then take another bag and do the same, then that's Wedge sorted. The last bag needs splitting; the bathroom floor is smooth and more importantly dry. I have my bank card with me to use as a separator. I tip a few out onto the floor—when I say a few I mean around four, maybe five hundred. This must be a drug dealer thing to see how good one's eye is for guessing weight and numbers. I have a few sandwich bags in the wrapping paper, but I only require one. I only need to count 500 out of the bag; what's left should be around the same, possibly more.

Ok so 427, 63 out—not too bad but not close enough. I bag up the ones I've counted and grab a few more out of the original packaging. I eventually hit the magic 500, seal the bags off and wrap them up. That was quick, maybe 10 minutes. I bag them all up and wipe everything down, leaving the bathroom exactly as I found it. I stash two thou in the airing cupboard and head down. Jay sees me and I do a discreet nod which he acknowledges with a similar gesture. The lads are out of sight and negotiating a sofa out of the lounge. Jay grabs the bag and sticks it in his rucksack which is in the cab of the Luton.

I spend the next half hour or so chomping at the bit. My burner isn't on and I've got deals to be done, then a penny dropped. I'm fucking moving so this address no longer matters. I run to my, soon-to-be Jay's van, climb in and reassemble the burner. It fires up and a couple of beeps come through. One is Wedge and the other is Cliff; fuck, what does he want? I opt to call Wedge first; fortunately, he answers, and for a change he has a good signal. I say keep heading in and we can sort a meeting place when you're closer. I'm running way too early and Wedge is at least an hour away from me. Thornton is a quick drop; assuming he's ready, I make a quick call to confirm his availability—it's good and he can link up almost immediately. I head back up to the airing cupboard and grab one of the smaller packages of 500. Heading back down to see if Jay can give an ETA. Jay says he'll be loaded within the hour, which is good timing on his end and the lads have done a cracking job loading up. It's fucking rammed mind you, but how the fuck did they fit my house into one van?

Jay knows the score and will sit tight until I return from seeing Thornton. I casually drive off but my nerves are jangling a bit as I need to return Cliff's call. I look at the missed call and press redial. It only rings once and he answers by saying "What you up to?". Being economical with the truth I say, "Flat out helping a mate move workshop". Cliff replies saying "Fuck that, sounds like hard work. How are you getting on with that work?". Feeling a bit of relief descending upon me, I say, "All good so far but I dare say it hasn't hit the end of the line yet, and I've still got a bit of surplus". Now when someone who's supplied drugs, calls you and effectively says, "How is it?", The alarm bells have to ring. It's because they know it's shit and he wants to know that none of it is coming back. I have to box clever and leave it open. If I give the impression that all is good then if it does come back in it'll be harder to return it, but if I leave it open it gives me room for negotiation because I now know that Cliff has his reservations about it.

I take this opportunity to ask about the other thing, saying "Any news on that other job yet?". Cliff replies saying, "Not yet, it's all planned once the Christmas presents are paid for". I say, "Ah, makes sense". Cliff says "Bye". I can never get to grips with Cliff's abrupt form of saying goodbye. Comes from nowhere, it's like he's said his bit and he's become bored of the conversation—fair enough, I guess it is business anyway. I'm closing in on Thornton's place. It's late morning and considering it's winter it's a bright sunny day. There aren't any shadows to hide in this time and the area is quiet, good in one sense but bad in another.

All the usual drills, time and time again, why can't I simply switch off and forget about the danger, it's exhausting. As I approach I see Thornton emerge from a local shop with a large bottle of milk in hand. He spots me, heads over and gets in. I drive off and out of habit I do a Cliff and say, "How are you getting on with that work?, I have a nine left if you need it". Thornton replies saying, "Yeah it's good, I may take you up on that, mine's nearly gone". Fuck I'm good, I managed to turn a question of concern about the quality of goods into a successful sales pitch. As Thornton gets out he says, "Thanks I'll let you know about that bit", and wanders off into the estate.

Feeling pretty good about things I head home, and checking my timings I contact Wedge to see where he is. Not great as he's still an hour away from me. Not a problem, it's not even twelve yet, so I make contact with Billy—maybe I can shift things a bit sooner, he's more than happy to meet up earlier. He'll be plotted up in his house so it's not exactly hard graft on his end. If Jay doesn't mind me not being there, I'll shoot off across town and offload to Bill and Wedge. I can't see it being an issue, as Jay has effectively been paid, the missus will be loving the prospect of a new home to set up and the lads will receive their drugs a bit earlier than planned. In my book that makes everyone a winner.

Approaching my soon-to-be old house, I smile to myself at the thought of not having to take the fucking battery out of my phone, and an even warmer feeling from the idea of nearly shifting everything a week before Christmas. This is a great success as the festive week is a hot time for police checks for drunk drivers. Although this doesn't affect me, the concern is always there. I pull up to see the van is ready to move and the lads have steamed into the biscuits. "How's it going?" I shout out, they respond saying "Good to go mate, Jay's doing the final checks". This is perfect, I go into the house to see how Jay is and he's doing a final sweep across the ground floor. He says,

"We're sorted bud, do you want to have a quick look around to make sure we have everything on board". I reply, "Yes sure thing mate, are you gonna be ok heading to the new address as I need to offload the last few of these things?". "Of course mate, you crack on," says Jay. I'm beginning to get that feeling of warmth, the one you get when everything runs like clockwork. It feels like such a long time ago, that I last felt this level of calm and confidence.

I head up to the airing cupboard and grab the last 1500, stick them in my coat pocket and head downstairs. I shake hands with Jay and thank the lads for their hard work, assuring them that the missus has a tip on the other end waiting for them. I get in my van and fuck off across town—this feels like a carbon copy of the coke run last week. Wedge is going to end up meeting me in Kwik Fit again and I'll be seeing Bill soon after. Daytime drug running is my preferred thing but I do prefer the cover of traffic and winter darkness. I know these conditions offer the police the same perks, but it feels safer. The fact is if they are watching, then it's already over, if they are not then the more cover I have the better.

I approach Kwik Fit and prepare to see Wedge. He's already on plot so will be jumping in with me this time—there he is, bless him; big old smile and a wave. I suppose nobody will think it's a drug deal; there's no way as this pair aren't exactly being low-key. He gets in and straight away says, "That coke's fucking great isn't it?". Replying with a blatant lie I say, "Oh yeah mate, I've heard nothing but praise, in fact, I'm sold out". Wedge grabs his giftwrapped pills and wishes me a Merry Christmas; that's nice and I respond in kind. He walks back to his car and I continue to Bill's place.

As I pull up to Bill's place I see a different car on the drive. It looks like a police car, so I drive by and park down the road, leaving the pills in the van. I get out and walk back up the road, towards Bill's. The car's a dark Ford Focus—not black, more of a charcoal colour, definitely filth; either way, I'm going in. What are they gonna say? I'm clean and seeing a mate for Christmas. I knock on the door and Bill answers; I must look perplexed as he immediately says, "What's wrong?", I look back at the cop car and say, "Whose is that?", "What the Focus?" says Bill, "Yeah," I say. I walk into the house as Bill says, "It's mine, I bought it the other day, I'm selling it".

Now there's a thought, I ask him how much, and Bill immediately says "Three and a half". I'm already interested; the car is exactly what I need, the perfect blender and it looks like a police car which ought to scare away the ruffians. I look at him and say "Done, I'll take it". Bill raises his eyebrows and says, "You didn't even negotiate!". "No need mate, I know where to come if it's a lemon". We head on in and sit down for a brew, half expecting to see Clive in the kitchen. I then realise I don't have the pills on me, so I let Bill know and shoot off back to my van and collect the goods, letting myself straight back in.

I arrive to a coffee and a logbook with a set of keys; I take a sip and say, "Can I put the cost of the car against the stock?"; Bill says, "I was banking on it". We do a quick bit of maths between us and come up with an agreed outstanding balance of £14,900. As good as this deal is, I'm playing a dangerous game, technically spending profits before they are in, but my profits over Christmas will be close to eight grand, plus a grand due in for the van from Jay. Yes, it's a calculated risk but one that needs to be done.

We spend an hour or so talking and as usual, I have to find the ideal momentary pause to say, "Right son, I'd best get back to the new house", which I do. Bill sees me out and we agree that I'll be back in a few days to collect the car. I take the car docs with me so I can sort out the insurance and stuff; it should be cheaper than the van which is a blessing, and now I have a car lined up I'll be offloading to Jay with a matter of urgency, and knowing Jay, he'll have money fairly soon.

I have a look over the car as I walk past—I like it. It's very clean, definitely a blender and something that I've not really taken into consideration is that I'll have a family car now. My wife doesn't drive, although she wants to. We're not in a position to afford it yet so family days out have been a bit hit and miss. This spontaneous purchase might take a bit of explaining though, seeing as I'm supposed to be on the sick and earning no money. I suppose the obvious blag is that I bought it with the money made from selling the van, even though the car is about seven years newer and in much better condition. Ah well, I suppose I'll have to roll the dice and see how it goes.

The drive across town was the same as all the others—fucking boring, and seeing as I'm clean I opt to give the missus a quick call in an attempt to find out how the move is going. We chat for a short while, and she says the lads are nearly done, they're just unloading the bedroom stuff. Fuck, I think to myself, that nine was in the garage, it's bagged and in a small toolbox but I wanted to ensure it didn't get opened or dropped. On that, I make haste in an attempt to get there to make sure everything is ok. It should be as I'm pretty certain Jay would have called and given me an earful if he's stumbled across it. Like it's gonna make a difference mind you, he's got 3,000 pills on board.

As I close in on the new address, once again I go through the process of dismantling the burner and stashing it in the van. The house is nicely tucked away on a private driveway with another three houses, and ours has a garage, which for me is a selling point. I drive up next to the entrance to see that Jay and his guys left already, giving me room to reverse in and park up. It's only just gone three, so the school run is due. I quickly inform the missus that I could go collect the kids if it's easier for her, plus I quite like the normality of picking them up. I never get the feeling that I fit in with any of the mums or dads that hang around. It's almost as if by default they all know one another and I don't.

I love being a dad, I just wish I could be there for them more. It's my head. It rarely feels as if it's in the right place, and even though I'm in a much better state mentally, I still find it hard to engage emotionally. I always have, I suppose it's a built-in defence mechanism, one that allows me to quickly emotionally detach if the need should arise. The kids love being in the van, sitting up front all high and mighty, not for long though because it's going, and we'll have a nice multi-purpose vehicle for drug and family runs. The new house is only a few minutes from the school. It's about the same distance from the school as the old house, just in the opposite direction.

I park up on our new drive and the kids run into the house to see their new bedrooms, almost pissing their pants with excitement. Equally excited but for different reasons I head straight for the garage to find that fucking nine that's been unloaded. They've kept it fairly neat and unlike the previous place, the landlord hasn't got any of his personal effects in there. I see the toolbox neatly positioned on a set of shelves at the back. I wander over and, making sure the coast is clear, I open the box a bit and look inside, see it's safe and sound. This one's got Thornton's name on it, so I take it out of the box, it's double bagged. I then stash it out of sight on the top shelf in the garage, removing the outside bag and any of my prints. The coke has just become the property of the previous tenant. Plausible deniability—one rarely gets to play that card.

I spend the next few days tying up loose ends. Thornton takes the last nine, I've got my new car and Jay has collected the van. This is mental, I've got everything done and dusted, and Christmas is still two days away. I've even got time to go do my Christmas shopping, which in my own true style will be done with an utter sense of panic on Christmas Eve, but I wouldn't have it any other way. It's standard practice. I used to do my Christmas shopping on the cross-channel ferry coming back from Germany on a block leave when I was based over there, so last-minute dot com is what I'm all about. Besides I never know if I'm going to be around for Christmas, so why waste time and money on stuff if I'm gonna be dead or banged up?

Chapter 4

A NEW YEAR BRINGS A NEW ADVENTURE

C hristmas went surprisingly well; the wife and kids were lavished with gifts and I did my best to pretend I was enjoying myself. Having a fat bill of nearly 60 large on my nut was weighing me down a bit, but all in all as Christmases go it was good. Long gone are the days of going on an all-dayer with the boys—getting on the lash from 11:00 and smashing it all afternoon in town. We'd be eagerly waiting for the office parties to rock up, then it was all hands on deck, ready for Christmas kisses with office girls and sexy Santas armed with nothing more than a sprig of mistletoe. God, I miss those days.

Rounding up the money went surprisingly well. Wedge owes a bit but nothing my profits won't cover. Boe tried to pull a fast one and return some but I fucked him off. I said it's too late and if he wants to start returning half of what he's taken on, then his fucking price is going up—that shut him up. Apart from that, everyone has paid up and, more importantly, Cliff's been squared away, plus a couple off of my debt. Terry's shot off on holiday for a couple of weeks and has kindly asked if I could hold onto his until he returns, which I'm happy to do. It's only three grand so I'll tuck it away somewhere in the garage.

Things have gone so well I'm waiting for the bubble to burst; I rarely get a good run for longer than a month without something going wrong. I think these happy pills coupled with the positive results of business are making life feel great, but how much of this is chemically induced by the anti-depressant, and how much longer do I have to be on them? The doctor recommended at least six months and besides, it's nice to have this reserve of benefits coming in to cover the bills. What I do need to do is start telling the missus that I'm doing some cash-paid security, as there's absolutely no way I can justify the money that's currently rolling in, if benefits are supposed to be my only income.

Historically January has always been a crap month. It's the calm after the storm; everyone is skint and all partied out, and it's during these times when all the mid-range dealers fuck off skiing or somewhere tropical. It's almost pointless even getting goods in, as anything collected will more than likely end up sitting there collecting dust. Consequently any money made during the festive season will have to be stretched out to survive on during the month of January and potentially even February, so what may initially seem to have been a very profitable couple of weeks, soon becomes an average take.

January draws to an end and as expected everything has been quiet. I'm beginning to wonder if this thing that Cliff mentioned is gonna happen, as he's told me fuck all about it, not even a hint. If it isn't going to happen then say so, don't keep me on the end of a line. I'm purposely not making any major plans as he said not to, and I understand why, but the lack of comms isn't helping. So I'm simply whiling away the days, waiting for something to happen. It's not as if it's a small thing. Smuggling drugs is a big fucking deal, and my involvement in drugs wasn't supposed to involve importation. The frustrating thing is, the money I'm earning now could easily pay the debt off in a few months, but Cliff is intentionally trying to keep my debt alive, by either saying he doesn't want the money in yet or lying and saying there's no work at all therefore delaying my payments. I'm not fucking stupid, I know he's taking the piss but at the same time a debt is a debt and one way or another it's getting paid.

January has been and gone, and we're now into February. Trade has the potential to pick up slightly but Cliff hasn't had anything in for a couple of weeks, and this fucking sucks as my funds are getting to a critical stage. My phone rings, but it's a number I don't recognise, so I cautiously answer by just saying "Hello". The familiar voice of Cliff responds, saying "This is my new one, we're on, you're going over next week". I fall silent; all I can say is "Yep ok". Cliff hangs up and I gather my thoughts. Fuck, what have I done? Suddenly visions of my family flash before me; I know I've been waiting for this call but I honestly didn't think it would happen. I need more details; I can't process anything with the lack of a script.

I call Cliff back on his new one, and he answers by saying, "What's up?". I reply, "Mate we need to catch up because I need more information so I can make the necessary prep". Cliff responds by saying, "It's all good, Skimmer will come to see you in a bit", and then he hangs up. "Fucking rude", I say to myself. Ok Skimmer's good; the voice of calm and reason from a firm that thrives on chaos. I'm looking forward to seeing him; I'm hoping he'll have all the details as I'm going nowhere without a detailed mission plan. My day has now taken a turn;

I need to start concocting some form of cover story to put the family off the scent. This is nuts, I can't do anything until I know the score. I need to calm the fuck down and wait until I've seen Skimmer, then I'll make my arrangements and formulate a cover story.

A couple of hours pass, and I'm being called by another unknown number. Assuming it's Skimmer, I answer with a slightly less sheepish "Hello", and the welcoming voice of Skimmer greets me saying, "Fancy a catch-up?"; I say "Yes please mate, I think that would be wise". Skimmer goes on to say that he's ready to catch up in about an hour, so we agree on a mutually convenient meeting place, and for once it's not the big Tesco's. I can sense that Skimmer has a lot to say but won't or can't at this stage of the game; it's clearly highly sensitive and seeing as Cliff's firm isn't usually bothered about talking in clear, this new level of being cautious makes me even more anxious than usual.

Waiting for the heads-up from Skimmer is killing me, but all I can do is wait patiently. This week is now a complete write-off—even if some coke does arrive I'm not taking it on. Pointless as I might not be here to get it out the door, which has presented me with another conundrum. If I'm now working for Cliff doing whatever it is I'm meant to be doing, I'm put in a position where I'm unable to trade. I'm fucking losing out here, and this needs to be addressed as I'm not going to be having a gun held to my head forever.

Skimmer drop calls me and I head towards our meeting place. As usual, I've recced the area and I'm plotted up locally. We've opted for a quiet country pub, which is ideal for this time of day—late afternoon and close to dinner time. Neither of us look like drug dealers and we're both discreet. I pull into the car park as Skimmer is parking up; I've clocked him, has he clocked me? The car park is about half full, meaning the pub should reflect that with customers. Not a problem, it's not like we're doing anything dodgy. I find a suitable space and reverse into it, still assessing my surroundings. I de-bus and head towards Skimmer, who by now has seen me. We shake hands and head straight in, approach the bar where Skimmer asks what I want. Somewhat preoccupied with checking out the fire exits, toilets, windows and customers, I say, "Coke please mate". I join Skimmer at the bar, but still no conversation as I'm now looking for a suitable table to sit at. I locate one in the far corner of the pub, next to the fire exit. I inform Skimmer that I'll grab the table before heading over and commandeering it.

Skimmer comes over with a couple of Cokes in hand and we embark on a bit of a catch-up, during which he expresses how shit he felt during the summer of last year. The fact that he expresses his thoughts is more than enough for me. He looks at me and in a sincere way he says, "Are you sure you wanna do this?". I look up and breathe out a sigh, saying, "I don't see I have a great deal of choice; I still owe £25 grand and this will help it drop". Skimmer looks down and shakes his head—he then goes on to say, "He's not paying you much mind". Feeling a sense of anger building I ask how much and he says, "£1,500 plus expenses". I sit back, take a deep breath and blow out, cringing in the process, saying nothing. Skimmer looks at me and says genuinely, "Look, Cliff needs you; there's nobody else he knows that he can trust enough to get this done, but you don't have to do it, he can't force you". I respond by saying, "No he can't, but I will do it, because unlike a lot of people if I agree to something, I'll see it out to the bitter end".

My initial anger subsides and I go on to say, "So all that aside, what exactly am I doing? I'm presuming you are here to fill in all the gaps?". Skimmer says, "I most certainly am. Ok so you're going over to Spain to pick up a couple of keys and bring them back." A sense of excitement sets in and Skimmer looks at me and says, "Why are you smiling?"; my response is "Because it sounds like an interesting prospect. How often do you get a chance to smuggle drugs in Europe?". Skimmer smiles and says, "Rather you than me". "So, what's the details then," I ask; Skimmer says, "Basically it's been arranged for you to meet up with a contact in Barcelona next Wednesday. It's a cash deal, and you're to bring back the two keys however you see fit; they don't care how, as long as it makes it over." I look at him and say, "Who's they?" and Skimmer immediately says, "I don't know". Of course he knows, he's merely not in a position to divulge certain details.

I have a load of questions to fire into him, things like: Do we have an exact meeting time? When and where do I collect the cash? Is Cliff gonna give me a float to work with? What car do I use? I'll be fucked if I'm using mine, so he'll have to get me a rental. Skimmer manages to cover all the questions in a more-than-satisfactory way. I guess a certain number of things will remain unknown. After all, it's another drug deal, so certain details will always be kept in the dark. We spend an hour discussing a few things and it eventually turns into us getting to know each other a bit more; we've never had this opportunity before as there's always been someone else knocking about or getting in the way.

I leave the pub relatively satisfied that I have all the details I need to know, meaning I can now focus on prep, the first task being to pave the way and lay down some heavy smoke to put everyone off the scent, especially my wife. Lying to people about my movements comes far too easy and it's not something I'm proud of, but the alternative is them knowing, or worse still them actually being ok with it. That doesn't sit well with me, so it's deception and lies all the fucking way. The only plausible thing I can concoct is the security ruse; this has never let me down and always affords me the luxury of discretion.

The other prep is logistics and finances needing to be covered, which will be courtesy of Cliff. I'll be fucked if I'm forking out and playing that game. If he thinks paying me one and a half grand is a respectable wage to do a job with this much risk then he can think again. I'll be ensuring I get paid more; how that will play out I don't yet know, but it will happen. My passport is good, so no problem there. I suppose the biggest thing is what car and how to stow the goods. Presumably the drugs will be in their original jackets and they're relatively waterproofed. My train of thought is stashing it under the car using magnets or straps. I guess the type of car will depend on how and where I stash it. I don't fancy having the kit in that car, as plausible deniability won't wash. I'll need to have a good think when I see the car; I need to get on Cliff's case possibly through Skimmer and get a car sorted ASAP.

Smuggling? I haven't really thought about it. I'm not looking at that stage yet. I'm the sort of person who tries to deal with things when confronted with them. The anti-depressants are helping massively. I'm not stressed or anxious. I know for a fact that if I wasn't on these things I'd be having a total fucking meltdown, and this is what worries me. My usual sense of self-preservation has been numbed, consequently my risk evaluation is offkey. I don't want to do this; the money doesn't even come into it. Even if I was in a good place and financially sound, no amount of money would tempt me to take a trip like this. This debt turned me into someone different; the want or need to die and my emotional detachment from the ones I love the most. It scares me that I would put a debt over my love for my family. What have I done?

Sitting at home, playing happy families is even harder than usual. My wife is pleased that I have a job working away as it means more money; well it would if I was getting paid, which means more fucking lies to explain the lack of wages from said job. Skimmer has arranged for me to collect a hire car on Monday morning. The costs have been covered, by whom I don't know. I've been told I'm having a Vauxhall Vectra; I can accept this as they are good blenders and there are shitloads of them on the road. I can only hope it's dark in colour. I've been informed that I'll be meeting a firm in London to exchange the money, and this is something I hadn't considered. To be fair that's how fucked my head is. I foolishly assumed that I'd be taking it over in English and paying in English but no, not a chance—it's fucking Spain, so it's euros all the way.

Expenses are tied up in the money being exchanged. Once the money is exchanged the deal is set for 40 grand for the two boxes; that's €20,000 each; fuck me that's a good price. Cliff will easily double or even triple his money, and the tight fucker's only paying me £1,500. How much is left for expenses will depend on the exchange rate. I'm gonna need at least £700, to allow for my cover plan to be implemented.

Skipping across the border at this time of year will need a reason. The more evidence I have for being overseas for a relatively short period of time, the better I'll fare if I get pulled by customs. I love skiing; always have since I did something called "Snow Queen" while in the army. It's classed as an exercise, but really it's two weeks skiing in Bavaria. My plan is once the money is exchanged, I'll head to Portsmouth and get the overnight ferry to Le Havre in northern France. I'll get some kip on that crossing as it's nearly eight hours. Once I land, I'll drive down to the Pyrenees mountains and spend Tuesday night in Andorra. The next morning I'll purchase a two-day ski lift pass. Wednesday, I'll drop out of Andorra down to Barcelona and collect the coke, stow it and head back into Andorra for Wednesday evening, where I'll check back into the same hotel for the night. Thursday morning, head back into France and head north for the same port, once again aiming for an overnight crossing, this time back to Portsmouth.

Looks great on paper, but my arse is giving it a full-on twitch. The amount of borders I'm crossing loaded up with money or drugs is slightly unnerving: UK to France, France to Andorra, Andorra to Spain and then back again. That's six chances to get caught with either money or drugs. If they catch me with the money, it's gone and so am I. If it's drugs, then it's the same outcome but slightly heavier consequences. Probably be best if I don't think about that. I'll just assume it's all good and worry about each stage as it's breathing down my neck.

I spend Sunday night packing my bags, which meant a trip up to the attic to retrieve my somewhat dated skiing attire. The kit was purchased back in the nineties and fucking looks like it, but it's a world apart from the kit we were issued while skiing in the forces. There's only one thing worse on the slopes than a five-year-old German kid who seems hellbent on taking your legs out, and that's a squaddie trying to catch up with the little bastards, because we think we can ski better than the little fuckers. It always ended in tears and usually resulted in our boss apologising to the ski staff or parents of the little rats, trying his best to not get us booted off the mountain. Either way, it was always good fun.

As the night drags on, I'm trying my damnedest to not let on to my wife that I might not see them again. It's hard enough hiding the truth about things over here, but I can't imagine how it would be if she received a call from me sitting in a French or Spanish jail. The guilt I carry just gets buried with everything else I'm hiding. Suck it up and crack on son; I'm sure it'll be fine. I eventually retire for the night, fully packed and prepped. I even manage to get a load of gaffer tape and straps to store the kit, once collected. If I'm honest I still don't know how I'm gonna do it. In my head it's simple, but in reality it's far from it. A couple of kilos of coke isn't that small, and can you imagine how much of a dick I'll look if it fucking falls off or comes loose as I'm driving through the port. Explain that away to Cliff; "Yeah mate, sorted", only to realise it's in the middle of the road back in Le Havre.

I didn't sleep particularly well last night. I guess the stress still affects me, even if I can't feel the full impact of it. I just feel as if I need to get on the road and detach from family life.

When I'm at home I'm totally divided, but as soon as I leave the house I feel alone, and when doing this that's the way I prefer it. It's almost as if they don't exist and I don't mean that in a bad way; it's purely my way of keeping them safe. This is the most important thing, because if I have to live in this world and do these things, then I have to be able to divide myself into two different people. The one that has a wife and kids and tries to act and behave accordingly, and the one that is so deep into drugs that has to act alone. The problem is the latter one has a direct influence on the former, making me a shit dad and husband; the two simply cannot coexist without dire consequences.

It's fairly early and the car hire place is local. I load my car up with my bags—one holdall and a second bag with my ski kit. I also load up my army slug, just in case I break down. I'll be meeting Skimmer before I head down to the Smoke to grab the dosh and he's giving me a fresh burner to use for this job and nothing else. I've informed all of my customers that I'm offline for a few days, so not to bother trying to call me. I say a final goodbye to the missus and give the kids a big hug, hoping that I'll be seeing them all again in a few days. I get into the car and slowly pull away, looking at them in my mirrors as I do; they haven't got a clue and that's the way it needs to be.

I pop the radio on and do my best to pretend I'm not worried, but my emotions are currently powering down, and I'm compartmentally putting them away until I need them again. As the emotions power down, the burner powers up. I call Skimmer and he promptly answers "Morning, are you there?". I respond, "Few minutes away bud"; Skimmer replies saying, "Ok mate, I'll see you before you pick the car up, I'm just around the corner". "Cool, see you in a sec". Time to grab the dosh and a new phone; I pull into a business park and slowly drive towards the hire place. Seeing Skimmer pull up ahead of me, I drive past and park up, I get out of mine and walk over to him. He gestures to get in, which I do.

"How's it going mate?" I ask. Skimmer immediately says, "Slight change of plan"; all of a sudden that stress I couldn't feel hits me like a fucking sledgehammer. Skimmer picks up on my body language and says, "It's nothing major. Cliff's partner in this wants to bring the money down and ensure that it all goes smoothly. It's because it's a new meeting and he wanted to make sure the money was safe". Oddly this lifts a weight from me as my responsibilities have been temporarily lifted. I look at Skimmer and ask, "So who is it?". Skimmer, trying to not show any emotions, says "It's Si". The car falls silent; is this good or bad? Si? I like it, but I didn't think he was game for working with Cliff; clearly, I was wrong.

I look at Skimmer and say "Cool". Skimmer, now looking a tad perplexed, says "Oh, I thought it would be a problem after last year". I smile and say, "On the contrary mate, I get on well with Si, we just don't interact that much". The truth is, I'm somewhat relieved; the kind of firms that Si will work with will be much better than the kind Cliff would associate with. Popping over to Spain to meet one of Cliff's connections would have been destined for me to be met by a loud-mouthed gangster in a bright yellow Range Rover. If you know, you know. Si's contacts should be a lot more discreet and besides, if he's overseeing the whole thing, that's not such a bad thing, as I know he's going to protect his investment. Or I could be totally wrong, the whole thing could all be Cliff's and Si is simply jumping on board. Either way with Si involved I know that at least the money exchange will go smoothly.

Skimmer hands me a phone and an envelope and says, "There's a ton in there to keep you going until you get the euros; as for the phone, all the numbers you need are saved; me, Cliff, Shriek and Si. Cliff said no matter what you do, do not call anyone else on that phone. The other number is Neil—he's your contact in Spain". "Neil?" I say. "Yeah, he has your number and will be expecting a call from you at some point tomorrow", says Skimmer. He holds out his hand and says, "Good luck mate". I shake his hand and, smiling, I say, "Cheers bud". I get out of the car and head back to mine. I get in and immediately take apart my burner, sticking it in the glove compartment. I leave the new one as it is for now and drive the last few hundred metres to the car hire place.

I pull in and park up, looking around. It's open but only just, by the looks of it. The staff are milling about moving cars, so I peer into the garage and see if I can see what might be my car. It's full of all sorts of Vauxhalls, Vectras, Astras and Corsas. I walk into the office where I'm greeted by a staff member and we go over the paperwork. It's all very familiar, as I used to work for a car hire company when I came out of the army. Not for long, mind you as I was advised to seek alternative employment when I kept bringing them back with cooked brakes. Ten minutes later I'm looking over a nice charcoal-coloured Vectra which is perfect—not even a year old. Not fast, but I don't need fast—I need reliable and grey.

I transfer my kit across to the hire car and lock mine up, leaving it in the customers' parking bay. I look at my car as I pull out, again wondering when I will see it again; even though it's just a car, it's now an attachment that I don't need to be thinking about. It feels like I'm mentally writing my last will and testament; everything I love, own and care about is about to become collateral and must be left in peace. I can't possibly go ahead with this job if I'm thinking about these things. I have to detach and focus on the road ahead because no matter what it brings, it'll be a new experience that will require 100% focus.

Chapter 5

BUREAUX DE CHANGE

Getting to grips with a new car doesn't take long and I've got a stack of CDs to keep me entertained. My kit's in the boot and, courtesy of Skimmer, I've got £100 in my pocket. I have my contract phone, but it's currently off, so all I really need to do is fire up the burner and give Si a call, to confirm where I'm going and what the plan might be. Feeling a bit uneasy and unsure of what to expect, I give Si a call. We haven't spoken for a while, as he was one of the lads I didn't fancy getting caught up in the net with that after last year's fiasco. Saying that I had received some sketchy information that Alfie got handed a three-and-a-half and Jeff got a four; I also heard that The Boy had managed to avoid a custodial and got a tag. Either way, they'll all be off the scene for at least a couple of years.

I climb onto the M4 motorway and head for London. Si's not answering, so I steadily head towards the big smoke. I'm not in a rush and I'm clueless as to where we are supposed to be meeting, anyway. London's not exactly small and it doesn't really matter where we're meeting; I just wanna know so I can ensure I'm not late. The ringing of my phone sets off a bit of anxiety. I see it's Si so I pick up and say, "Morning mate, how's things?". Sounding fairly upbeat, Si replies, "Yeah all good, are you all set for this job?". "Of course" I reply; I then go on to say, "I've just left, where are we heading for?". Si answers,

"Aim for Kingston upon Thames, I'll send you a postcode where we can meet and have lunch. We'll talk more when we're there". I respond, "Sounds good to me, see you in a couple of hours".

Ok so I have a destination—that's a good fucking start. My phone beeps and the postcode lands in my inbox. I've borrowed a satnav from a mate but I've still got my European atlas though, just in case I fall out with the tech and launch it out the fucking window. These satnav systems are new to me and part of me doesn't trust them as much as a map, so I tend to operate both. I type the postcode into the satnav and it brings up my route, which is just under two hours away—not bad, giving me an ETA of just after 11:00. I'm presuming Si will be arriving at a similar time, and loaded up with dosh.

This part of the deal is out of my hands, so I'm hoping it's quick and painless. How the fuck do they change up that much money? There's no fucking way it's going into the bank, surely, and how much do they need to change to get the correct amount? They need 40 bags in Euros, and surely the rate will fluctuate, either coming up short or a bit higher. Fuck it, it's not my problem; the only way this will be my problem is if they only give me the 40 grand for the coke, and if that happens the job's off. I need expenses (exp)—end of story.

I've reeled in London fairly quickly, and there's not a great deal going on upstairs as my mind is a bit preoccupied. I've not yet considered my part of the deal yet; I know I'll have to figure out how to stash a load of money in the car, but until I see the way the money is bagged, it's hard to think of a discreet place to put it. Forty grand is still gonna be a lump to contend with, but I'll worry about that en route to Portsmouth, which is a relatively short journey from London. I wanna be on the ferry no later than 20:00 because that puts me in France at about 04:00 the following morning. This will give me all day to drive to the Pyrenees, which is a fucking trek-and-a-half. It's a good 10-hour drive and about 1,000km—a piece of piss. We used to drive those distances from Fally in Germany—going home to spunk a month's wages for a night on the piss in the UK. I was a classic weekend millionaire; no wonder I'm shit with money.

I'm approximately 20 minutes away so I decide to call Si and see how he's getting on. The phone rings a couple of times, then he asks, "Are you there, mate?". I reply, "About 15, 20 minutes out". He says, "Nice one brother, I'm here, waiting for you, see you in a bit", and he hangs up. Well, that's good news; he's there and all being well he'll get it sorted before I get to him. I have to admit that the satnav has impressed me—it was bang on with all the information, and so far hasn't dicked me around. I close in on my location which is a residential area. I keep an eye out for Si, which is pretty fucking pointless at this stage as I don't know what he's driving. I can almost guarantee he'll be in something half-decent. After all this is a business meeting; granted it is for drugs, but it's still a chance to flex with other firms. First impressions go a long way and do make a significant difference in these first-contact meetings. We're not handing over a score for half a bag. These are serious organisations, arranging for the exchange of bigger lumps of money and they'll no doubt be connected to the firms overseas.

Gotcha! He's out of his car, a Merc—I fucking knew it. He has a passenger with him, who I recognise as one of Si's mates. I don't recall his name, but as far as I know he's sound. Si's on the phone so I slowly drive past and park up a bit further down the road. I sit tight for now, observing in my wing mirrors, waiting patiently for Si to finish his call. He drops the phone down from his ear into a pocket and he looks in my direction—this is my cue. I get out and head towards him, smiling; this is like a bit of a role reversal and I'm suddenly feeling like Wedge must do when he sees me. It never dawned on me that Wedge was nervous when he saw me, but this is how I'm feeling.

We shake hands and surprisingly Si gives a man hug, which isn't what I was expecting. He says, "We're all good; they've given me another postcode, somewhere in town. It's a café where we can chill out and wait". I say, "Ok nice one, have you seen them yet?". Si responds, "Not yet, apparently they need to double-check the exchange rate first to get the correct amount back; it's a back door job so the standard rate doesn't apply". I look at him and take the opportunity to ask him about the expenses; I say, "Sounds good, how does it work with expenses? Cliff said it would be covered once the money changed". Si responds, "Yeah it's covered, I've been told that the usual rate with these guys is about 1.4 euros to pounds; I'm giving them 30 bags so we should get back at least 42 grand, the coke is 40 leaving you a couple to cover costs."

I'm thinking that's a fucking result, so I say, "Sounds good, is the price definitely fixed on the coke?". Si quickly replies, "It should be, but if anything changes I can Western Union over a few quid—it's not ideal but it's a backup plan." Feeling a bit relieved, I say "Cool, then I'm pretty much sorted, what time are we meeting them?". Si says, "Now—let's fuck off." We both head back to our cars; as I get in I see Si's mate run towards me. I drop the window and he leans in to give me the postcode of the next meeting place. I stick it into the satnav and head off.

It's round the corner, just a couple of minutes' drive. I'm hoping the parking is ok as London is usually a fucking nightmare. I've spotted the café; it looks good and not too busy. I suppose I need to have faith in these guys; it's their local area and they'll know what's best for meetings. It's just that London is so busy and chaotic, but this area looks fairly affluent. Nice cars and large sums of money are the norm. Forty large in euros might raise a few eyebrows though.

I find a suitable parking space, hoping it's free, but I never fucking know in London—it's like a different country. They've got red double yellow lines and I'm quite sure they're worse than yellow ones, so the whole thing confuses the shit out of me. I walk towards the café as Si and his mate approach the doorway. I can see Si has a rucksack in one hand and is on the phone as he goes in—more than likely trying to ID the contact that we're meeting. I join Si and we walk in to be greeted by two well-dressed lads; typical London boys in trousers, shirt and shoes—this makes me feel like a right scruffy fucker. I'm wearing a pair of trackie bottoms and a sweatshirt—as first impressions go that's me fucked.

We all shake hands and sit down. Almost immediately Si discreetly passes his rucksack to one of the lads, who then gets up and departs. It's started. We all start to look over the menu with an eye to grabbing some lunch; good timing as I'm starved. I forgot to eat on the way up here and the smell of the food reminds me that despite what's going on we should try to enjoy the odd moment here and there when the baton is in someone else's hands, because very soon it'll be my fucking problem, and it'll be a hell of a long time before I get to hand it over.

We all engage in conversation, but when I say "all", it's more Si and the lad that remain here as a form of security. He won't know this but I know that Si is already visualising the best way to fuck him up if he tries to have him over. Part of me is kind of hoping it does go wrong at this stage, but then again I don't fancy being pulled into one of Si's kidnappings. He's got his fucking mate here for that. I'm listening in and the general feeling I'm getting is that it's definitely a pissing competition, so I simply glaze over and my mind wanders off—can we just get the euros and be out of here? Thank fuck the food has arrived and quickly consumed, along with several drinks, yet we still wait. The guy who's sat with us is calm—he clearly knows that this is a potentially lengthy process.

He's not letting on what that process is though. They are clearly making on the rate somehow; maybe a backhanded commission, it doesn't matter as we're all here to make money—it's not a fucking charity. One, two, three hours pass and Si is clearly becoming slightly stressed. He looks at me and says, "Let's pop outside a sec". I get up and we head out. Si does look a bit preoccupied, so I ask, "Are you ok? Is it supposed to take this long?". Si responds, "Yeah, they said it might take a fair few hours, the problem I have is I need to get back by five". "Oh I see your dilemma—look, if you trust these guys, then I've got this if you need to shoot". Si looking slightly relieved then says, "Are you sure? I wanted to make sure it was all sweet before you headed off". I say, "It's not a problem mate, I'm gonna be doing a lot more so I'm happy to pick up the ball and take it from here". Si looks at me, holds out his hand, we shake and head back into the café.

We both look at the lad that's left behind, whose confidence and bravado faded ages ago. Si says, "Any news?"; the guy responds, "Yes he's on his way back, he'll be about half an hour." Si looks at him, in fact, he looks almost through him and says, "Ok I'm gonna get off"; looking at me he then says, "My mate will take it from here". The buck has been officially passed and I can feel the virtual weight on my shoulders. The last few hours haven't been too bad, but suddenly shit got real. Si gets up with his mate in tow. We all shake hands and they shoot off, leaving me and this guy, whose name I don't recall, left alone to chat.

The lad looks at me, saying "Have you done this before?". I respond, trying to sound confident, saying, "No, but I've been involved with a few things for a while". The guy looks at me and chuckles to himself; he is about to say something when his phone rings once, and he says, "We're up". He gets up and walks out. I follow him, assuming that's the plan. We are greeted by his mate and, feeling relieved, I see the rucksack in his hand. He says, "Sorry for the delay, they're funny as fuck about how the money comes. I had to go and arrange it all. If it arrives any other way they either won't accept it or worse still they might change the rate in their favour to compensate". I can relate to this; who wants to count out 30 bags if it's not presented neatly? "What did we get in the end?", I ask; he responds saying "I got you the agreed rate of one point four— you got 42 bags". He hands me the rucksack. I take it and it feels considerably lighter, in fact it feels fucking empty—I panic a bit and look inside.

Hang on a minute, where the fuck's the money? The two lads look at each other and smile; clearly they can see the look of concern in my eyes. If they only knew the amount of shit that I've been through, the last thing I need is another bill on my head. They say, "Mate, the euros are in 500s". Wait, 500s? What the fuck, I didn't realise they went that high. The guy who handed me the money says, "Have a look". I respond saying "Ok, hang fire, I'll do a quick count". I go back into the café and head for the toilets—fuck it, I'll use the disabled one. I go in, lock the door and sit down; I reach into the bag and grab the envelope that's rattling around at the bottom; it's not sealed so I open it and remove the contents. No fucking way! Purple notes and sure enough, "€500" written clearly on the front.

I count through them; the magic number is 84, which will give me 42 bags. I flick through and count the notes. I'm still in a state of disbelief. I count again and one more time—bang on. Feeling much better about the situation, I head out and see the lads standing there, waiting patiently. Fair play—that's the sign of a good firm, and how fucking stupid must I look!? I thank them and say goodbye, not knowing if I'll be doing any other business with them; I wouldn't mind as they are on it and definitely my kind of people. I get into the car and sling the bag on the back seat. I'll sort that out in a bit. I quickly call Si and let him know we're all good. From now on it's radio silence to everyone except Neil, who I need to call tomorrow at some point. Next stop Portsmouth.

Chapter 6

EUROPEAN ROAD TRIP

ortsmouth is about an hour away from London, give or
take a few minutes. The ball is now firmly in my court
so I need to start planning a few things. The first one is
where to stash the cash; my initial thought was the car boot
lining, but that's when I was expecting a larger package in
smaller denominations. Now though, this one will go almost
anywhere. I reach behind to see if the back of the driver's seat
has a gap. It doesn't! That's what I liked about my Cossy. The
Recaro seats were designed in a way that you could easily stuff
things into the lumber support, so it was worth a shot. Am I
overthinking this? Surely I can just pop the envelope in my bag,
I mean if they're gonna search, they're gonna search. I have to
consider two things; I need to protect the money at all costs,
but in the eventuality of getting caught I have to consider
damage limitation. I need to put the money somewhere in the
car so that it's well hidden, but at the same time if it ends up
being found I can deny any knowledge of its existence.

This can't be done whilst driving. The port is only a few
miles away, so I keep an eye out for somewhere to pull over,
thinking that a garage would be good so I can fuel up prior to
departing. Closing in on the port I see a fuel station—perfect!
I pull onto the forecourt and up next to a pump. I fill the car up,
but it didn't need too much, just over £20. I pop into the shop,

grabbing a few snacks and a drink for the other side. I pay the cashier and head back to the car, then I pull away from the well-lit area of the fuel pumps and park along the side which is a tad more discreet. The boot lining is now sounding favourable so I pop the boot and head to the back of the car. I lift the lid and have a look inside; my slug and bags look a bit lonely, but the wheel arch cover looks good and has PVC carpet-type material around it, so there should be some cavities in there. I stick my head in and have a look to see if it has an edge, which it does. I pull it away from the top, and surprisingly it pops off relatively easily, revealing a decent-sized gap where the metal arch sits—perfect! I hastily open the back door of the car and grab the rucksack, then more importantly the envelope from the inside. I have a quick look around and being mindful of the time, I transfer the envelope from the back of the car and into a cavity next to the wheel arch. I then carefully replace the trim, trying my best to make it look like it hadn't been disturbed. Again looking around, I head back to the comfort of the driver's seat and proceed to Portsmouth.

That's the money stashed. The next thing I need to consider is my reason for going abroad. Skiing is the obvious one, but on my own, that's fucking weird. I've always liked to use my time served in the army to my advantage. The good old M.O.D. 90 got me out of so much shit while I was serving, but unfortunately my get-out-of-jail-free card was handed in to Bovvy years ago. This is why I bring my doss bag; it's not quite a forces ID but it's enough to give an indication. So the story will be that my skiing trip is planned to meet up with some old army pals that are already there. That I'm just joining them for a couple of days skiing and a night on the piss. Not only plausible but a fucking good idea.

I'm banking on the 20:00 ferry not being full; it's February so I'd like to think not. In the past I've always managed to rock up at the port's travel office and buy a ticket for the next available ferry. This purchase will be one of the few made on my debit card; I purposely do this to leave a digital trail, not only for my defence if it goes tits up, but also for my wife, as she will clearly see that I am going abroad when I said I was. With any luck this will successfully put her off the scent that I'll be smuggling coke over the channel, which when I think of how close I am to this, rattles my nerves somewhat. But right now I need to get the money out of the country. One stage at a time—plan ahead yes, but focus on the moment.

I close in on the port; trucks are everywhere but not that many cars. I reflect on my decision to travel from here rather than Dover. I like a longer crossing because it reminds me of my childhood; we used to holiday in France a lot and we always did a long crossing. I guess it'll take my mind off of the gravity of what's really happening. The journey there is a simple road trip, but the journey back, that's a whole new thing. Two boxes of pure worth €40k, coming in at a value of nearly double that over here. The more I think of it the more I worry about the return journey, and more to the point about the channel crossing.

The 20:00 ferry from Portsmouth to Le Havre is sorted— thank fuck for that. If that was full I'd have had to drive to Dover and get the short crossing, which I just don't fancy, and the beauty of this crossing is, you can get a cabin. I drive away from the booking office and follow the signs for the correct boat, blindly following the vehicle in front. My nerves are elevated and I don't know why. I suppose I was expecting this bit in the morning. I'm in a queue of about five car lengths from the passport office and a man in a high-vis jacket is walking along the side of the cars, leaning in and talking to the drivers of each one.

I calm myself as he approaches, drop my window and say, "Good evening"; he replies in English "Good evening sir, do you have your passport and tickets ready?". I respond by showing him and saying, "Yes all sorted"; he quickly looks over them and says, "Ok thank you sir, if you can proceed to the passport security check and through the customs zone which is indicated by the signs on the lane you're in". I smile and say, "Thank you", then secretly shitting myself, I raise the window and drive to the passport booth, where I can see two French customs officers sitting and manning the two-sided booth.

Calm is the key; I have to convince myself all is good— I'm going skiing with the lads. In the split seconds between arriving at the booth and handing over my passport, I mentally convince myself I'm going skiing, by visualising myself on the slopes. In a strong French accent the customs officer says, "Good evening sir". Fuck it, I respond saying, "Bonsoir monsieur"; he smiles and takes my passport, looks at me and then at my passport, then says, "What is the purpose of your visit?". I look at him, put on my finest bullshit and say, "I'm skiing for a few days"; he responds by saying, "Where are you looking to ski?". Fucking hell mate, grilling me, so I respond by saying, "Snow depending, I'm aiming for Andorra". He then says, "Oh you should be fine, there is always plenty of snow there". I smile and say, "Oh thank you, I was concerned because it's my first time skiing there". He hands me my passport and says, "Goodbye and enjoy your holiday"; I hit him with a bit more French and say, "Merci monsieur, au revoir". Fucking nailed that, but my high is very short-lived as my next hurdle is customs. I cautiously approach, looking for some kind of structure designed for searching people and vehicles. Nothing—there's no fucker here, but I do see some more high-vis jackets that are clearly signposting the vehicles into lanes.

Feeling relatively calm and relaxed, I pull up into a lane and switch the car off. I can see the boat slowly docking in front of me. Looking around, I again wonder how many of these vehicles are loaded up with money or if I am the only one. I get out and stretch my legs, using this as an opportunity to scan the area. A few minutes pass and the ferry is docked; the vehicles begin to unload with a mixture of cars and lorries. My mind is still wondering how many of those are loaded up with drugs and illegals. There's been a substantial influx of illegals coming in since the Afghan war; this has got to be a good thing as it's keeping customs busy looking for people and not drugs.

I get back into my car as the waiting vehicles are given the signal to move, starting up along with most of the others. You always get some weapon that decides to go and take a shit just before they load us up, blocking the lanes and stressing the ones stuck behind. Fortunately this isn't the case, or at least not in my lane, so I begin to move forward, slowly gaining speed as I approach the ramp that leads onto the ferry. I slowly move onto the back of the boat—I'm officially committed, there's no going back now. I'm directed towards the front of the boat where I pull up behind another car, switch off the engine, apply the handbrake and leave it in gear. Old habits—I've done this crossing so many times, and although this crossing is still in the channel, it is winter and could still give us a bumpy ride; handbrakes can and do fail.

Leaving the car and the money on the car deck, I head off upstairs and have a quick recce, but all I really want to do is get my head down. Giving a sense of nostalgia I walk around the various decks, taking everything in, but it's all tainted; I can't enjoy the experience, not like this. I head for my cabin on the lower decks; they're relatively easy to find, considering they're located in a maze of well signposted corridors. I pop the key in the door, hoping that I'm not sharing with anyone; not sure why I'd think this but it's a two-man cabin and I'd assume space is a premium. I pop the door open and thankfully I'm not faced with a hairy-arsed truck driver. I walk into the cabin which is fucking tiny, but I've slept in smaller—try the gunner's seat on a Challenger tank. It's ok until your commander, whose legs double up as your backrest, starts messing with his rancid smelly cock that's not seen soap in weeks. Either way, I'm sleeping regardless.

I sleep very lightly, but it suffices. I can feel the foundation of the ferry shudder as it reverse thrusts and manoeuvres towards the dock. I can hear the ferry tannoy sounding various alarms and notices to proceed to your vehicles; feeling slightly panicked I quickly wash and get ready. It's almost as if yesterday was a dream and I've woken up to the reality of my situation; where the fuck did I go wrong? How did my life end up like this? Feeling like I'm on autopilot I head back to my car, hoping it hasn't been broken into; it won't have, but it's where my train of thought is. Constantly waiting for the next disaster, the next fucking tragedy. The cars are good and I get in as the ferry drops the doors of the bow. Vehicles start up all around me, and I join them.

One by one the cars in front of me unload. It's barely 04:00, but I'm wide awake and eager to get on my way. Once I'm committed, all senses of reservation and doubt are gone; it doesn't mean I have to like what I'm doing, it simply means I'm doing it. I've successfully smuggled the dosh onto mainland Europe. I casually drive off the boat and onto terra firma; "Welcome to France" I say to myself, although I was technically in France once I'd had my passport checked back in Portsmouth. I leisurely drive out of the port, remembering to drive on the other side of the road; the side of the road I learnt to drive on when based in Germany. I'm as comfortable on the right as I am on the left. I tap my next destination into the satnav; Andorra la Vella—yep just over 1,000 km. I've got a tank full of fuel and €42k— here we fucking go.

Leaving Le Havre behind me I pick up one of the main roads and get onto what is the French equivalent of a motorway; two lanes with a max speed of 130kph, that's about 80mph. It's pointless calling Neil yet, it's way too early and I don't fancy upsetting the Spanish connection by calling at 04:30. I'll cover some ground and maybe call him once I get past Paris; I'm not going through Paris, just around it—fuck that London was bad enough yesterday. I stick on a CD and get stuck into my journey.

Something I hadn't accounted for was the toll roads, which only accept coins, smaller notes or cards. My card has limited funds available as I've generally lived off of the cash earnt from you-know-what. There is money in there from my benefits, but just enough to cover the costs of the hotel and lift pass that I'm gonna get for my cover story. I'll need to get some change in a garage. I'll dig into one of these 500s and sort it out in a few hours. I'm happy to pay for a few toll fees on my card for now, so when I refuel in a few hours, I'll kill two birds with one stone.

Driving south I clear Paris in just over three hours; as I pass Orleans my fuel is looking good with about half a tank left and it's still not even 08:00. I'm still conscious of when to call Neil; I don't wanna leave it too late, but hang on a minute, France is an hour ahead of us and I'm going from the clock on the car, so it's nearly fucking 09:00 hours! I feel like I've lost an hour and a hint of panic sets in as I mentally dial in the new time. Fuck it I'm calling Neil, but is that his name or what? I don't know if he's Spanish, English or fucking Chinese. The phone rings, is picked up and Neil says, "What's going on la?". For fuck's sake, it's a fucking Scouser! I say, "I'm all good mate, on track for tomorrow", Neil responds, "Which way you going, la?". Feeling a bit fucking concerned, I explain to him my route through Andorra, but I'll be fucked if I'm telling him where I'm staying. I've heard a lot about Scousers, so the chances are he'll be plotted up waiting to rob me if the rumours are true. Neil then goes on to say, "If you're going through Andorra can you grab me a sleeve of ciggies? Number One please, la". Cheeky fucker! However, taking into consideration a future working relationship I say, "Yeah no problem". I then ask him if he has a meeting place arranged to which he answers, "Yeah la, head for Fuengirola; when you get closer I'll meet you by the zoo". I say, "Cool no problem. I'll call you tomorrow when I'm closer". He finishes off by saying, "Yeah la, don't forget my ciggies", and hangs up.

Fuengirola? Where the fucks is that? I was told by Cliff and presumably Si, that the meeting place was Barcelona. Either way my plan is set, so I continue on my way towards the Pyrenees mountains and Andorra la Vella. I've been driving for four hours straight and the kilometres are flying by, but I'll have to stop and fuel up soon, as I'm down to a quarter of a tank and I could do with a toilet stop as well as something to eat. Next *Aires* is about seven k's away—that'll do nicely. The thought of a coffee and a croissant sounds quite appealing, and I mean a proper fucking croissant—not these shitty UK imitations you get in Tesco.

I pull into the *Aires* and next to a fuel pump; I'm gonna brim it now and then once again in Andorra cos I don't want to be fucking about filling up in Spain. Bollocks, I need to get the fucking money out of the boot; luckily there are no visible cameras so I pop the boot lid, reach in and carefully remove the boot lining that covers the wheel arch and money. There it is, that's the first time I've seen it since landing in France, and I'm somewhat relieved that it's still there. I grab the envelope, pull a note out of it, and look over my shoulder, checking for any onlookers. I once again place the money back into the cavity next to the wheel arch. I shut the boot and get into the car, pulling forward and parking in a space outside of the shop.

I enter the shop, thinking about the croissant and coffee; I head over to the machine and see it's coins only. I can't see it accepting a note of this size, so I opt to go pay for the fuel first.

I walk up to the cashier and say "Number trois, merci". I always thought my French was good until I speak it in France to a French person. I go to hand her the note and she looks at me, muttering something under her breath whilst shaking her head. I say, "Ça va madame?"; she looks as if I've just shot her fucking dog and says in English, "Do you have another note? This is too much". Fuck I didn't even consider this; a nifty is enough to raise the alarms back in the UK and this is more than 10 times as big, so no wonder she's pissed off. I'm gonna clean her till out. I attempt to look sorry and say, "Je suis désolé", which I'm pretty sure means "I'm sorry".

She half smiles, takes the note from me, rings it in and hands me my change. A €200 note, a €100 note, some normal-sized notes and a bit of shrapnel. At last, some money I can spend! I head over to the coffee vendors and grab an espresso— only €1 so that's a bargain. Croissant time; I pop over to the patisserie and grab a couple of croissants and a pain au chocolat. I haven't got the heart to go back to the same woman, so I aim for another cashier, with the intention of hitting her with a €100 note.

That went remarkably well and my French was spot on, or at least I think it was. Time to head for my overnight stop in Andorra, which I'm looking forward to. I'm about halfway so this part of the journey should be quite pleasant; I've got oodles of time so no need to rush. I've made successful contact with Neil, and arranged to see him in Fuengirola. This plan is slowly coming together, but I'm still not thinking about the return journey—I don't want to.

The Pyrenees mountains are a beautiful sight as they loom up in the distance, but I've had a few stops so my timings have slipped. This isn't a problem, it just means I'm losing the light and I would have liked to see the mountains as I drove towards them. But it's fucking dark and I can't, so I just stick the stereo on and blast out a bit of dance music to liven things up a bit. My fuel will probably be ok until I hit Andorra la Vella, but I'm now onto smaller, less economical roads, so filling up may be a good idea. I'm not going out of my way, it's a case of "if I see a garage I'll stop".

Fortunately a garage appears in my sights, where I stop, fuel up and successfully offload a €200 note. The final leg now, heading into the Pyrenees mountains and ultimately Andorra la Vella; this journey will take a good few hours, if it's anything like the Bavarian mountains in Germany. Much more fun to drive, though. It's dark and the roads are slow and winding. I'm often confronted with larger vehicles like coaches coming the opposite way, taking a wide berth to clear the corner. It's winter and the ski season is in full flow, so there must be a good drop of snow up there. As my altitude increases the temperature drops, then patches of snow begin to appear. The patches of snow increase in size as the roads get even more winding; still I have plenty of time so I'm simply enjoying the drive. This would have been so much more fun if I had my P1 Scoob; probably not the most discreet car to use for smuggling though.

I can see the glow of my destination getting closer; Andorra la Vella is like an oasis in the middle of the mountains—a tax-free haven for big spenders. My final approach comes with a sense of relief; the time is fast approaching 19:00 hours, and I need a good meal and a kip. It's like every stage I go through on this job my nerves increase. I keep telling myself that it's just another deal and to treat it the same way, but I just feel as if I'm out of my depth.

There's no shortage of hotels—in fact it seems like that's all there is. I drive around a bit and locate a hotel that is near the ski resort—not hard as this whole place is one big resort. After a few minutes of driving around, I find one that seems ok; I'm not looking for an expensive one, all I need is a bed and a shower. This one will do; I park up in what I assume is the hotel car park, get my bag out of the boot and my road atlas off of the passenger seat to look over tomorrow's journey, and then head in to see if they have any rooms for the night. This is where I could come unstuck; I'm aiming to pop over the border and be back within the day. I'm only gonna book for one night, then when I get back tomorrow I'll book for another night, leaving on Thursday morning and giving me the whole day to drive back up to the ferry port. I'm unsure if I should use the same port or not, but that's not yet my concern, so I'll see how I feel on my way back.

I check in using my card; the price is fairly reasonable but doesn't include breakfast. I head up to my room and throw my bag onto the bed, which is small but a definite upgrade after last night's cabin. All I want to do is eat and get my head down. Showered and feeling fresh, I call for room service; there's a limited menu and out of everything the pizza is looking favourable. The food is a while so I take the opportunity to look on the map and see how close Fuengirola is to Barcelona, and by scanning through the index I locate it, the page and the grid reference. Are you fucking kidding me? It's in the Costa del Sol, that's over 1,000 km away—a 10-hour drive. Barcelona is three hours; this has fucked my whole plan up. I'm calling Cliff.

I ring his burner but it's off, for fuck's sake. Fuck it I'm calling his contract and I don't give a fuck what he says. If he had known about this before I left, I would have asked for more money. I grab my clean phone out of my bag, switch it on and wait a few seconds. A few beeps come in and it's from the missus; she's just checking in. I respond and reassure her everything is ok and I'll call her when the job's completed, which by the looks of it will take longer than planned. I can't believe Cliff would do this; oh hang on a minute, it's Cliff, this is what he does. I call his clean phone from mine, and he answers sounding a bit concerned, "What's up? I thought I asked you not to call". I respond, "Well I thought I was going to fucking Barcelona"; he responds saying, "What do you mean?". Trying to remain calm I say, "Come on mate, the guy I'm meeting has asked me to meet him down south. It's not what we planned". Cliff then changes his tone and says, "Well, you're a fucking commodity so just do it". This sends me into a fucking rage, "A commodity, is that how you see me you piece of shit, why don't you find another commodity to do this then. Go fuck yourself", and I hang up.

I'm fucking fuming. If Si wasn't involved in this deal then I'd be seriously considering turning around and going home. My phone rings, it's Cliff. I answer and say, "What?", he says "Look I didn't mean to say that"; is this an apology from Cliff? I respond by saying "I don't care, you said it so you meant it, but I'm not the sort of person to back out of an arrangement. However, if the terms change then so should the payment. I want more money". The line goes quiet for a bit; Cliff is clearly not happy with the situation. I couldn't give a rat's cock— he's throwing me into the fucking meat grinder here, so it needs to be worth my while. Cliff says, "Ok, I'll chuck another bag on top, is that ok?". I reluctantly agree and say, "It'll have to do but I'm not happy with this. You knew I was going down there, you just decided to withhold that information. My whole cover plan was built around what you told me; it's now fucked. There's no way I can do that journey in one day". Cliff responds saying, "I suppose so". Yeah just as I thought—he doesn't give a fuck. I say goodbye and switch my phone off; just in time as there's a knock on the door with my pizza.

I set my alarm for 06:00; faced with another day's driving I need to get an early start, plus I have to top up the fuel and get Neil his fags. I'm aiming to break into another €500 note as well, so I hope Andorra will be slightly more accommodating. I shut my eyes and think about tomorrow's drive. I've only ever been to Spain a couple of times and that was skiing in the Sierra Nevada mountains. Looking at the map I see I go past there, but inland and not coastal, which could be a plausible reason for being down there. As I slowly drift off to sleep I have a series of thoughts flashing through my mind. Feeling anxious, but somewhat relieved that my happy pills are working enough to take the edge off of the stress. Two and a half grand for this job, plus the expenses money; seems like a good wage, but I'm pretty sure I could earn more from my own thing, which incidentally is now fucked, because there's no way I'm gonna get back for Friday as planned. I finally fall asleep, thinking of my family and how they'd feel if they knew what I was really doing.

I wake seconds before my alarm goes off, shutting it down before it gets a chance to annoy me. So today is the day; another fuck off drive, and part of me is looking forward to it. I'm half curious about the climate in Spain at this time of year; will I notice a difference as I drop down from the Pyrenees and into Spain? All of this is irrelevant at the moment, as I've still got to negotiate Andorra's customs, which I'm led to believe are clued up due to the amount of people buying tax-free goods.

As far as my head goes I'm still on autopilot, hyper-vigilant and constantly looking out for danger. I leave the hotel and head for the car to drop off my kit. It's still dark, not yet 07:00 and if my original plan was still in play this would have presented a problem for me, as I would still need to purchase a ski lift pass and as far as I can tell they don't open for another hour. Fortunately, or unfortunately depending on your point of view, this no longer matters as I'm now heading to the Costa del Sol, for at least a day. I don't know whether it's worth hanging on for a bit to get the pass anyway. Fuck it I'm gonna sit tight; the shops aren't open yet and I have to grab those ciggies. I'll go grab breakfast and kill time for an hour.

I spend the next hour watching the sunlight slowly illuminate the slopes; man I wish I was skiing, there's a fair bit of snow and I bet it's lovely up top, but that's not the kind of powder I'm here for. I've eaten some kind of breakfast; very continental but does the job. I head on over to the ski lift pass shop, and thankfully it's open. I have a look at the tariff, and it would appear to be relatively straightforward, so I opt for the cheapest day pass available. Thirty-eight euros for the day; fairly restricted on where I can go, but seeing as I'm not even donning a pair of skis, it'll fucking do.

I see a shop where I can grab Neil his fucking fags, so I head over and make the purchase using one of the €500 notes. Right, so that's the admin done; now best to top the car up and head south. I sling the ciggies on the back seat, and quickly check if the money is stowed properly. All good—I then find a petrol station as I head out of the resort, so I fill up and proceed south and towards Spain. I know Andorra is small so the border should be relatively close. There it is, much closer than I thought with no queue and apparently no staff; there's just a little cabin and a barrier that's raised.

I cautiously drive up to the cabin and look around as I approach what must be the physical border between the two countries but I can't see anyone, so I crack on through. That's another border nailed, meaning I'm technically halfway, and so far no dramas. My burner is on and it's nice and quiet so I guess I'll do my best to enjoy the drive south. I've entered my destination into the satnav and sure enough it's just shy of 1,100km, but what a cracking route all the way down the Mediterranean coast! I'm gonna try and switch off and enjoy this.

The drive out of the mountains and towards the Mediterranean coast was all good, with no dramas and I can already feel a definite increase in temperature, not summertime heat but UK spring-like warmth. I've even got the windows down, taking in the fresh air; I'll need that as the drive goes on. A couple of hours pass and I'm getting close to the originally proposed meeting place of Barcelona, but I now think this was never the case. I continue south, seeing signs for the likes of Valencia and Benidorm.

The kilometres are flying by; a few hours pass and I'm passing Valencia, which signals me for a fuel stop and a spot of lunch. When in Rome and all that, I go for a big fuck off plate of paella, which I eat in true squaddie fashion, meaning fucking quickly. I head back out to the car and continue on my way. Looking at my satnav ETA and dialling in any stops, I'm attempting to figure out an accurate time that I'll land at Fuengirola. I'm definitely gonna stop every couple of hours for about half an hour, which puts me in a time frame to arrive quite late, between 22:00 and 23:00. I don't fancy doing a deal at that time; I think the best thing is to let Neil know when I'm due and see what he's thinking.

I call Neil, who picks up and says, "Morning la, how was the skiing?". I reply, "Oh it was lovely mate, I've got your ciggies"; Neil responds by saying, "Cheers la, I'll get you squared away when I see you". I thought that would be nice but didn't want to come across as a tight git and besides it's not my money, so I say, "You're all good mate, these are on me". I go on to explain my rough timings, trying to ascertain if we are doing anything tonight. Neil then says, "It's ok la, when you get here, I'll get you into a hotel and we can chat about things tomorrow". Now feeling a definite sense of relief, I say, "Nice one bud, I'll call as I get closer".

The odd thing about this kind of deal is when the inevitable is delayed for whatever reason, it feels like your life has just been extended a bit. It's the sort of feeling you get if you are given a sudden day off of work. The time is ticking away and as it approaches 16:00 I'm passing the iconic sight of Benidorm—high rises next to the sea. I've seen pictures of it and it's been on TV but it really is a sight when driving past; wouldn't go there mind you, fuck that.

The hours and the kilometres are whiling away and I'm surprisingly relaxed. I've fuelled up again; I should have got a fucking diesel but the petrolhead in me can't bring myself to do it. The satnav is telling me my ETA is 22:16 and I've still got over two hours to go. It's dark and the temperature has dropped and I can't see them but I'm sure I'm passing the Sierra Nevada mountains. I'm still blasting out the tunes, with the heater on full blast and all the windows down to keep me awake. To be fair I'm quite enjoying the moment, thinking would I rather be stuck in a shitty nine-to-five? As it stands right now, not a chance, but it has been a long day and the thought of a nice hotel in the Costa del Sol sounds very appealing.

Yes! Signs for Fuengirola, I'm just under an hour away. I call Neil and update him on my ETA, he says to head for the zoo as planned and to call him when I'm five minutes out. This has been a mammoth couple of days; 2,000km in 48 hours, fuck me that's going some. As I approach my destination I'm trying to visualise what Neil will look like; but I can't, so it's pointless trying. Five minutes out and I call him; he answers and informs me that he's standing on the corner by the zoo. I continue on my way, and I'm relieved to see two things; the first is the satnav saying, "You have arrived at your destination" and the second one is a big, tall fucker in a long, dark coat standing by the corner of the zoo—that has to be him.

I slowly drive up to the zoo and just pass the guy in the coat, still not totally sure if it's him, when I hear "Yes la, welcome to Fuengirola" in a strong scouse accent—that's him. I get out and walk up to him, we shake hands and have a brief chat, then he says, "If you follow me I'll take you to your hotel", getting into a small Spanish-plated car and driving off with me in tow. Several minutes pass and we're on the coast; it's hard to make everything out as it's dark but it looks like it could be the sort of place that would be busy in the season. He pulls up outside a large, plush hotel and gestures for me to park up then meet him inside.

I find a space opposite the hotel and park the car in a bay facing the Med. I grab my bags and his ciggies and head into the hotel lobby. It's a four-star place; fuck I can't afford this! I look at him and was about to ask if there is anywhere cheaper, when he says, "Ok la, I've booked you in, this is on me as you've had a long drive, get some rest, and in the morning once you've had your breakfast, give me a shout and we'll have a chat about the plans". I thank him for his generosity and give him the ciggies; he smiles, thanks me and heads out of the hotel. I head up to my room; feeling shattered I hit the sack and wonder what tomorrow will bring.

Chapter 7

HURRY UP AND WAIT

Y ou'd have thought sleeping in a relatively luxurious hotel would have been a pleasant experience, and it would have been had I not woken up with the realisation that today is "the day". My little busman's holiday will soon be ending abruptly. Consequently I awoke not feeling well rested but stressed to fuck. Fortunately my room has a sea view, giving me a decent look at the Med. I peer out of the window and look up and down the coast, clocking my car outside in the process. Everything looks very calm and quiet, with a few people floating around as well as some dog walkers, but other than that it's fairly dead.

I wander downstairs to get some scran; I'm on the third floor and can't be arsed to take the lift. I'm occupying my mind by trying to enjoy the feeling of being in a high-end hotel; I'm busy taking everything in and looking forward to the breakfast. If the rooms are anything to go by then it should be magnificent. I walk into the restaurant and give the member of staff my name and room number, they usher me to a seat and almost immediately bring over a pot of coffee. I take a moment and pour a coffee, adding a touch of milk; I know full well what I'm doing, I'm treating this like my last meal before I collect the coke. Once I'm loaded up, I go straight into patrol mode for two days while I return to the UK.

I quietly sip on my coffee which is really good, not like the shit we get in the UK. Looking around I get up and head for the breakfast bar; naturally it's a continental breakfast, but I did spot some scrambled eggs and what look like sausages. I load my plate up with food and head back to my seat, where I make an attempt to not eat like a squaddie, but no matter how hard I try I always end up eating like a fucking pig. The food is ok but my head is elsewhere; I suppose now's the time to start thinking about how to store the drugs in the car. With this in mind, I finish off the food and coffee then quickly head back up to my room to retrieve the car keys.

It's approaching 08:30 and I take the opportunity to text Neil. "Morning mate" I write, and leaving that for him to respond to, I head on down to the car. As I exit the hotel I instantly feel that the weather is definitely milder down here. I should have brought some shorts or maybe even my swimming trunks, but I doubt I'll have time for that even if I did. I walk towards the car and have a good look around and under it, looking for a recess or appropriate location to store the coke, but much to my dismay it's not looking particularly good. There's nowhere underneath where I can stash it, so maybe in the engine bay or inside the wheel arches. Fuck all—I'm fucking shafted.

This is a major issue for me because it now means the drugs will have to be in the car— more specifically the boot. I wonder if the cavity where the money is stashed will do; maybe a key on each side. I pop the boot and have a proper look, taking the opportunity to put the money in my pocket. I don't fancy leaving it in the boot anymore; you never know who's operating in the area and although Neil seems to be ok, I don't know if this is a set up by Cliff to get me robbed and hit me with another bill. I'm pretty sure he knows that if that was the case I'd likely have to put one in him.

My phone rings and it's Neil; I pick up and hear him say, "Morning la, how's the hotel?". I reply, "Yeah it's nice mate, better than the previous two nights". He then says, "I'll be there in a few minutes and I'll see you outside as I need to check your motor out". He hangs up, leaving me wondering what's going on. I walk over to the edge of the beach and wonder how I might be feeling if I wasn't under this enormous stress; I guess it's hard to say as it's all I've known for the last 10 years or so.

As I'm taking in the sea air I sense the arrival of a car; I look round to see Neil—he's a big old chap, but funnily enough he's driving a small car, a little FIAT—it's fucking tiny. He gets out and walks over to me, again we shake hands and he says, "Right let's have a look over the car". He walks around, alternating his attention by looking at the car and then me. I don't know him that well but he looks a bit concerned; he says, "Is this your car?" I answer, "No mate it's a renter", again his face shows concern. He looks at me and says, "Mate it's your profile, you're ticking all the wrong boxes". He then goes on to list all the wrong boxes that include how I look, duration of stay in Europe, rental car and a few other minor details. He stands at the back of the car and says, "Pop the boot la"; I lean into the car and pull the lever, the boot pops and I hear him chuckle. I walk to the back of the car and see him looking at my slug; he says, "Who did you serve with?". I smile and say, "Third and Second Tank Reg". Neil smiles and says, "I'm ex-infantry".

No fucking way, he's another squaddie! As if by magic the whole dynamic of our relationship changes for the better. He says, "Come on, let's go for a walk and talk". We head off along the seafront; Neil then says "Look la, if you load up with coke, it's highly likely you'll get a tug at either customs, the toll roads or one of the borders. What did you have planned?". I take some time to go over my proposed plan, which prompted Neil to ask, "Why are you doing this, la?". I breathe in and sigh, saying, "I've got no choice bud". I then spend the next few minutes filling him in with what happened with Alfie last year. Neil then says, "Look, the coke's not here yet, I'm waiting on a call for a load". He looks at me and sincerely says, "I'm gonna do you a favour. I'll put yours in with ours and take it over the channel for you, no charge". I look at him with a sense of relief and disbelief and say, "Are you sure, that's fucking spot on, how can I make it up to you?".

Neil looks at me and says, "Well, Trev and I have been looking for a third man to help us out over here, are you up for it?". Well, I wasn't expecting this, but I think it would be best to let him know a bit more about me, so I say, "I'm interested for sure, but can we catch up later and have a chat, let me know more about my role and maybe I can tell you a bit more about me, so you know who I am and what I'm all about". Neil agrees and says, "Sound la, I'll grab you at 19:00 and we'll go get some food and go to a club. Oh and don't worry about the hotel, I'll cover you for another night. See you later!". He heads back to his car, squeezes himself into the driver's seat, pulls away and heads off along the coastal road.

Should I be skeptical? I now have to weigh a few things up; should I trust a scouser with two keys of coke that doesn't belong to me? Ordinarily not a fucking chance, wouldn't trust anyone, but he's served so that tells me I can certainly trust that element of him over the scouse bit all day long. The next dilemma, do I tell Cliff and Si that I'm no longer bringing it over the channel? Cliff will most likely try and drop my price if I do, but until I know the full story I'm saying fuck all. Once again my life has been extended. So I'll simply chill the fuck out and enjoy the day.

I've come to realise that during the winter months down here in the lovely Costa del Sol, there's absolutely fuck all to do. There are plenty of shops but I'm not in a position to enjoy that, nor do I wanna be floating around unnecessarily getting picked up on any CCTV systems, so I spend the majority of the day chilling out in the hotel room with the occasional walk out to take in the fresh sea air. Even though Neil has offered to take the coke over for me, I'm still confronted with the dilemma of whether to take him up on it. I think a bonding session with him this evening will help to influence my decision one way or another. The highlight of my day is calling Cliff and informing him that there's been a delay and I've been told to sit tight. He isn't happy, hence it being the highlight, but there's nothing he can do. He asks if the money is ok, to which I say "Of course". I do say that the expenses will be running low, as I need to eat and fuel the car for a much longer journey, which he appears to just shrug off.

It's fast approaching 19:00 and I'm ready for the off. Neil's first assessment will be his timekeeping; if he's served he'll be waiting for me at 18:55, so I head down to the hotel lobby at 18:50. As I exit the lift I'm greeted with the sight of Neil already plotted up in the corner; he's occupying the exact same vantage point that I'd have selected. Scouse or not he's passed with flying colours; this guy has definitely served. He gets up, we head out of the hotel and both of us get into his tiny fucking car.

We spend the night bonding, talking about where and when we served; turns out we were both over in Germany at the same time, which prompted a shitload of NAAFI-related war stories. Turns out he even got into drugs in the same way that I did. So many parallels, it's mental; the thing that got me even more was when he explained that his mate Trev is also ex-forces— he was a Para which is great stuff, as these guys are class. On the face of it this is more or less a mercenary set-up—just dealing drugs and not killing fuckers. Part of me gets excited at the prospect of working with like-minded people. I've spent all these years working with civvies to be let down time and time again, and finally I've come across Neil, another ex-squaddie with a similar outlook as mine. I've yet to meet Trev but from the sounds of it, he's the real deal.

The majority of the night is spent in a Thai restaurant, and after several courses of really good food, Neil convinces me to go to a club. The Spanish clubs aren't the same as UK clubs; they're more like brothels that would be found in Amsterdam or the Reeperbahn in Hamburg. Great atmosphere but not my cup of tea. I spend an hour or so taking it all in, and Neil is definitely taking it all in too, as he's got a couple of girls hanging off of him—he must be a regular here. I'm curious about his lifestyle because we spoke about family and connections. He has an ex with kids and his girlfriend over here is Colombian; I'm presuming that she could be the connection. He's clearly not giving a fuck about any of that though, and when he looks at me and says he'll be back in a bit, I use this as the opportunity to make my excuses and leave. I thank him for the evening and we agree to catch up tomorrow for an English breakfast. I walk out leaving him to his own devices. I have to admit, I do feel slightly envious of his ability to switch off everything and enjoy the pleasures of what life has to offer. Maybe one day my debt will be repaid and I can start to live again.

I sleep well, and despite a slight hangover, I feel pretty good, more to the point I'm confident that I can trust Neil with the gear. However, I'll have breakfast with him first and find out what's going on. I'm pretty sure I can't plot up here forever; I don't mind if I do but at €200 a night, I'm pretty sure Neil's funds will expire sooner or later. I purposely dodge the hotel breakfast, as I'm keen to sit down with Neil and have a proper cook-up. I'm banking on ironing out the details of the deal at the same time, as we didn't really go into any details last night. Even though I trust him, I'm not handing over the money, not until I see the coke.

We've arranged to meet at about 10:00, so I've got about half an hour to kill. A steady walk along the seafront will do for now; it's still relatively warm and no matter how I dress it up this all feels quite surreal. I can't seem to get my head into the right frame; I have so many mixed emotions about what I'm doing out here, but I feel oddly at home and for a long time, part of something special. Looking at the time, I head back to the hotel and as I close in, I see Neil's motor parked up next to mine. He's clocked me; he gets out and comes forward followed by another guy, a bit older and not as big; I have to assume it's Trev.

Approaching each other, Neil immediately introduces us saying, "This is Trev". Trev and I shake hands. Trev, still holding a firm grip on my hand, says, "Tanky eh", I smile and reply, "Para, been eating any crayons recently?". Neil laughs and says to Trev, "Satisfied?"; Trev grins and says, "Yeah". Clearly Trev had his doubts about me and I like the fact he felt the need to double check if I was the real deal or not—I fucking would. Neil says, "Let's walk to the café, it's only down the road on the seafront". So the three of us head off for breakfast.

During the short walk, we take the piss out of each other, each of us claiming regimental superiority over the others; this is bonding, squaddie style. All this aside I'm still itching to know what's going on, so I say, "Any updates on the job yet? I'm not too fussed, I just need to keep the lads back home informed". Neil says, "Well, my usual contact is waiting to get a load in for me, which is already confirmed and the deal is done; the deal for yours is being done separately as your guys are looking for a different quality". I look at him and Trev and say, "Ok, sounds good, do we have a confirmation on price? The lads have only given me a set amount with no room for movement". Neil says, "Yeah the price won't be any more than 20 on each, what could happen though is if I go through the person I'm thinking of there will be a commission on top of €500 on each one". Shit, that's gonna wipe me out! I say, "Ok mate, if that's what we get then so be it, my issue is that they've only given me a finite amount of expenses and that cost will wipe me out". Neil says, "Don't worry, I've got you". Now that's what I like to hear, "Thank you", I say. Neil says, "Anyway fuck that, I'm starving let's eat". We head towards a café which says, "English breakfast" on the sign; we all trundle in, take a seat and enjoy a proper English breakfast.

I actually felt quite at home eating breakfast, as for once I didn't feel like the only pig at the table and Neil nailed his in half the time—fucking hell he can put some food away! During the short time we were eating, I established that Trev used to be a bodyguard for a few big names back in the 90's, and this gave me a chance to talk about my own experiences in the industry. More importantly, Neil has given me the full script about the plan; he's literally waiting for a phone call for mine. His has already landed and is being prepped for transit. We'll be meeting his guy once mine is picked up, and from what I can gather he's due a call imminently. All being well I'll be on my way back to the UK fairly soon.

Chapter 8

YOUNG GUNS AND COCAINE

How many more days will I be kept waiting? I get up and go through the motions, half hoping that today is the day. The other half of me is trying to savour the fact that I'm in Spain chilling. Breakfast was ok—continental with some token sausages. Even though it's not a scratch on yesterday's food, it is technically free, so I should stop fucking moaning and be grateful. I mean, if this was Cliff running the show I'd more than likely be eating fuck all! I head for the exit to take my morning stroll, walking around outside to get some fresh Mediterranean air and you know what? I'm actually beginning to quite enjoy the routine.

As I suck in my first breath of fresh air, my phone goes off. I look who's calling and it's Neil so I answer, with the standard greeting of "Good morning, mate". Neil responds saying, "We're on! We have to be in Madrid for about 18:00". Fuck, this is it—once again reality kicks in and I'm brought back down to earth with a massive bump. I ask, "What time do we need to get off then, I'm guessing pretty soon?". Neil responds, "Yes la, in about an hour. We want to give ourselves plenty of time to get there, do the thing and fuck off up to France—the Prof will meet us in Madrid". The Prof is Neil's runner; he's not been mentioned that much, but there's no doubt I'll be bumping into him fairly soon. Neil and I finish our chat, and he'll be with me just after 10:00, so I'd best go sort my shit out.

For the last time I head back up to my room. I want to ensure the money is good and that I have enough there, which there is—I simply need to see it with my own eyes, which will avoid any issues with people saying it's light. I do love these €500 notes, which I have since learnt from Neil are commonly known as Bin Ladens, because you never see the fuckers. The other thing I've learnt is that they are commonplace in two main circles: dodgy politicians and drug dealers. I'm not sure which is worse! I slowly flick through the money, hitting the correct number of 82 notes; 40 bags for the coke and one spare, probably the drink for the people I'm getting it from. Either way, I'm satisfied it's correct, so 40 bags get sealed off and the one remaining is left floating.

I have one last look around my room before grabbing my stuff and heading down to reception to check out. I have that all-too-common feeling of being deployed on operations; fully prepped and ready for things to go wrong, because let's face it, they usually do. I load up the car, putting my bags in the boot and the money back into the arch liner. I lock up and sit on the small sea wall, waiting for Neil to arrive; I'm presuming he'll be with Trev. I sit there contemplating how I ended up in this situation and where this new path might lead me. Neil has been doing this for a while now and he says it's no riskier than dealing in the UK. I want to believe this but everything will always appear to be ok until your fucking door comes off the hinges.

The clock hits 10:00 and sure enough Neil is here, with Trev sitting alongside him. I can also just make out the figure of a girl in the back. He's in a different motor now, a bigger one; clearly he's readying himself for a trip. They jump out and we all have a quick chat, Neil says, "My girlfriend's cousin lives in Madrid and he's gonna sort your two things out. He wanted 41 bags but I got it down to 40 with a €500 commission because we're family". Two things spring to mind. The first one is a relief to find I'll still have a Bin Laden left, plus some bits for my journey back. The second is more of an "Oh shit!" feeling. Neil's bird is Colombian, so reading between the lines, her cousin must also be Colombian. This means I'm dealing directly with the Colombians; this is a coke dealer's dream.

We all set off on our drive to the capital of Spain, a place I've never been to so it'll be an interesting experience. The drive is long and slow, with plenty of stops. We're not really travelling in convoy as we're doing our best to limit any interactions between us. I'm learning how to operate as a part of a team again, so I'll follow their lead and keep the comms down. I'm probably about 10 km or so behind, which isn't a problem, but I'm beginning to feel glad I have this satnav with me. Neil has sent an address for me to aim for which is not central, but even if it was I wouldn't have known, because it's getting dark and I've still got at least another 30 minutes before I get there. The road to Madrid is long with no pretty coastal route to take your mind off the reality of what's happening. It's like a fucking mountainous desert and Madrid is smack bang in the middle.

I receive a call from Neil; "How are you getting on la?". I reply, "Yes mate close, around 10 minutes out"; "Good, when you get there you'll see a McDonald's, park up and we'll see you in there", says Neil as he hangs up. Oh my fucking God, please tell me I'm not doing a deal like this in Maccy D's?! Surely not. But it's not my call, so I fucking hope they realise

91

that I will be checking the coke to see if it's any good. That ain't happening in McDonalds, or is it?

I pull up in a good space and see the meeting place opposite me, so I head on inside and see Neil, Trev and Neil's missus standing by a pillar, chatting to a couple of young lads. None of them are eating, so I go over and say hello. They all look over; the young lad looks a little bit nervous, as does his mate. Neil introduces us and we all shake hands, slightly alleviating the obvious buildup of stress that's been brewing. Neil says, "This is Antonia's cousin Adam, he's going to sort things for you". So now I know Neil's girlfriend's name. I look at Adam and say, "Ok no problem, how is this going to work?". Adam looks at Antonia and speaks in Spanish to her, she then replies and he nods. This is not good. I say, "No hablo español". Neil starts laughing and says, "He's waiting for a phone call, we'll be going to his friend's apartment to sort it out". Nothing changes, all the way to fucking Madrid (also known as the Mad one) and even the Colombians have to wait for a phone call! I thought this firm would have it on tap.

None of us bother eating—we're all hanging around like a bunch of fucking teenagers, and even Trev looks bored. Funny because he looks like he's itching for a fight; that'll be the Para in him. Adam's phone rings and he looks uneasy, he says something to Antonia and she says, "Ok we go, we follow him in cars". Man that accent; it's not Spanish, it has a certain edge to it and the feeling of being in a movie springs to mind. We all head out and into our respective cars; this time I need to follow Adam and his mate, with Neil and Co behind me. I appreciate that this is my deal but I'm really hoping that they are joining me, or at least Antonia is so she can translate for us, plus I get to hear that accent again.

It's only a short drive from the burger place. It's dark and we are in a residential area full of three-story apartments. I fucking hate dealing in flats; no exits if it goes tits up and too many floors and neighbours to contend with. Adam parks up and I find a space close by, but I decide I'm leaving the money in the car—fuck taking it up into a flat! I don't give a fuck who they are, I need to see two good keys of coke before they see the dosh. Neil and Trev join us as we head into the building. "Please be on the ground floor, please be on the ground floor", I repeat to myself. We go up one then two flights of stairs— now the top floor— fucking great. Five of us are standing by the door as Adam knocks. I'm looking around at the other doors opposite and down the stairs; Neil and Trev are doing the same.

The door opens and another young lad appears, inviting us inside. Adam still looks nervous and his friend isn't faring any better. This tells me they aren't even middlemen, they just know some people who can access some weight. This makes it even worse because the trust is now being based on second and third-hand information. I'm trusting Neil and he's trusting his missus, who in turn is trusting Adam, and he's got to have faith in the guys he's meeting. Fuck knows how far these two keys have got to go. There are a lot of people in this deal, and that's a lot of things that can go wrong.

We all head inside. Neil and Trev are scanning as they enter, Trev still looks fucking mean. The entrance is small; there's a bedroom on the left, a small bathroom ahead, and the lounge is through a door on the right. The lad that opened the door walks in, followed by Adam and his pal, then me. I see an oblong-shaped room with a sofa on the right. A skinny young lad is sitting there under a quilt. He's definitely fucking carrying. What would appear to be his girlfriend is sitting next to him. Another young lad is sitting on a single armchair opposite. I walk past all of them to the other end of the room where a dining room table and chairs are situated. There's a kitchen opposite, a separate room with no door. I discreetly sit down while peering into the kitchen to assess any hidden dangers, things like machete-wielding Colombians. As I sit down, Neil says, "Can I use your toilet?", then walks back out. He's clearly checking the toilet and the bedroom in the same way. Trev is just standing in the corner, looking intense— probably should have fed him some crayons earlier.

Neil reappears and the room settles—three ex-squaddies and six young Colombians, never a better mix for trouble. What the fuck now? I look at the guy sitting on the sofa, and say "Hola, are we good?". He just looks at me confused and laughs then the girl sitting next to him says, "He doesn't speak English". I look at her and smile, saying, "Thank you, so who's the person I'm doing the deal with?". She looks at the guy sitting on the armchair, saying something in Spanish, presumably translating my question. He then looks at me and says, "You have money?". For fuck's sake, either they speak English or they don't! I wish they'd stop fucking about. I look at him and say, "It's a fucking long way to drive if I didn't", and smile. Trev cracks a grin and Neil shakes his head as if to agree with me. The lad just shrugs his shoulders and looks confused, so I say, "Si". He gets up, puts on a jacket and fucks off; I look at Neil and then Adam, who in turn look at each other. Adam frowns and nods his head in reassurance. I'm hoping this means it's cool and he's gone to get it, but for all I know he's bailed out on us.

Looking around the room, none of us are moving, especially the guy on the sofa; it's not cold yet he's under a fuck off quilt? I look at Neil and Trev and they are on it; for all I know they might be carrying themselves—I might be the only one who isn't. I'm now thinking about the coke; it's been a long fucking journey and I'm finally here, doing the deal and with Colombians. I have some kit down in the car that I have to retrieve, so I look at Neil and say, "I'm popping down to the motor a sec, I need to grab a few things". Neil says, "Not the dough la, not yet". I reply, "No, fuck that bud, I've got a blade and some tape to repackage the coke". He nods as I walk out. Fucking flats! These kinds of flats are all the same; as I head down and out to my car, I can conclude that no matter where these flats are in the world, you can always smell food cooking and it's usually a stew of some kind.

I pop the boot and pull out the Halfords carrier bag which contains all the stuff I need. I empty out the bits I don't require and keep the packing tape and a blade, the same fucking blade that I was gonna do myself with last year. The knife isn't to attack or hurt anyone with, it's so I can cut into the block and dig some coke out. I have to check it's ok, otherwise it's not being accepted. That might not be an easy thing to do though, sitting in a room full of young Colombians and informing them that their coke's shit. I'd like to see how that plays out.

I head back up to the top floor, catching a whiff of the neighbours' dinner en route. I gently tap on the door and it's opened by the guy who appeared last time. We walk back in and it's refreshing to see nobody is tied up in the bathroom being cut up with a chainsaw. I say this because this is exactly the scene it reminds me of; very tense with a lot of paranoia. I regain my position of sitting by the table, look at Neil and say, "Any news?". He just nods and says, "Not yet la". We all spend what must have been the longest hour of our lives waiting for the door to go. Eventually the lad returns with two more guys. Fucking hell how many do they need for this deal? They're on eight now.

The new arrivals head over towards me and hand me a bag; I look inside and can see two packages. I'm looking for a couple of key indicators—a rubber jacket and a stamp—then I'll check the coke. I sit down at the table and get the two blocks out. They're wrapped in brown tape, which is good as this is the same tape I'll be patching it back up with. All eyes are on me—no pressure—somewhat intimidating. It's the same feeling you get when you go to a café in Amsterdam, buy some pot and roll a joint in front of the locals; they grew up on that shit and you get the feeling they're laughing at you.

I look at the two blocks, about the same size as an old VHS cassette case, same dimensions. I look around the room, get my blade out and cut away a triangle on what I hope is the top of the block. I cut through the various layers, to be met with a rubber jacket—good news. I can feel the tension in the room as I proceed through some shrinkwrap-type material to eventually be faced with a shiny white substance. I look at it and cut away, a slightly larger opening eventually revealing a print on the top which looks like a fish or a dolphin; doesn't matter, it's got a stamp. I cut into the coke, sensing everyone looking at me. I guess we all want this coke to be good, otherwise we've all wasted our time. I go in about a centimetre deep and pull a bit out. It's good; it smells right, looks right and it has the correct feel to it— nice and oily. I look up and see everyone is eagerly looking at me. I nod and say, "Bueno"; I know this is Spanish for "good", so hopefully they'll get the gist. One down and one to go, I get stuck into the second block. This time the room feels a lot more relaxed. Thankfully it's the same, so I patch them up roughly. I say to Neil, "Mate I'll get the dosh, back in two, I'll wrap those properly while they count the money". Neil nods and I head out saying to the lad who gave me the coke, "Un momento". Yes I know it's fucking Spanish, but it's better than walking out the door and saying fuck all.

This deal is pretty tense, and the worst part is about to happen. The money and drugs will be in the same room. If it's gonna go tits up, this is when it'll happen, and I don't fancy our chances against eight of them. I head back up with the money in my pocket, listening carefully for any noise in the apartment as I approach. As I enter I walk past Neil, hand him the last Bin Laden and head back over to the table where the coke still sits. I check it again, making sure it's still the same stuff, which it is, so I pull the envelope out and hold it up to see who wants to take it. I say in English "I've checked it and it's correct. You can count it here with me if you like". In other words, don't you fucking dare think you can count it elsewhere and then say it's light.

The lad heads over and goes into the kitchen with Trev behind him, which makes the guy look a bit uneasy, but needs must; Neil is still on oversight. I start the mission of repackaging the coke for transit. A few layers to patch up the triangular hole then it's time to start wrapping it properly. I've got two rolls, so plenty to work with, As I'm wrapping the coke, Manuel is counting out the Bin Ladens. Those notes have been with me for what feels like an eternity, and that day in the café in Kingston seems such a long time ago. I've just exchanged 40 bags for a 10-stretch in a Spanish nick.

I'm satisfied the coke is safely wrapped and Neil gives it the nod; after all it's his firm carrying it over for me. Manuel reappears with a smile on his face and you can immediately sense the atmosphere change in the room; even the skinny fucker with the gun cracked a smile. We all shake hands and we get the fuck out of there—quickly. I head straight for the car and pop the drugs in the boot; they are in the Halfords bag and I'm not gonna fuck about here—I'll sort them once we're out of the area. I approach my car to see a large white van parked nearby; Neil approaches the driver and speaks to him, so this must be the Prof. I get a sense of excitement, as the prospect of offloading the coke is a pleasant one.

The feeling was short-lived, as the van pulls away and drives off. Neil comes over and says, "That was the Prof, he's loaded up so is going to take yours off you when we get to Coquelles in France. We'll head out of Madrid and see how far we get; we might need to plot up in a hotel before we go over the border, as there's less traffic at night and I can almost guarantee you'll get tugged". I can feel my confidence slightly dropping at the thought of the return journey, but putting on a brave face I say, "Yep no problem", which is becoming a default fucking answer for me. We set the satnav for Coquelles in France; fucking hell 15 hours and 1,500 km. It's already past 21:00, so there's no way we can do this drive in one hit.

I head off, following Neil and still mindful that I'm not yet clear of the area. Neil's driving carefully and I'm not too far behind. The drive out of Madrid was ok, with no major traffic and no sign of police. The run has officially started; 15 hours up to northern France, with two in the boot. I'm fucking starving as well. I give Neil a call and say, "Mate are we likely to stop as I'm starved and need to fuel up". Neil replies, "Yes la, I'll do the next garage". We continue on our way along the main route out of Madrid and into the darkness of the Spanish wilderness—well that's how it feels anyway.

It's not long before we come across a service station so I pull up next to a pump and fill up. Neil walks over and says, "How's your expenses lasting?", I quickly tot it up in my head and conclude that the money I have left won't cover the costs. I say, "It'll be close, mate". Neil puts his hand in his pocket, hands me a purple one and says, "I got them to drop the commission in the interest of future business, so this is yours". A sense of emotion hit me; the feeling that after all these years, I've finally met someone who really does get it. I say, "Mate that's so good of you, thank you". Neil smiles and says, "Part of the firm now, la".

Chapter 9

HOMEWARD BOUND

It's getting late—too fucking late for driving around with this in the boot. Fortunately Neil is of the same mindset because as I'm thinking it, he's pulling off the road and into a rest area that has a motel. It looks shit but that doesn't matter. We pull in and he goes into the reception area; I wander over to speak with Trev, who is now out of the car. I ask, "What's the plan, mate?"; Trev replies, "We're gonna plot up here for a few hours then crack on. Neil wants to be on the road early as we need to be in Coquelles by 21:00 tomorrow". Sounds ideal—I'm trying to figure out a plan in my head about stashing the coke in the boot lining. While I'm pondering on this, Neil returns and throws me a key; "Here you go la, we'll get some kip and be on the road at about 07:00". On catching the incoming key, I say, "Yep, sounds good". Neil walks up to me, hands me a phone and says, "Use this for the rest of the journey; it's Trev's phone, we bought it today and we only need one in the car, so fuck your other one off and if you need to contact the lads back home, use this one". I look at the phone and say, "Nice one, do you have a charger and is there any credit on it?". Neil says, "Yeah mate, here you go". He then says, "The plan tomorrow is to follow the Prof up to the border—we know a little road that misses out the main checkpoint. It takes longer but it's worth it as it's never manned. Once through it's straight up to Coquelles; we just have to be careful when going through the péages on the toll roads, as there are often police there pulling the likes of us".

With this in mind I head into my room to get some sleep, switch on Trev's phone and put a few of my numbers into it, including Skimmer's and Cliff's. I then dismantle my old one—I momentarily consider binning it but think that leaving a burner from the UK in a Spanish motel might be a bit daft, so I opt to pop it into my bag. I clean up and hit the sack, thinking of the gravity of the deal I've just completed, but also considering the journey that sits before me. A good 13 or so hours up through Spain and France, to link up with the Prof and finally offload the coke. With this in mind, I suppose I'd best let Skimmer know the plan. It's far too late now, so I'll call him in the morning.

I'm woken earlier than expected by my new phone ringing, an unfamiliar ringtone on what I soon realise is a Spanish network provider. I answer and it's Neil; he says, "We're ready la, are you good?". Fucking hell mate, poor comms, I'm still in my scratcher—so I say, "Give me five and I'll be outside". I put the phone down and sort myself out quickly, and I mean quick; I leap out of bed and start getting dressed. I flick the quilt to make the bed, catapulting the burner into the wall in the process, which fucking explodes with the battery flying out. I quickly reassemble it and crack on. I'm outside in less than five minutes. It suddenly dawns on me that I still need to conceal the coke in the boot. Looking around I see there's a fair bit of movement; it's still dark but I'm not risking it. Neil, Trev and Antonia arrive from another entrance and walk towards me. Neil says, "You don't fuck about do you?"; I smile and say, "Tankies mate, we're the best". Neil and Trev shake their heads and laugh under their breath—I know what they're thinking. Tankies aren't known for being elite, we're known for being slack and scruffy, and they'd be correct. I say to Neil, "Mate, I just need to stow the goods for the journey, can you give me ten minutes?". Neil says, "Sorry la, the Prof has already gone and we need to escort him through the borders and the péages; we won't go nuts but we have to catch up with him as he's been on the road for a few minutes already, and the border is about an hour and a half away". I look at my car and consider stashing the drugs here, but instead I opt for another option and say, "Ok mate, I'll follow you for now until I see somewhere convenient to pull over and hide it".

We pull out of the motel complex and onto the road that heads towards the border. We've still got an hour or so of darkness, so I start scanning for a suitable spot. The road isn't lit but as I cruise along I can tell we are surrounded by wooded areas, and these have got smaller roads turning into them. I take the opportunity to pull off the main road and drive down one of these dark side roads, no artificial lighting but a slight ambient light as the sun is getting closer to showing itself. I see a small layby and pull into it, knowing that every second I'm sitting here fuck arsing about, Neil is getting farther away and closer to that secret road that misses the main border crossing out, the secret road that I will not find if I lose Neil.

I pop the boot and hastily get out of the car, looking around for any other cars or people; it's still relatively dark so any oncoming vehicles will be seen well in advance by their headlights. I rush round to the back and open the lid, reach inside and pull the lining away from the arch, periodically looking up and around as I do—fuck me, this is moody as fuck!

I grab the first key and stuff it way down inside of the lining and it seems to fit fairly well, so I grab the other and shove it in next to it but slightly higher, again looking up and around. I then grab the lining and push it back into place—fuck it won't sit flush, I'm getting more stressed knowing Neil is now gonna be fucking miles away. Why the fuck didn't I do this last night when I had time? I decide to use guerrilla tactics and start whacking the fuck out of it. Eventually the lining sits flush—that'll fucking do. I slam the boot, get back in the car and get the fuck out of there.

Feeling slightly better that the coke is well stored, I start trying to catch up with Neil, mindful that I don't wanna get caught speeding. Fuel's good, I'm a bit hungry but that can wait. I've been driving for nearly an hour now; the sun is coming up and still no sign of them. I grab the phone and go to make a call; fuck it's off so I switch it on and wait for it to power up. It kicks into action and I see a message on the screen saying, "ingrese su pin", which I have to assume means "enter pin". For the love of God, what the fuck is the pin? It's a new phone so I enter the generic pin of "0000"—nope—bollocks! I need to get this phone to work. I enter another possibility—"1234"—still no luck. This is not good, I must think fast, the border is getting close and I need to catch up with them, or at least get some directions for this alternative crossing.

Lightbulb moment—I'll call him from my other phone, thank fuck I didn't chuck it! I pull onto the roadside and go to my bag in the boot, retrieve the old burner bits and head back into the car. I get back on the road, knowing that I'm losing ground every time I stop. Once my phone is reassembled, I call Neil immediately. Fuck his phone's not active, he must have changed phones for the new one, makes sense but that doesn't help me. I then risk entering another generic pin, "9999" and a new message comes up, "ingrese el código PUK". For fuck's sake, I haven't got that PUK code, this will have to be displayed on the box that contained the SIM.

All right, remain calm; the main thing is getting the coke across the Spanish border and up to France, even if I have to risk the main border, but flapping like a fucking chicken isn't going to help. With this sound advice in mind I continue on my way. I have to contact Skimmer and give him an update; I call him and he answers, saying "Hello mate", I respond saying "I'm calling from my skiing trip". Skimmer asks, "How you getting on?", I say, "Yeah all good the snow was great and I'm on my way home, I've lost contact with my tour guide and he was gonna help out with my luggage, do you have an alternative number for him so I can get hold of him?". The phone goes quiet for a short time and Skimmer says, "Yes mate, I'll text it to your clean, but don't call from it, use a phone box". I thank him and finish the call.

I now switch on my clean phone; it's not been on for a day or so, so no doubt a few messages will appear but nothing, that's fucking disappointing. A text soon beeps from an unknown number, it has a contact for Neil, I type the number into my old burner and switch off my clean phone. I now desperately need to find services and a public pay phone. I pass a sign saying "Francia 13 km". Balls, I think I'll have to do the border. I visually check the car and hide away all the fucking phones except one, my clean phone. The car is relatively clean, but I dread looking in the boot, I've got a feeling the boot lining is trashed, but it's too late now, I'm on the border.

I steadily approach the back of a long, messy queue of vehicles, all converging to form a more orderly queue for the passport checks. My arse is definitely going here; the money was one thing but the coke, this is making me seriously rethink my decision-making process. As I get closer I can see the Spanish guards waving the majority of cars through. It's just after 08:00, so I guess the Spanish must have a rush hour of sorts, this must be why Neil wanted to leave at this time. The customs and passport control are flat out. I'm about four cars away from the checkpoint and once again I put myself into that place. I pop the radio on and listen to some music, it's all Spanish but it'll have to do. I drive up to the checkpoint, my passport on the passenger seat, I'm trying not to think of the ten stretch in the boot, the guy looks at me and waves me along. I steadily drive through, smile and politely wave, thanking him as I do. I then put my fucking foot down and try to make up some ground.

All I've got to do is catch Neil—they must be fucking miles ahead of me now; they said the Prof needed to be at Coquelles for about 21:00, so that must be my deadline. I've got just shy of 1100 km to go and that's gonna be a good 12 to 13-hour drive, what with a couple of fuel stops. Well I've got half a tank, so I can take a lump out of it; I'll fuel up, grab a snack and call Neil at the same time. Let's fucking go, I speed up to about 140 kph, a bit over the limit but not tearing the arse out of it. I'm trying very hard not to call Neil from my other burner and I won't be calling him from my clean one. I'm hoping that the route he took would be slower, as it was a diversion off the main route, but the truth is I don't know; the thought of this makes me instinctively press the loud pedal a bit more and my speed increases to 150 then 160.

Services ten clicks out—that'll do. I've been hammering this thing for a couple of hours and we all need a break. I pull in and fill up, using the smaller notes I have left. I've got about €600 left including the last Bin Laden. I pop into the shop and grab some food to eat on the hoof, then with some small change in hand I head out to a phone and make the call to Neil, hoping he'll pick up. It rings off, so I try it again, this time he answers saying "Who is this?", I say, "It's me, your favourite Tanky". "Fucking hell la, I thought we'd lost you", Neil says, sounding genuinely relieved. Feeling a whole lot better, I answer, "No mate, the phone you gave me needed a PIN and it locked on me; I don't suppose Trev has the PUK code?". I hear Neil speak to Trev and he says, "You're fucking lucky la, he still has the box and the code here along with the PIN". I get the burner out, open my text messages and say, "Ok mate, fire away". Neil relays both the PIN and PUK codes as I type them into my phone as a text message. I then say, "How are you getting on?". Neil responds, "Yeah we're good, we didn't come off at the border as it made sense to queue in the traffic, we're about three hours from Paris". I say "Ok mate, can you text me the name of where we're going?"; Neil replies, "We don't have a meeting place yet, just head for Coquelles and we can go from there".

Being mindful of the time and potential distance between us, I get back in the car and make haste, but before that I switch the other phone on and enter the PUK code followed by the PIN. Hallelujah, it's alive! Once again I dismantle my burner, feeling thankful I kept it—I'd have been right in the shit if I hadn't. I get back on the road and steam into my journey, feeling slightly troubled that my ETA in Coquelles is now after 20:00, and for some reason Neil is two hours ahead of me. He must be fucking tanking it, but then again he isn't loaded up with coke.

I put my foot down, again bringing my speed to 160 kph. I don't want to be speeding, but given the alternative of carrying the coke over the border, I have to risk it. I'm trying to get my ETA down, and it's becoming a fixation. Seeing the arrival time gradually getting earlier, I'm now due before 20:00 so I ease off a bit and bring the speed down a touch. One forty should do it, but this speed is annihilating the fuel so I'm gonna have to stop again soon and top up. It's like formula one, calculating the amount of pit stops and fuel loads. Each time I stop for fuel I lose ten minutes' drive time and this means I have to catch up by booting it— it's a shitty, vicious circle.

I'm on a quarter of a tank and I have just over 100 km left before I need to crack into this purple one. After the last headache in a French fuel station, I'll use the change as I don't have time to be piss arsing around with stroppy cashiers. The Spanish ones didn't seem to give a shit but the French seem to have a real issue with them. My current ETA is a few minutes before eight so I'm good for my timings, but I still don't fancy running my chances.

I pull into a service station, fill up and head into the shop. I grab a drink and a few snacks, then feeling under pressure I join the short queue and wait patiently for my turn. Clock watching, this is dragging; 15 minutes have passed on this pit stop and I'm still fucking waiting. I've still got over three hours of driving and it's approaching 17:00. I can feel the stress levels beginning to peak as I finally get to pay for my fuel. I hand over my last €100 note, the cashier rings it through and I get a few coins in return. No stress, I've still got the Bin Laden to get me the rest of the way home—better still I may end up with some change for my time.

Back on the road, next stop Coquelles and to offload the coke to the Prof—I just hope he's gonna be there. I was thinking about how I put things across to Skimmer and whether or not I should let him know the coke will be going over with another firm, but then again they've been waiting for nearly a week now and the most important thing for them is it fucking lands. If Cliff wants to start moaning I'll remind him that he has trusted me to get the job done and, I quote, "He doesn't care how you get it over" is pretty much what Skimmer told me, so I'm using my initiative on this one and as far as I can tell, the risk of taking it over myself far outways the risk of handing it all over to Neil's firm.

My phone rings, it's Neil. "Yes mate," I say. Neil replies saying, "How you getting on, la?". I reply, "Not too bad, just refuelled and I'm coming around Paris, about three hours out". Neil says, "You might want to put your foot down la, the Prof is getting ready to make the next move and he needs to be ready by 20:30, 21:00 at the latest". Fuck, I look at my satnav and the ETA has crept up to 20:30. I say to Neil, "No stress, I'll be there for 20:30". Neil says, "We're in a Buffalo Grill at Coquelles, it's the only one, I'll send you the details".

How the fuck did he get to be three hours ahead of me? He must have been fucking flying. More to the point, was the Prof going at the same speed? He's in a van! I put my foot down, now slightly panicking that I might just miss my boat with the Prof; 160, 170, it's getting dark and I'm definitely not comfortable at this speed. An hour at this speed and my ETA hasn't dropped, it's still saying 20:30, so I ease off a bit and drop it down to 160, that's a ton in English money.

The road ahead is long and straight; at times I climb the odd gentle hill and drop down over and continue. Visibility is dropping off and I concentrate on the road ahead as I climb another gentle hill, still doing a steady 160. As I hit the brow of a hill I see a sight that instantly makes me regret my decision to put the hammer down—it's a French police car on the roadside. I gradually ease off, hoping they haven't got a speed camera on them. I'm about 100m out and as I pass by my speed is a respectable and legal 130 kph. I casually look across and try not to look like I've just shat my pants. I'm past them and I'm looking in my rear-view mirrors, hoping they don't move. I'm gaining a bit of distance and it appears that they haven't followed me—thank fuck for that!

My relief is short-lived as in my rearview mirror I can just make out the image of the police car slowly catching up. I'm not going to outrun this car, even though French police cars are shit, but where would I go? The coke's in the fucking boot and it's not possible to ditch it. I'm thinking fast; the car gets closer, but no lights on, so maybe they're just heading off and I'm jumping to conclusions. Remain calm, let them pass by and crack on, but the police car is right on my arse now and not going around me, then the lights go on. Shit, this isn't good! Relax, it's gonna be a speeding thing, they don't know about the coke.

I indicate and steadily pull onto the roadside, putting my hazard lights on as I stop; I switch off the car and try my best to remain calm, telling myself it's a speeding thing, not a drug search. The French officer walks up alongside the car and I drop the driver's window, saying, "Bonsoir, monsieur". He peers into the car and has a look around, he then says in English, "You were going too fast, the limit is 130 kilometres and you were doing 160, why is this sir?". I then say in a combination of broken French and English, "Je suis désolé monsieur, I have to catch a ferry to the UK and I had broken down earlier. I was trying to catch up and didn't realise I was going so fast". I fucking hope he buys it; he looks at me and says, "Ça va monsieur, you will have to pay a fine for speeding, it is €90". Feeling relieved that it's an on-the-spot fine, I reach into my pocket and it dawns on me that the only note I have left is a Bin Laden. Now there's no fucking way I even resemble a dodgy politician, so producing a €500 note is going to look bad, and it did. I sheepishly hold the note up and try to smile politely as I do, but the reality is I must look a right tit. The officer looks at me, shakes his head and says, "Non monsieur, this will not do", and looking back at his colleague who is still sitting in the car, he asks me to wait one moment, then walks back to talk to him. He soon returns and says, "Ok sir, you follow us", and walks back to his car.

What the fuck, I'm done. I'm now considering doing one, but I can't see it being any good. I won't have enough time to lose them, get to the boot and offload the coke. Ditching the car will mean they'll find the coke and attribute it to me anyway, either way I'm fucked. I may as well see it out and should an opportunity present itself, I'll take it. The police car pulls out in front of me—I switch off the hazards and follow them. They still have the lights on. My mind is blank now; I'm back in the present and not thinking about anything else; all I wanna know is where the fuck am I being taken? We drive for a painstaking several kilometres—all the time my head is calm. I glance at my ETA for Coquelles and it's now 20:45. This means fuck all as it's possible I'll be locked up in a French police cell, and if that's the case I won't be there to hand over the coke anyway. With this in mind I don't bother calling anyone, as that will only incriminate them.

I'm oddly beginning to think about what a French prison will be like. I hadn't considered that—I was thinking if it goes tits up, it'll be in Spain. The police car pulls onto the roadside and onto a slip road that has an access barrier. I follow, positioning myself safely behind them. The passenger gets out and walks up to the barrier, unlocks and lifts it, the police car drives through and the officer gestures for me to do the same thing and I comply, politely waving as I slowly pass him. The slip road leads onto a smaller country lane like a B road; as the officer passes me the thought occurred to me that they might be taking me somewhere quiet to rob me. I'm not sure if this is how the French police operate but if they think I'm loaded up with €500 notes, it may be worth their while.

We head off again; the car still has its flashing lights on, but my nerves aren't feeling too bad—once the adrenaline kicks in and I know I'm committed, I go with the flow. I always seem to be on some kind of ride that I can't get off. Not unlike a child's first time on a merry-go-round—looking at their parents each time they pass, confused and looking as if they should be having fun, but with an obvious look of utter terror in their eyes—they only realise that it was meant to be fun when it was all over. That's my fucking life.

The road is dark but is well-lit by the flashing blue lights on the police car. I see a complex of buildings appear on my right; as we approach it the police car indicates right and I do the same. We pull into a police station and the car switches off its blue lights. I'm officially fucked. We both pull up to a gate that is closed; a few moments pass and the gate automatically slides to the right, giving us access to the site. It looks like some kind of HQ, but I'm past caring now, as my arrest for smuggling coke is imminent, another fucking disaster to add to the catalogue of things that could have and have gone wrong in my life since leaving the army.

We drive into the complex, down a small road and curve around to the right where a main building and car park is revealed. There are several empty spaces with writing in them, I'm not sure what it says but I'm told to park in it. This has to be a search bay; I guess there's a chance they may not find it, I've not had a chance to look since this morning but I'm pretty sure it's well hidden, but I'm also sure that the arch lining is a fucking mess. Maybe I can go down the route of plausible deniability but I fucked that one by not wearing gloves when handling the coke.

The officer that I spoke to earlier walks up to the car—I remain seated inside and drop the window. He says, "Do you have a card?", I look at him as he looks over to the building where a cashpoint is situated. I look at him and say, "Yes", simultaneously pulling out my bank card. I then say, "I don't have enough money left on here because the repairs on my car earlier cost a lot of money". Obviously this is a blatant lie but I know that there isn't enough on the card; what's left is for the missus to live on and I'm not leaving her short. The police officer again shakes his head and then says, "Ok, you follow us". What the fuck is going on now?

The police car drives off with me in tow, back to the gates and heads down the road in a different direction. Right now I'm confused but I'm also sure that they aren't gonna search me. With this in mind I do feel a sense of relief. We continue along the road and once again the police car pulls off the road and onto a slip road, this time taking us back onto the main motorway, and from what my satnav is saying it's the same one. This time the police car puts its foot down, still with the lights going and me close behind. I wonder if I gave them the €500 note, they'd escort me all the way. I'm so far behind now I've surely missed my boat with Neil, but I'll have to worry about that when I'm done here—whatever it is that I'm meant to be doing.

Several kilometres pass and we eventually arrive at a service station. We pull in and the police car stops just shy of the pumps. The same officer gets out, walks up to me and says, "You buy fuel". I look at my gauge and it's just under full but I'm not about to let that stop me; if this is the only way to get rid of the filth then I'll stick a bit in. I pull up to the fuel pump at the same time the police car plots up over to my right on the exit slip road. I cram €10 in and head into the shop, make a beeline for the cashier and she says "dix euros". I shove the €500 in her face, smiling, probably looking more deranged than happy. She shakes her fucking head and says "Non"; I nod mine and say, "Oui"— I don't give a fuck, she's taking this fucking note. She digs in and says, "Non", I dig in further and say, "Oui". She then gets up and fucks off out the back somewhere—oh my fucking God, please someone take the fucking note so I can at least try and make it to Coquelles to offload this coke!

The cashier returns with another member of staff; the other staff member says in English, "I am sorry but we cannot accept this unless you spend more". I look at her and smile, I run over to the display and randomly grab chocolate and crisps, looking at them in the process. I keep grabbing shit off the shelves until they look happy. Eventually the cashier cracks a small smile and says, "D'accord, monsieur". I know this means ok so I politely hand her the note. I then say to the supervisor, "Madame, is it possible to have €90 change? I have to pay a fine to the police". I point outside to the police car patiently waiting. She responds by translating this to the cashier, who then kindly hands me a load of notes, including the correct amount to pay my fine. I thank them and, carrying a ton of junk food, return to the police car, where they gesture at me to sit in the back.

I plonk myself in and drop the food on the seat next to me. I then say, "Je suis désolé, they didn't want to take the money so I had to buy lots of food". The police officer smiles and says, "Yes this is the problem with these notes". He hands me some paperwork to be signed, which I sign quickly without even reading it. I then hand him €90 and say, "quatre-vingt-dix, monsieur"; he looks at me and smiles saying, "This is funny, I speak to you in English and you speak to me in French"; I smile and say, "Oui, J'aime la France, mon arrière-grand-père était français". The officer takes the €90 and smiles, saying, "Your

French is excellent". Trying not to overdo it, I return the compliment. He then says, "Ok monsieur you are free to go, please remember the speed limit". Feeling genuinely relieved I thank him and his colleague and head back to my car.

Once again I'm on the road. The police are nowhere to be seen and I'm now cruising at a respectable speed of 130 kph. I've lost 40 minutes and my ETA is now just after 21:00 so I call Neil, who answers and says, "Where are you now?". I reply saying, "Getting there, had a bit of a delay but I'm back on track, not gonna be with you till after 21:00 though". Neil says, "That's ok la, the Prof isn't gonna rush off now, he's gonna do his bit in the morning so we'll wait for you here", and hangs up.

A huge wave of euphoria passes over me as the good news settles in—I ease back on the pedal a bit more and relax. The day isn't over yet but fuck me it's been right up there with the most stressful, as it's been relentless from the off. I put the music on for the first time today, and crack on with the journey; plenty of fuel and no shortage of shit to stuff my face with. It's time to reel in Coquelles—one last push and I can finally offload this beak.

Half forgetting I'm still rammed to the hinge with coke, I continue on my way with Coquelles getting ever closer. I suppose I'm still counting my chickens about the close call I had a couple of hours ago. If they only knew what they had— two keys of near pure, right under their noses, all they had to do was pop the boot and I'm sure they'd have seen it, or at least the hash job I made of hiding it, but they didn't find it and I'm still here, trucking on into the night, heading northeast.

Coquelles is just a few clicks out and by the looks of it the Buffalo Grill is more or less on the edge of the area. Ordinarily, I'd drop a call or give a heads-up, but this time I'll turn up and just hope they're still there.

Coquelles is surprisingly well-lit and the Buffalo Grill is easy to find. I pull into the car park, scanning it for Neil's car and more importantly the Prof's van. The car park borders the whole place with limited spaces; I spot a van that could be the Prof's down near the bottom of the car park, in a pretty dark and secluded spot. I see a space nearby and reverse into it; I get out and as I do I look over at the van and swear I can hear noises coming from it. Ignoring this I opt to head in and meet up with the rest of them. I walk in and, finally feeling relieved, I look across and see Neil, Trev and Antonia sitting at a table, drinking and laughing. Judging by the way they are enjoying themselves, they probably haven't had a day like mine.

I approach the table and Neil slides a lager over to me, saying, "Here you go la, how was your journey?". Do I tell him or not? Fuck it, it'll make for a good conversation, so I proceed to tell them what an eventful day I've had. The look on their faces says it all and Neil says, "Probably be a good idea if you don't tell the lads back home about all of that. Personally, I'm well impressed that you managed to keep your shit together. I don't know many people who could still be here and not be fucking crying or bleating about how stressed they are". I reply saying, "Oh, I was definitely stressed"; Neil then says, "Yeah but you didn't lose your shit, and whatever you did was obviously the right decision because you're here". Taking solace in Neil's words I then say, "Mate can I please go and offload this to the Prof, so I can relax?". He smiles and says,

"Yeah la, he's in the back of the van sorting the rest, so just knock on the back and chuck yours in; he'll probably shit his pants so knock loud to make it worthwhile". Trev starts laughing and says, "Yeah, shit the prick up". "Charming", I think; I get the feeling that the Prof probably isn't cut from the same cloth as the rest of us.

Eager to mag to grid the coke I head outside, leaving my drink for when I return. I go to my car and retrieve the coke from the wheel arch, still in a semi-state of disbelief about it still being there. I put them into the Halfords carrier and head over to the van, which now clearly has someone in the back. I can hear the Prof moving about, obviously very busy. I opt to discreetly knock on the side of the van—it suddenly goes silent—the Prof is definitely bricking it, I can picture him in there, frozen—his mind racing trying to figure out who's banging on the door. I let him sweat for a little bit and announce myself. There's movement again and the back door is partially opened; the Prof pops his head out and says, "Fucking hell mate, I shit myself", I say "Yeah I know". Trying to hold back the laughter I then pass him my bag and say, "Two more for you bud, thank you". The Prof snatches the bag from me and slams the door shut. "Moody fucker", I think to myself, clearly he has no sense of humour.

With the baton once again passed on I can now relax, so I head back to the bar and take up my seat next to the others. I look at my drink and take a big fucking sip. It tastes like shit— warm and almost flat, but fuck I needed that. I say to Neil, "What now?", he goes on to explain the rest of the plan and when the goods will be available to pick up. This gives me an idea of my next move and, more importantly, I can update

Skimmer with the plan on the other side. I am a little nervous because although the goods have been passed, they are still financially my responsibility, which makes me very nervous. This is how it sucks—no matter what option I take, there will always be a level of accountability. Some people don't give a toss and would run or turn into a rat to escape the responsibility of what they have to do, but I can't and more to the point won't do any of those things—it's wrong on every level.

We're going to plot up in a motel tonight; there's a cheap one around the corner, and I've got enough left in the expenses to cover my own costs. We'll be getting an early-morning ferry from Calais that leaves at about 05:00 or 06:00. Neil wants to get on the piss but I just want to go to bed—I'm so fucking tired and I'm desperate to speak to the missus and kids. I let them know that I'll be calling it a night and I'll see them in the morning. Neil says, "Meet us at Calais la, I'll be there at 06:00; the ferries are regular, and it's only a 10-minute drive". I say, "Sounds good, see you there". I neck what's left of my drink and head back out to the car. The motel is in the next car park so I drive over, feeling two kilos lighter and a lot less stressed. I park up, head in and grab the cheapest option. It's €55— that'll do nicely.

The room is shit—made of moulded plastic units with a stupid fucking cubicle for the shower, but it matters not. I have a quick shower and dive into the bed, a bed which I have no doubt is somewhat more comfortable than the one that I could have been sleeping on in a French prison. I take some time to relax and then I text the missus, informing her that I'll be back at around lunchtime tomorrow. I've been gone almost a week, but it feels like a lot longer. She's glad to hear I'm ok and I wish I could have spoken to the kids, but even with the hour's difference, it's still a tad late. I eventually fall asleep feeling quite content, thinking about the next time I have to take on the baton; presumably this will be at some point tomorrow in Windsor, which is a right result as it's on my way home.

I wake early feeling relatively well rested, mindful that we are aiming for the 06:00 ferry. I have a standard squaddie shower, do my teeth, check the room and get the fuck off; no more than five minutes tops. I'm in the car for 05:30 and already dialling Neil's number; he answers saying, "You shit the bed la?". I respond, "Mate I don't fuck about, how you getting on?". He replies, "Yeah we're just leaving, should be at the ticket office in about 10". "Me too, see you in a bit", I say, hanging up in the process. Calais is easy to find and well signposted from here, but I've bonded with the satnav and I feel that it would be a shame to not use it for the last few 100 km. I put in Calais ferry port and yep, it's 11 minutes away.

Calais is always rammed—trucks galore and yet again I can see why Neil chooses this time to cross; it's fucking nuts, and I'm curious if the Prof will be crossing at the same time with the coke. I close in on the port and drive straight into the car park, where I see Neil's car already there. I can see him and Antonia sitting in the car; it's still dark but the whole port is lit up like a fucking Christmas tree. I head straight into the office and catch Trev as he walks out; I say "What ferry did you book, mate?", Trev says, "The next one to Dover, just ask for that", and walks out. I go up to the desk with what's left of my euros, around €320, and purchase my ticket, relieving me of another €115. Fuck me, it's nearly all gone! Just enough left for fuel and a breaky on the boat, maybe a duty-free gift for the missus and kids.

I head back to the car; Neil has already left and I'm hot on his tail, feeling a bit of deja vu from the days of going on leave. I don't think I've been through Calais since then but it doesn't appear to have changed that much. I follow the signs and pull up behind a row of cars, all waiting for the next boat to England. I get out and again have a scan, looking for Neil and the Prof; I think I see Neil but no sign of the Prof. He's in a van but it's not commercial. For peace of mind, I need to set eyes on him, so I head down to what I think is Neil. I approach the car and see them all sitting inside; Neil drops the window and I ask, "Is the Prof on this crossing?"; he says, "No mate, he's cross-loading everything to the guy that's doing the channel for us. I can't even trust the Prof to not get pulled on this crossing, so we have a special setup for this. I've got a courier who travels from Belgium on a regular basis, he knows some of the customs staff and they wave him through. He has to wait for the shift that knows him to come on, then they wave him through with no dramas". I look at Neil and say, "Good stuff, what's his ETA over there?". Neil says, "Should be later, but it has been known to take a few days, he won't cross unless it's right". That's fair enough I think, so I say, "No worries mate, see you on the boat". I wander off and back to my car, feeling a little bit uneasy but once again I'm already committed, fucking praying the coke makes it to Blighty.

The cars all start up and row-by-row embark onto the ferry. I'm trying to wonder how I'd be feeling if I still had the coke on board. We head onto the back of the boat and are directed towards the front; I'm about halfway down this time and conveniently next to a stairway for the upper decks. I get out and have a gander to see where Neil is, but he's nowhere to be seen. He's a fucking enigma—seems to appear and disappear at random—typical scouser. I join the mob of people and head to the upper decks. I guess Neil will already be eating his breaky knowing him, so I follow the signs for the café, eventually locating it. I join the queue of passengers, looking at what's on offer whilst looking for Neil. I grab a coffee and breakfast; it looks a bit fucking ropey but will do for me.

I can't see Neil anywhere, I've almost finished my food and still no sign of him. I'm pretty sure he got on the boat, then the thought occurred to me: "Did he get on, or has this been one big fucking scam?". I begin to feel that all-too-common feeling of anxiety and stress building in my gut. I'm trying to remain calm but part of me thinks I've just been had over. Si will fucking kill me. I can't take another loss, I still owe 25 bags and you can guarantee that they won't add 40 on; they'll add the profit as well, putting me back up to about 100 grand. I'm sitting here sweating fucking bullets but then I hear a familiar sound—"Hey la, what's happening?"—Jesus, I've never been so happy to hear a scouse accent!

I look behind me and, trying not to show the obvious sense of relief, I say, "How's things?". They rock up and sit next to me, fucking loaded up to the hilt with duty-free. Neil says, "Had to grab some ciggies for the boys, you know what I mean, la?". I simply smile and take a sip from my coffee; we'll be landing in about 40 minutes so I sit back and relax. We have a chat about the day before and all agree that the meeting with those lads a couple of days ago was a bit too moody and we probably won't be going back. I tried to find out if Neil knew if the Prof was actually leaving today and he didn't give much away, but maybe he just doesn't trust me with those kinds of details yet.

I have to get some air so I head out onto the decks—forgetting how cold it is back in the UK compared to southern Spain; heading towards the front of the boat so I can get a view of these legendary white cliffs of Dover, It's still dark so there's not much to see, however the lights of the port have created a glow. It's a welcoming sight, knowing that I'll soon be back on English soil. Again my thoughts are on how might I feel if I was still loaded up; I guess it would be a very similar feeling to yesterday when I was sitting in the French police station, waving a Bin Laden.

Dover is now only a few minutes away and the ferry begins to shudder as it manoeuvres into the port. The familiar sound of the intercom requesting all drivers to return to their vehicles doing its thing. I head back to the car, and having lost Neil I'm once again scanning around for him or one of the others—it shouldn't be fucking hard to spot them, he's fucking massive. Trev's angry as fuck and his missus is Colombian peroxide blond, but no joy so I'll have to text them when I get back to the car.

Almost the last leg and I'm rather excited about the next bit—customs. I'll be keen to see if Neil's prediction of my profile is correct and if they do pull me over. The ferry shudders to a standstill, the doors open up and the cars head off in an orderly line. I text Neil to call me, and within a few moments he does; I say, "I'm guessing I should head on home then wait for a call, mate". Neil says, "Yeah la, the Prof has messaged and he's coming over tomorrow, so you can come to us on Monday to grab your shopping". At least I know, so armed with this information I pop my address into the satnav and proceed towards customs. The customs setup in Dover is busy but a well-oiled machine; as I approach I drive into a well-lit undercover area with a couple of HMRC staff standing directing the traffic. Either we get waved through and we're on our way or get ushered into the search centre on the left.

My turn now and feeling very relaxed knowing I'm clean, I steadily pull up to the guy and lower my window. I politely say, "Good morning", he responds in kind and then says, "How was your trip away?". I reply, "Yes good thanks, skiing in Andorra with some old army mates". He smiles and waves me through. I fucking knew it; the good old army blag, every fucking time. I drive off, leaving the customs behind me. I've done it, I've made it back to the UK with no issues! I appreciate that I still need to collect the coke, but that's a different thing. I head on out of Dover and back home at long last. What a trip!

Chapter 10

REBUILDING THE BUSINESS - A 2nd TIME

It feels a bit odd, being back home after my week in Spain, with no time for any kind of decompression because I'm thrown straight back into family life. Don't get me wrong, I love family life but I'm still finding it difficult to fully engage while this fucking debt lingers on. I'm waiting on a call from Cliff who apparently is quite happy that the coke has taken a safer route—Skimmer must have sold the idea to him. Si remains quiet and he'll stay away from the mechanics of everything until he feels the need to get involved. I'm also having to consider my options regarding business—this opportunity to work with Neil and his firm is great but it'll put me up against it with my own work, so I feel I may need to take someone on. This does leave me in a spot though as there's nobody I can immediately think of that I trust enough, but if I'm to take on this additional work I'll need someone to help me with my own business. My own setup will generate more funds than any wage I'm paid running for another firm, but it's all money into the pot to help get rid of this fucking debt.

My phone rings and it's Skimmer; I answer and say, "Hello mate". Skimmer replies, "How was your holiday?". Trying to ensure that I maintain some kind of plausible code, I say "Yeah all good, the conditions appeared spot on and the snow was good, we did have a change of resort, but all went well". Clearly impressed with my ability to encode that transmission, he then says, "Quality, do you know what the next move is as he's asking". When Skimmers says "he", he's naturally referring to Cliff, so I respond with "Waiting on a call, they said that it could be the same day, if not it'll likely be a couple of days after". I then go on to say, "Can you reserve me some work as well, as I missed out on a good earner last week". Skimmer says "Yeah, of course, let me know your numbers later".

This is good news, so I act on it immediately and start ringing around to get an idea of what people need. They had fuck all last week so I'm hoping it'll be a biggy, and seeing as I'm picking the shit up, I'll have a definitive ETA to keep the boys happy. My phone goes again; Jesus it's Cliff, what the fuck does he want? "Yes, mate" I say, still making a point over the commodity insult he delivered while I was plotted up in Andorra. Cliff says, "Thank you for getting that sorted, I'll put the money against the tab". He then says, "Are you looking for any more work running around?". I take my time, mindful that Cliff's offers of work are usually underpaid and overworked— last week being a prime example. I say, "Potentially, I'm pretty busy at the moment, what are you looking at?". Cliff says, "I need a new runner, the other lads are focussing on other parts of the business and I was curious if you fancied it". Interesting, but why me? Surely he has plenty of bodies to choose from? So I say, "Can do mate, I'll see how it goes with everything else, what's the payment?". Cliff promptly replies, "Five hundred a week". I spend a moment considering what I'm taking on along with everything else. My thought process is this: The more he needs me, the less shit he'll dish out, and as it stands I'm very quickly becoming an asset, especially if I'll be working with Neil as well. I say, "Fuck it, I'll do it for a while, but I'm gonna take on a body at my end to help out, so it might not always be me doing it—take the five off of the bill each week". Cliff says, "Yeah, I was going to", and laughs; this laugh for a change wasn't out of malice but was real humour, so I laughed back, calling him a dick in the process.

Ok, my mind is set—I need a wingman and I need a good one because I'm gonna be getting busy, working my own shit, Cliff's and whatever the fuck I'll be doing with Neil over there. There's only one person that springs to mind and that's my old mucker Hassan; he's ex T.A. and I make sure he's reminded of it as well; weekend warrior, SAS and all that bull. Joking aside, he's a bit of a free spirit and I know he's never been shy to have a little bit of a sniff. He used to come to see me on a Friday night years ago when my oldest was just a baby. The wife would be sitting in the lounge watching TV, and we'd be getting slowly wired by having a sneaky line out of the kitchen cupboard. I just hope he's around. Hassan also carries the additional advantage of being rather large; he's well into his bodybuilding and he's a pure unit. He got me into door work and CP security when I first came out. We both got introduced to coke backstage at the Oasis gig in Knebworth '96, looking after multiple VIPs. It was fucking heavy, life-changing stuff, and part of why I ended up getting involved in this shit.

I scroll through my phone and locate his number which never changes, same as his address—he's lived there since time began. I used to pop around on leave; he lives on one of the top floors of a high-rise and I used to show off my marksmanship skills by taking out pigeons on the roofs below with a single shot from his air rifle. This used to piss him off as he usually took a few more shots, but that's T.A. for you. I make the call, slightly worried that he'll not be up for it, but he's the only person I can think of that I trust enough and I've known him since the days of knocking around in the arcades in town, back in the 80's. Hassan picks up and says, "Yes mate, how are you doing?". I respond by saying, "I'm all good, bud", neglecting to tell him how much shit has happened over the last year or so. I then say, "How's work? I may have something for you if your balls are big enough". Hassan responds saying, "Come on, you know they're fucking big". I can't deny him this, as I've never seen him back down and with over 10 years on the doors, he's not afraid of a tear up. "Good", I respond, "as there will be some well-paid, high-risk work with me, doing my thing if you're up for it". I know Hassan that well I can almost hear him smiling, and without hesitation, he says "I'm in". We arrange for a catchup the following day to go over the details and sort him with a burner—the call ends with me on a proper high.

Tuesday comes and goes, and I'm developing a little bit of anxiety about the next stage of this job but I'm pretty sure that it's ok; if it wasn't I'm positive Si or Cliff would be barking down the phone at me. I had a good old sit down with Hassan and he's on board and kitted out with a nice new burner. I've let him know that as soon as I receive the contacts I'll send them on—the plan is to divert Hassan onto Cliff's customers along with a select few of mine, not too many at this stage but the ones that I feel would reduce the distance we both have to cover. I've told him the wage will be 500 a week, but it'll only happen if we are working. No work, no wage—he gets it. The eventual plan is that if I am overseas with Neil, then Hassan can hold the fort for me.

A few hours pass and I'm about to write the day off when my burner goes. It's Neil, thank fuck for that! I answer, "Yes big fellah, how are we?". He replies, "Yeah la, we're on, head on down to the castle when you're ready". I'd almost forgotten that he was a scouser! I say "Ok mate, I'm on my way, do you have a meeting place?". Neil says, "Yes la, head central and my mate Lofty will meet you". Lofty? Where the fuck do we get these names from? I'm presuming he'll be tall, at least I'll have an idea of who to look out for. Neil then says, "I'll text his number now—speak later—let me know if you get any problems", and he shoots off.

My phone beeps and Lofty's number soon arrives. I save it under the aforementioned name, adding it to all the other bizarre names saved in the burner. I've decided to hold on to the satnav for now; my mate doesn't need it and I've become quite attached to it. The way things are going I can see myself getting one soon, 'cos he'll be wanting it back and I definitely need one, as the Mark 1 map is rapidly becoming obsolete. Windsor is about 80 miles away so If I fuck off now, I'll be there for about 15:00; an hour of fucking about with two more to get back here; my ETA is about 18:00 so I call Skimmer and let him know my rough timings.

My ducks are in line so I embark on the penultimate leg of this journey; the missus is all good, she knows I'm busy and as long as the bills are being paid, I don't think she's overly concerned. The two-hour journey doesn't last long and the sight of the castle is quite something from the motorway. I'm about twenty minutes out so I call Lofty, but the phone rings off so I give it a few and try again. I fucking hope he's reliable. The phone rings and Lofty answers, "Yes mate, how far out are you?"—fuck me another scouser —hardly surprising though, if Neil is one he's likely got his mates involved. I say, "About 15 minutes mate, I'm in a dark Focus, whereabouts shall I aim for?". Lofty says, "Head for the central car park and I'll jump in with you and show you the way". Sounds good to me, so I tell him that I'll see him soon and crack on to the car park.

Winsor is very pleasant, bigger than I'd expected and flooded with tourists and off-duty squaddies. I'd blend in if I wasn't so fucking fat; I can't pass it off as a serving soldier now, no fucking chance. With too much beer and not enough exercise, I've successfully transformed from a squaddie into a lazy, fat dealer—a lazy shit. The car park in question is easy to find and surrounded by buildings, souvenir shops, bars and restaurants. I park up and have a look around; the place is flooded with cameras but as this is the Queen's gaff it would be, and probably not the best place to be dealing large amounts of cocaine. While I'm pondering about it, an expectedly tall lad approaches me and gets in the car. He says, "Let's go, the coke is ready for collecting", so under his direction, I drive off and away from the area, and eventually into what has to be the shit part of Windsor. Fucking hell, this isn't what I was expecting— council but rough with it.

We pull up to a house and head on in, walking into a room where another three lads are sitting. Unless they are part of the firm then I'm not fucking interested in getting involved with them. Lofty points to a lad who's sitting in the corner with a joint in his mouth and a screwdriver in his hand, attempting to dismantle a large stereo speaker. Lofty says, "This is Muggy, he's part of the firm". Muggy goes on to tell me that he's just got out of jail that morning, and how shit it was. I'm thinking I don't like this; it feels way too hot and a million miles away from the set up in Spain with me, Neil and Trev, and surely if he's just got out of the jug then he'll have eyes on him. Lofty fucks off into the kitchen then reappears with another speaker and hands it to one of the other lads. He then disappears, returning with another for the other lad—they're all sitting there slowly dismantling them, removing the backs and as they do they produce a slab of coke, followed by another two. So that's how it came over, I like it! I'm presuming that mine will be amongst these; the ones I've seen so far appear to be a slightly different shape and I'm not taking one of those because they might be shit. There is also the chance they might be much better, but it's not my stuff so I'll take what's mine and not fuck around with taking chances.

I ask Lofty if mine are with these, and he says, "Yeah mate, come out here and let me know if you can see them". I walk through the small lounge, past the lads who are busy pulling slabs of coke out of speakers and into the kitchen, where I'm met with the magnificent sight of a lot of coke, more than I've ever seen before anyway. There are another four speakers on the deck and about twenty or so blocks on the side, all of them wrapped in brown tape, which is fucking annoying and although I'm sure they are a different shape, it's quite hard to tell. I'm gonna have to look for the ones that I've rewrapped and, more to the point, cut the fuckers open and find the obvious triangle that I cut away to test it. Which again seems like ages ago but was less than a week back.

I ask Lofty for a sharp knife or Stanley blade to start cutting open blocks—Lofty points towards a kitchen drawer and says, "Crack on, mate". This house is making me feel slightly uneasy, I don't want to be in here any longer than a few minutes but I've come so far to get this shit here so I need to see it through properly. I start carefully cutting through the blocks of coke, mindful not to spill any and they all look the same. I'm about to cut into my third when one of the lads in the next room says, "Is this them?". I walk in and can clearly see the difference from the others and say, "Yes mate, that's them, thank you". They are a different shape but only just and I can even see where I've repackaged them in a rush—what a fucking hash job! I ask Lofty for a decent carrier; he rummages around the kitchen drawers and produces a nice-looking IKEA bag—that'll fucking do. "Thank you mate, I'm gonna get off, it was good to meet you." Lofty responds saying, "Yeah, you too la. Neil says he'll be in touch soon". I head out and towards what still reminds me of an unmarked police car, subconsciously scanning the area as I get in and drive back towards the motorway.

My return journey mirrors the outbound one, only this time I'm calling the likes of Skimmer to arrange the dropoff. Shriek is the man to see and he'll be local to me when I arrive. The last 80 miles and this job is finally done, but the last leg is the one that always worries me. The chances of being caught feel as if they are increasing as I go through the various stages of dealing, and this has been a fucking beast of a deal, the better part of 4000 km for an earner of two and a half-grand. I must be fucking desperate, which indeed I am and I will continue to be desperate until this debt is paid. With the amount of work I'm taking on, I'm hoping that it'll be paid off fairly soon.

The last few miles and Shriek has been told to be there, and I've made it quite clear that I won't be seeing him in Tesco's or any other supermarket. He didn't like it but I feel that I've been running this coke for ages and now I'm making the decisions on where to offload it. I arrive at the arranged meeting place just after 18:00, feeling rather smug about my estimated timekeeping. I finally drop the coke into Shriek's hands and drive away feeling light, liberated and definitely happy I pulled it off. The baton is once again passed on and I dare say I'll be getting back a watered-down version of it tomorrow—this will be a day to put Hassan on the road and see how he gets on. I call Skimmer, he quickly answers and I say, "Done mate, I'm gonna shut down and spend some quality time with the family". Skimmer says, "Fair play mate, you made a good call using their network, I'll call you tomorrow when we're ready". "Thank you", I say and take the phone apart. Now it's time to relax with the family, or at least try.

I wake up feeling surprisingly positive, and so I should be. I've recently completed my first successful trip to smuggle cocaine. It does feel as if I've elevated myself to a different league: importation, heavy stuff, dancing with the big guns. I'm still going through the motions of being a husband and a dad, my focus firmly fixed on business. I know that once this debt is paid, I'll be making some big decisions to move on and get out of this business. I gather my thoughts and head out of the house, my intentions being to get Hassan out of his bed and see how he works. I'll be getting him to see Cliff's lads, the contacts of which I'm still waiting for and I'll put him into Wedge, Billy and Thornton—I'll cover the rest.

Groundhog Day is the best way to describe my morning routine, the same fucking shit every time. Get out of the area, build the burner, stress out a bit in case anything has gone tits up and then breathe a sigh of relief when it hasn't. I used to get a buzz from this shit, but not anymore though. That all went when I signed up for the coke market. My phone powers up, bearing in mind it is still early for most dealers to surface, especially Hassan; he likes his bed, his body clock spent so long doing the late shift with door work that he's never really changed it, but from now on it's strictly daytime shifts.

The phone remains silent, so I take the initiative and text Skimmer: "Call me when you get a chance". I also text Hassan: "Get up, you lazy fucker". I spend the next hour or so speaking to my lot, prepping them for a visit and they are happy for Hassan to come see them. Billy is a bit sceptical but accepts that I am on the up and staff will be a part of the process. My phone lights up and it's Skimmer; I answer, "Yes mate", he replies saying, "Yep, we're all good, Shriek will call you soon and he'll give you the contacts when he sees you, about half an hour". Ok here we go, I call Hassan's phone and he answers, barely able to speak. I say, "Stand by, I'm putting you on immediate notice", and as if by magic he wakes the fuck up and says, "No problem, where?", I respond by saying "Wait out".

That's how it should be done, and I know Hassan will be literally dashing around, frantically getting his shit together; it's his first day of work, can't be late now can he? It's not long before Shriek is on the phone, and as I look at it ringing I'm hoping everything is in order and more so, that the quality is good enough for my punters. I answer the phone and Shriek says, "We're ready, I'll see you where I saw you last night in about 20 minutes". Fucking hell he's learning, but I'd prefer to not use the same place twice in a row, so I say, "Yeah ok, but just down the road a bit". Shriek agrees and we both head towards our meeting point. I'm there in ten and en route I direct Hassan to a location close by, so I can offload his share of the goods, still unsure of how much I'll be getting on behalf of Cliff.

This is how I like it: organising things, getting my shit lined up, and Hassan knows how I work because we think in the same way. I've got a good feeling about this, and I shouldn't get too confident because something is guaranteed to bite me in the arse, but I can't help feeling more positive about Hassan's ability to get the job done. I move in and plot up near my pickup point—it's all good, quiet but not too quiet. I can see up and down the road, so I decide to get out and be on foot when Shriek arrives; I just hope he's on time as I don't wanna be hanging around like a fucking idiot. I casually wander along the road, trying my best to not look suspicious but ultimately looking very suspicious in the process. Shriek approaches from my front and he pulls over, looking way too serious. I get in and say, "Fucking hell mate, you look so angry", he half smiles and replies, "Oh, stressed out—we've been smashing this stuff for hours, I'm fucked". I laugh and only because I know exactly what he means. He hands me a rucksack and goes on to explain what's what; "There are two big bags in there, one has a box and a half and the other has two". A sudden warm feeling comes over me—I'm Cliff's biggest customer, the two are for me, so unless he only has one customer that makes me quite valuable and far from a fucking commodity. I take the bag and say, "Do you have the numbers?". Shriek hands me a small piece of paper with the contact information on it, I then say, "Are any of these cash customers?". Shriek replies, "No mate, we'll be collecting the cash, Cliff just wants you to drop the coke". "Good stuff," I say, this makes my life so much easier, as it's half a fucking job. I get out of the car and head back along the road to mine.

I drive out of the immediate area and call Hassan; he's advised me he's on plot, so I head directly for him to lighten my load. Hassan's parked discreetly on the perimeter of a B&Q car park; he's on foot so I head towards him, he locks in on me and adjusts his direction enough for me to not have to fuck about pulling into a space. Hassan gets in, we firmly shake hands and I say, "Are you all set mate?". Hassan, grinning like a Cheshire cat says, "Yep, what's the plan?". I pass him the rucksack and say, "If you can, pull the larger of the two out of there and what's left is yours to deliver. There's a key and a half". I hand him the paper and then say, "This should have all the info you need", but having not looked at it I can only hope it does. Hassan looks over the paper and says there are four drops, reeling off some names that I'm not familiar with: AJ, Spooks, Dil and Kanes.

Looks easy enough, although we don't know where the fuck these lads are yet. I say, "Mate I've got a few bits to offload myself, how do you want to do this, you wanna do two runs, this one then the next one or load up now?". Hassan looks at the weight and says, "Let me call them now, to see where they are and if they're ready". I fucking love this guy, the soldier in him is kicking into action, even if it was a part-time one, much better than no time at all. A few minutes pass and Hassan has finished his calls, slightly abrupt, but fuck it he's just become a drug dealer and being nice to strangers isn't really part of the job description—well not Cliff's lads anyway. Hassan says, "One of these lads is fucking miles away, but he has the smallest load, one is central near where I live, I'll take it all and put some of it down at mine while I offload the bigger stuff, then I'll come back and replenish".

Feeling more than satisfied with Hassan's plan, I drop him back to his car, while he loads up another key and a half for Wedge, Billy and Thornton—half a box each. I'll do the rest and I'll ensure that Hassan gets more than 500 for this—he'll be getting a fat bonus if this goes well. I'll be seeing Boe— don't think I'll risk exposing Hassan to his idiocy at this stage of the game—usual bullshit, he's asked for half a box and he'll fucking complain on Monday that he's had headaches and blah blah blah.

Once again I'm feeling the pressure of responsibility as Hassan heads off on his mission and I head off on mine, another 40 large on my bill and I can only hope the quality is worth the money—I guess I'll only have myself to blame, as I'm the one who picked it up. Reading between the lines though, I can easily work out how much it's been hit; Cliff's produced at least three and a half from the ones I collected, presuming Cliff and Si had one each. If I were to call Skimmer and ask how much he has left because I might need more, then I'll know exactly how good it is. I'll not do this yet though; I'll make sure Hassan is home and dry first then I'll do a bit of digging.

Time moves slowly when there's coke being shifted. I've done my drop to Boe and that was piss easy, I'm waiting for Hassan to call, but we did agree on radio silence until it was a job done. I can't go home, so I aim for town; maybe Hassan and I can grab a bite to eat when he's done, have a debrief and close down for the night. Knowing roughly how long these things can take and that Bill will be getting the kettle on, Hassan has at least four hours of running. Wedge will travel which is always nice—he'll be even more nervous when he sees the size of Hassan's fucking arms, and Hassan is wearing one of his tighter, tight tops.

After what feels like an eternity, my phone rings and it's Hassan; "Yes mate, are you ok?". Hassan says, "All good oppo, high and dry, heading back to the ranch". Feeling a sense of relief, I say "Nice one mate, I'll meet you in town, dinner's on me". It's the least I can do, as he's done me proud—Hassan is the first person that's been on my books that I can say rivals the Russian, and that's saying something, because the Russian was fucking good.

Chapter 11

PREPPING FOR ANOTHER RUN

O nce again I find myself patiently waiting for the next move. Hassan has been smashing it like a true soldier and I've been doing my best to whittle this never-ending debt down with Cliff. Over the last couple of weeks I've managed to shave another three off, so that brings it down to a nice and well-rounded 20 bags. Seven months of pure fucking stress working this debt off—80 bags! I can only imagine the things I could have done with that. Hassan has managed to build up a good rapport with Cliff's customers and he's beginning to build bridges with a couple of mine, but I haven't introduced him to Boe yet as that will more than likely get unnecessarily emotional. Hassan can get a bit angry from time to time and can be taken the wrong way, so all things considered, he's done well.

My phone rings, triggering me in the usual way but weirdly, seeing Si's name on it is, for once, quite a refreshing sight. I answer it, again feeling chilled and positive and say, "Hello mate, what's up?". Si replies, "All good, are you ready for another holiday?". I reply "Fucking right I am, what's the plan?". Si says, "We've got a few things to put in place first, so come see me at home and we'll go over it". I know where he lives or, at least, I know of a house that he is in regularly and says it's his home. It is quite possibly just a meeting place, as

Si's the sort of person who wouldn't let his address become public knowledge.

Heading towards Si's place is making me jumpy and for no reason other than what happened last year; there will always be a sense of self-preservation that kicks in when it comes to this kind of meeting. I disconnect my burner and leave it in the car before approaching the house, which is in a residential area close to the main road. One way in and one way out—not my choice of access routes but Si would likely shoot or fight his way out of anything, whereas I would be a tad more discreet, having multiple options.

I knock on the door and Si opens with a smile. "Come in, brother", he says; I say nothing but return the smile and enter the house. The last strange house I entered was full of Colombians, so this should be relatively stress-free. I go into the lounge and sit down, then Si sits opposite me and says, "Good shout on using Neil to carry the goods over, I was fucking panicking that you'd get tugged at customs". I respond, "Yeah mate, he seems to be good stuff and has brought me onto his team, I'm hoping it'll secure you and fuckface a better route for getting your work over". Si laughs and says, "How is that debt going, anyway?". I reply sarcastically—"It's going". Si has a little laugh then begins to explain the plan. "So we're gonna climb on board with Neil—his courier has asked if the coke can be stashed in a better way to get it over the channel, as he had a close call on the last run. We've made up a couple of false-bottomed boxes to take over to Coquelles so we can prepack the coke into them. Neil will then fill the fuckers up with car parts to disguise the cavity at the bottom".

I say, "Sounds good, but how are the logistics gonna work?". Si responds, saying "We've sorted you a hire van for next week. Once you've got that, head over to my mate's and load up the boxes—they're in his garage, I'll give you the address in a bit. We'll give you the dough before you go, then you truck on down to Windsor where Neil will change up your dosh. He'll explain the rest from there—as far as I can tell, you'll be heading on over and he's gonna catch up the next day". I sit back and mull it over then say, "Cool, I'm presuming the boxes are all good and of the correct dimensions". Si looks at me, and in a slightly sinister way says "Yes", as if to say "How dare you suggest I didn't do my homework!". We shake on it, and as we do I ask, "What's my commission on this one?". Si says, "Cliff will sort it out for you".

Well, here we go again then, back over to Spain next week. I can't fucking wait! I've not spoken to Neil in over a week so I call him to get a handle on the plan. He answers promptly, saying "What's going on la?"—Scouse accent, never gets boring. "Busy mate, I'm popping over yours next week, what's the score?". Neil responds, "You'll be doing a bit of work for us but nothing serious, make sure you're kitted out as before and you'll be fine". This sounds good to me—I can hardly wait—I guess I'll bring my ski kit and slug again then. I say, "No worries, sounds intriguing"; he says, "Nah la, it's normal fucking bullshit logistics REMFS work". I say, "Cheeky fucker, I'm not an REMF!". He laughs and says, "I know la, but someone's gotta do it". We have a chat for a bit and agree that I'll contact him next Thursday when I head down to his neck of the woods. My next plan is for me to load up Hassan, leaving him to run things back here while I re-supply over there.

The weekend comes and goes, as does the majority of the week. I've loaded up Hassan to keep him busy and for once everyone seems to be happy and content, even the missus— I've been feeding a bit more money into the house—not much mind, but as the debt decreases so does the pressure. I've told her that my security contract in Europe is doing well and I'll be doing a few more days, so I'm hoping it's enough to keep her off the scent. Having Hassan on board is fucking delightful— he's taken a huge amount of stress off me and he simply cracks on, I love it! The smokescreen is successfully deployed and my family are all in good stead; I'm so much more relaxed doing this, knowing that I don't have to do the channel. The rest as far as I'm concerned is shits and gigs, and in a weird way I'm enjoying the idea of what lies ahead.

It's time to get the van so I'm heading towards a different car hire place this time, but it's the same fucking script. I drive in, park my unmarked, head in to do the paperwork and drive out in a Merc Sprinter. I've got Si's mate's address in hand and it's only a short hop away, so I promptly head over there. I've still got the old faithful satnav, which I've now come to realise I couldn't do without. I've still got my map but the satnav is definitely the way forward; it will however be my undoing if I get nicked, since the addresses on this thing will bury me and potentially whoever I've visited. I approach Si's mate's house, reverse onto the drive, park up, get out and pop open the back doors of the van. Si said not to bother knocking as they'll all be out; that there will be a bag in the box containing the correct amount of money for the exchange; to load up and fuck off as quick as poss. I lift up the garage door, only to be confronted with two fucking humongous boxes! Are we smuggling coke or people?

I look them over, immediately noticing a dark rucksack, presumably the bag of dosh. I peer into the box and reach down to retrieve the bag. I can see that the bottoms are false, but it's cleverly done as the boxes are deep—deep enough to not notice the difference from the outside. I quickly check the money and for once it looks like it's in good order, so I sling it into the front with my stuff. Next I go to lift a box into the van—fuck me they weigh a ton! I have to manoeuvre one up onto its edge lengthways and walk it towards the van, but as I do this the false bottom falls away revealing the cavity. I like it—plenty of room for kit. I replace the false bottom and continue to load the boxes onto the van again, ensuring the bottoms are correctly fitted. I opt to leave the lids off and place them at the front of the van against the bulkhead. The two boxes barely fit but they just go in lengthways, taking up most of the floor space.

With the boxes secured, I get back into the van and do a quick checklist; kit, comms and money are good. It's time to start this mission, so I hit the fucking road and head straight for the motorway. The difference I feel this time is unreal—so chilled, actually enjoying it. Windsor's an hour away; I give Neil a heads up and he says to call him when I'm close, as we need to head to Kingston first to sort out the money. I climb onto the M4 and start the first leg of what could be my greatest adventure. I've got a feeling that the stakes are gonna be higher, but as I'm now part of a team, the risks are shared. I've got limited accountability and for a change, I quite like it.

142

A little over an hour later and with no issues with traffic, I begin to close in on Windsor. I've given Neil the heads up and he's said to head for Lofty's yard. I can vaguely remember where it is, but trying to not make any unnecessary calls I do my utmost to find the address without breaking radio silence. Much to my relief I find the address—it was easy enough because it's the only area that I would class as a shithole in an affluent area such as Windsor, so not too hard to find. I have a quick recce of the area, and feeling fairly confident that it's all good I park nearby, stash the bag of dosh under the seat and head over to the house. There are a couple of cars parked outside; one of them is Neil's car, the same one he was in last time we worked together. He must be spending a fortune on expenses, such as hiring cars all the time—it does make me curious about how much he's making. Going by the amount of coke that was being pulled out of those speakers the other week, it's got to be a fair bit.

I cautiously approach the front door and gingerly knock, not too loud but loud enough. I know what it's like to be plotted up in a house used for dealing and have the door go—there are certain knocks that can send you into a near meltdown—reaching for the hardware or flushing the evidence. A few moments pass and the door is opened by Lofty, who smiles and says "Hello". I return the compliment and walk in, only to be greeted by Neil, who says, "Let's have a look at these boxes, shall we?". I do an immediate about-turn and walk back out, saying, "Yes mate, let's go". We walk away from the house, with Lofty staying put. I deactivate the alarm, unlocking the back doors in the process. Neil climbs into the van, I stand at the back looking in, he has a rummage around, and whilst leaning into the box, his voice sounding faint and muffled, he shouts, "Sound these, la". Not really giving too much of a fuck, I say "Yeah mate, they should do the job".

He climbs out of the van and says, "Right, if you follow me, we need to go to Richmond to get the money exchanged. My other lot are pissing around with the rates and they'll only give 1.3 on the pound, but you need 1.4 to have enough to make the purchase". I'm beginning to realise that this is quite a big setup and Neil must have multiple things going on; this is definitely a level way beyond what I've worked at. I reply, "Sure mate, what's the crack after that?". He says, "So once you've got the money changed, head on over to Coquelles again. You'll need to park the van up in a specific car park, hide the keys on it somewhere and leave it there". I say "Ok then what?"; Neil then says "Get the train from there to Paris—I'll give you the Paris address in a sec. There's a Spanish renter parked up in a hotel car park—the key is hidden on the back wheel. Grab that and head on down to Fuengirola, then check into the same hotel as last time. Use some of the dosh you have on you to cover your costs—I'll replace it when I arrive the next day".

I'm loving this—a proper road trip—I say, "Sounds good to me", and ask "How long has the car been parked up for?". Neil looks at me and says, "A few days—Trev was doing something with it so it should be fine". My mind is beginning to race slightly. What has Trev used it for? Is there a marker on it? What's in the boot? I guess if I'm part of this firm, then I need to accept certain things as they are, and stop fucking stressing. Neil hands me a piece of paper; on it is a list of addresses and a vehicle make, model and registration. Looking it over I confirm what I'm seeing with him and say, "Ok the first address is the car park for the van; the second is the hotel where the car is parked in Paris; the car is a red Golf with Spanish plates, situated on the third floor; the parking ticket is on the dash and has been paid for". He looks at me and says, "Yes la, spot on". He then says, "Come on, let's saddle up and get you on your way".

Neil walks over to his car and I shout out, "You got an address for me?". He turns and goes into his phone, I approach him and he reads out an address which I text into my phone. He says, "Follow me, only put that into your satnav if we lose each other". I reply, "Ok mate, understood". I head back over to the van, close the back doors and get in. Neil gets into his car and heads off—I pick him up as he passes. The great thing about working with squaddies is that they understand the principles of how a convoy works. A military convoy is a well drilled discipline; if you fuck it up you get a boot in the back of your head so it's a quick and steep learning curve. He maintains a realistic speed, knowing I'm carrying around 30 grand on me, and after being pulled into a French police station last time, I've learnt my lesson about speeding whilst loaded up.

Richmond isn't that far and it's around lunchtime, so not a lot of traffic, but none of this is particularly relevant as I'm more curious about this money exchange. Where are we doing it? A bank? A travel agent's? I'm assuming it's Neil doing the exchange for me. While I'm mulling this thought over, Neil indicates and pulls into a parking space next to a long row of shops, restaurants and cafés, very much like the ones Si and I sat in last month. He gets out and walks over to me, standing by the driver's door as I drop the window. He says, "Ok, see that shop in the middle? It's a convenience store—the one next to the café with the seats outside". I look over and clock the seats on the pavement under a canopy outside. I then look at the shop next to it which looks like a general store, the kind that sells all sorts of shit. I look at Neil and say, "Seen"; he smiles and then says, "Right, so head in there with your bag, and as you walk in you'll see a small bureau de change on the left with a guy behind a counter. He'll be expecting you as I've just called him and given him the five-minute heads up". I then say, "Ok, so do I just hand him the bag and fuck off?". Neil looks at me and says, "For a Tanky you're a quick learner". I look at him and raise one eyebrow—he knows what I'm thinking—"Twat".

Neil walks back to his car and gets in, as I simultaneously get out of the van carrying the rucksack full of money. I casually walk over to the shop entrance, still unsure of what to expect, scanning up and down the road as I enter. Hoping the shop isn't busy, and keeping my head down I enter and look around inside. It's a standard setup, apart from the counter being shielded by a protective booth—a bit like a bank. The guy behind it nods at me and I approach. Popping the side door open, he reaches out with his hand below waist height and I pass him the bag as discreetly as possible. He takes it, retracts his hand, closes the door and says to come back at 14:00. I acknowledge this and head out of the shop, feeling slightly uneasy but having faith that what's going on must be a well-used and efficient system.

Neil clocks me as I exit and walk back to my van—he then pulls away and I blindly follow. We only drive for a few minutes before he pulls into a car park; I follow and park up slightly away from him. I get out and walk over to him. A big smile on his face, he says "Right la, let's sort the phones out". We head towards a shopping precinct, casually chatting about random stuff, locate a Vodafone shop and walk in. He beelines straight for the cheapest phones, grabs two, goes straight to the counter and pays for them in cash. This shouts drug dealers, but I'm sure he knows what he's doing; we then head back out of the shop. At this point I'm feeling like a right fucking sheep, following Neil everywhere. I decide to say, "What's the crack with the phones then mate, shall I offload that Spanish burner you gave me last time?". He says, "Yeah mate, bin that—use one of these until you land in Spain, then we'll all grab new Spanish ones before we start working". I reply, "Ok, good news —I'll jog it on, I'll shut down my UK burner and switch off the clean one. I'll need to check in on a couple of things from time to time though". Neil says, "Yeah, that's not a problem".

Although I've been told to return to the shop at 14:00, Neil has said that he's waiting for a phone call once the money's sorted. In the meantime I'm already mentally planning my timings, primarily considering that I need to get the money over the channel as well as two hand-crafted boxes—boxes that will raise some eyebrows if they decide to look inside. I'll be going over on the Dover-Calais ferry this time, so I have all of this in mind, along with travel timings. I might have to plot up on the other side of the channel, and more than likely I'll be in that same, shitty hotel in Coquelles. I'll see how it goes; it doesn't appear like there's any urgency to get to Spain and all the expenses are being covered so fuck it—I may as well try and relax and enjoy the process.

It's approaching 14:00 and Neil's phone rings. My sense of relief is quickly followed by disappointment as he hangs up after saying, "There's been a small delay—another hour". Feeling a bit frustrated but at the same time accepting that these things happen, I ask him what the delay is. He responds, saying "It's quite normal, they have to go to the bank and do a mass exchange. The money needs to be pre-ordered from the bureau and because he's doing us a favour and obviously he's earning on it, he has to go to a couple of banks to get the rates he needs". It's all beginning to make sense now so I say, "Right, I get it". Neil says, "We may as well get some scran". I've not even had a chance to respond and he's already walking into the first place that has food.

We take a seat and mull over the menu. I'm making the assumption that Neil is paying, even though I've brought my own finances, unlike the last time. My money is a little bit better and I've brought a backup grand with me, my aim being to change some of it on the boat. It feels quite nice, actually. After everything I've been through—the stress, the debt and all the other shit I've had to deal with, I'm finally beginning to feel like I've got some money again. I have no intention of breaking my neck paying Cliff back, not as long as he's paying me a poxy two grand, especially for this level of work. I've not even discussed with Neil about money from him—is he paying me to do this or have I been roped into this while Cliff and Si get looked after? The truth is, I'm not too bothered. Weirdly enough, the experience is all I'm fussed about—payment comes in many forms. I'm still looking at the menu and Neil says, "What're you having?". I look at it again and blindly and somewhat randomly choose the first thing that jumps out at me.

I say, "Club sandwich, please mate". He looks across at the girl behind the counter and shouts, "Eh love, two club sandwiches and two chips please". He looks at me and says, "You wanna drink?". I immediately respond, "Yeah, coke please". Neil again shouts out "... and two cokes. Ta, love".

We spend an hour sitting, relaxing and enjoying our food, whilst I'm subconsciously thinking of the passage of time. Two false-bottomed boxes and over €40.000 will be stashed in the van. I've not even considered where I'll be hiding them and I'm presuming that they will be in Bin Ladens again. I'm hearing Neil talk but I'm not really listening—my mind keeps wandering and as the clock ticks—I do feel a tad more stress creep in. I don't like to come across as rude, but I want to get on the road and at least into France, and all this waiting around is doing my nut in.

Neil's phone has rung several times but not once has it been from the money man. It's just gone 15:30 and finally the call we've been waiting for comes through. The phone stuck to his ear, a big grin slowly spreads across Neil's face—he's clearly receiving positive news. He looks at me and silently says "You're on". This phrase takes me back to last month, when he gave me the same news about the coke deal in Madrid. It's like pulling a trigger that fires me into action—I love it! We both get up; I head for the door and Neil pays the bill, leaving a substantial tip, or that's what it looks like. We exit the café and go back to the car park, Neil saying, "Follow me back there; I'll plot up outside on overwatch, he's expecting you again". "Cool", I say and get into the van.

We head off back in the reciprocal direction, and literally moments later Neil is pulling over into a space outside the shop. I have to continue further down the road to find a space big enough for the van. I pull over, check my mirrors and get out, locking the doors as I walk away. Once more I approach the shop on full alert, while Neil sits in his car, making sure the coast is clear. Again keeping my face down, avoiding being seen on any CCTV I walk into the shop. Thankfully it's empty, apart from the same guy that I saw earlier. Getting a bit of deja vu, he looks at me and nods. I walk up to the counter and he passes me an A5 envelope, clearly rammed to the hinge with Bin Ladens. I take it, say "Thank you" and exit the store. I walk outside, not even acknowledging Neil, and walk straight over to the van. I get in, start up and fuck off.

Looking in my mirrors, I see Neil pull out and follow me. My phone rings and predictably it's him—I answer by saying, "Hello mate, I'm all good here". He replies, "Have you checked it yet?". My response is, "I will once I'm out of the area". He says, "Ok, there should be slightly over 42 large in there—he got the rate at 1.41". That's good news—an extra cent times 30 large. I take a moment to work it out and I come to the conclusion that I can't, so I decide to wait until I pull over. Neil says, "Ok la, you're on your own from now on; radio silence until I see you at the bottom". I say, "Ok bud, no worries, see you in a couple of days—I'll be doing the other side tomorrow, gonna plot up once I hit the mainland".

I head on out of Richmond and put Dover into the satnav. As I enter the details, I see a convenient layby to pull into so I can check the dough. It's quiet so I pull up to the very end of the layby, park up, leave the engine running and check my mirrors. I pop open the envelope to see the familiar sight of €500's. Pulling them out, I also clock three green ones— €300. I start counting the purple ones—84 is where it needs to be. Trying to take my time, whilst periodically checking my mirrors, I flick through the money. First check, 83; trying to be calm and still checking my mirrors I go again, not worrying about the green ones. Second count—84; I double check it— 84; that'll do for me. I put the purple ones back into the envelope and stick the €100's into my bag. Looking around the van, I think now would be a good time to stash the money. After a good look around the driving compartment and weighing up the possibility of stashing the money in the rear, I look down at the heavy-duty rubber flooring around the area by the transmission tunnel. It lifts up where the base of the gear stick is located, so I stuff the envelope under the rubber flooring and push it all back into place. I like it—it's not particularly dark but I can't see any sign of anything under the mats. Feeling rather confident, and temporarily oblivious to the fact that I'm still hauling two fuck off, false-bottomed boxes, I stick the music on and head for Dover.

Closing in on Dover always reminds me of the return route back to camp. Whether it was a bank holiday mad one or a block leave, you were almost guaranteed to bump into other squaddies that were based over in Germany. You can guarantee it was always the latest possible ferry as well—talk about cutting it fine! First parade at 08:30 and we'd be getting the 23:00 ferry, leaving zero margin for error but we always made it. Well, most of us did and those that didn't would normally be covered for by the lads. The switched-on ones would press their kit and polish their boots before going but the slack ones wouldn't, so you can guarantee I'd be frantically polishing my boots and pressing my kit with ten minutes to go, before rushing out of the block across the parade square to the squadron office for inspection.

I drop down the hill and into Dover port; it's early evening so not particularly busy, in fact it's surprisingly quiet—this isn't particularly good as I prefer the port to be busy. Common sense says that if they are busy they'll need to push the traffic through in order to get everyone loaded up, but if they're quiet then boredom would surely give them more time to look over more vehicles. I've already got my cover story rehearsed; my in-laws moved over to Spain last year and have excess kit so I'm helping them to bring a load back to go into storage. It works for me and in my own delusional way I've convinced myself that the HMRC will buy it.

I park up and steam into the ticket office, and taking the delay we had last time into consideration I opt for a semi-open return, coming back no later than a week, which is next Wednesday. That should be plenty of time, if not then I'll worry about it when the moment comes. One hundred and fifty euros later, I get back in the van and drive towards the ticket inspection booth. My nerves are now beginning to elevate as my next bit is HMRC. I hand over the ticket which they swiftly process, then without hesitation I head towards the HMRC checkpoint.

It's dark and I'm feeling nervous, yet relatively confident that they won't suspect anything. I clock the recognisable Hi Vis vests and dark uniforms of the HMRC—fucking hell, here we go again. The customs officer approaches my side of the van and starts the usual script; "Evening sir, how are you?". I politely reply saying "Very well, thank you". He then asks, "Can I have a quick look in the back?". I immediately oblige by switching off the engine and walking to the rear of the van. I open the doors and the interior light switches on, revealing the two fuck off boxes in the back. He asks, "What's in the boxes?". I get into the van, gesture that they are empty and start to reel off my well-rehearsed story about relatives, too much stuff, blah blah blah. The customs officer replies with "Ok thank you, have a safe trip". I smile with a genuine sense of relief and say, "Thank you, have a good night". I get back into the van, conscious of the €84.000 below my feet, start up and fuck off—sharpish.

Fucking hell that was all right—that huge sense of euphoria still coursing through my body— it's times like these that seem to justify my involvement. Short moments of victory that seem to keep me pushing further into this world—the feeling that I might actually be really good at this smuggling lark. I'm directed to join a relatively short queue of traffic in lane "A"; all being well I'll be first on and first off. I know I can relax now as there won't be any further checks on the French side, or at least there shouldn't be. I'm gonna leave the dosh in situ for now—it's well hidden and I don't really need to be carrying it around on the boat. My plan is for a quick scran and a bit of fresh air; by then we should be approaching Calais.

In my boredom I rummage through my bag and its various pockets to see if there's any random cash knocking about. I've been known to tuck things away and forget about them, and this travel bag has pockets everywhere. Feeling through the pockets, I locate my backup grand and dig out 300 quid to change on the boat; I don't intend to touch it but it'll be nice to have at hand, just in case. Alarmingly what I do locate is a small, metal tin. What the fuck, it's my pot tin! I take it out and crack it open. Shit, it's not empty—enough for a joint and more than enough to fucking sink me if it gets found. I quickly grab a pair of boxers out of the bag and wipe the tin all over, as well as the lighter inside, removing any of my prints. I then stash the tin under the van seat, so if it gets found I can go for the plausible deniability. It shouldn't matter, as the van's being dumped at Coquelles and will be coming back empty. Although this is all a bit late, I'd rather be cautious. What I should do is fucking bin it right away, but I quite like the idea of a victory joint on my way home next week—if I make it, that is.

The boat slowly docks and the incoming vehicles unload. Not long after, we get the green light to load up; I start up and thankfully lane "A" is the first to drive on. Looking around there's not a lot going on, maybe 40 or so smaller vehicles, but saying that, there are a lot of trucks. Once again I blindly follow the car in front and drive along the lane towards the ramps to load up, periodically looking down at the floor, making sure the money hasn't magically moved. It hasn't, but part of me is thinking what if there's a hole in the floor and it's fallen through and is now lying on a road somewhere near Dover? Paranoia.

I drive onto the boat and I'm guided to move in as close to the vehicle in front as possible, then asked to switch off the engine and apply the handbrake. All done—now it's time for some food and an hour's rest. Again I check that the money is secure and hide my bags on the floor, conveniently covering the area where the money is stashed. Feeling a bit uneasy, I leave the money where it is and lock the van, then walk around it and individually check every door is locked. They are and, feeling satisfied that the money is safe, I head for the stairs and what will be a bit of a break, as I mentally prepare for the next leg of these overseas operations.

Chapter 12

ANOTHER EUROPEAN ROAD TRIP

Money changed, belly full of food, lungs full of fresh air—I'm feeling good as the clock approaches 22:00 local time and we slowly shudder into Calais port. The tannoy goes off and, like sheep, the drivers all head down towards their respective vehicles. Feeling unnecessarily anxious I walk towards the van, hoping it hasn't been targeted by thieves. Yet again the same old ridiculous paranoia is triggering my anxiety, and as any sane person would know, the van hasn't been fucking targeted and the money is still there— exactly how I left it, not 90 minutes ago.

From my position I'm within sight of the ferry's bow doors, so will most likely be one of the first off. The ferry jolts to a sudden stop as it moors up to the dock and, within seconds, the doors begin to open and the crew fires into action. I'm not feeling too smug yet, but I reckon I can safely say the money is now on the European continent. Like the grid at the start of an F1 race, the engines all fire up and the drivers prepare to move. Thumbs up and we're off! As we all slowly move off the boat I remind myself: right side of the road. I say it a few times over to ensure it sinks in. Whilst we gradually drive off, I input Coquelles into the satnav and head for the same area that I stayed in last time. Apparently, I can leave the van at the train station car park and pay for a long-stay ticket, an arrangement that will simplify things tomorrow when I head south.

As I clear the port, I know Coquelles is only a few minutes' drive, but I don't think the train station is as close. Either way it's gonna be a matter of minutes to get to, and as far as I'm aware I'm not on any timescales tomorrow. I just need to get to Fuengirola, and to achieve that it's gonna be a mixture of trains, taxis and another car that has been parked up somewhere in Paris. All of this and I'm carrying a fuck ton of money—I love it! Just a few minutes to go and I'll be there. The area does become familiar as I clock the complex where the Buffalo Grill and hotel are located. As I pull into the hotel car park, it's at this point I decide to dig out the money and stick it into my travel bag.

I look around the dark car park and, not seeing anybody around nor anything that concerns me, I lift the heavy rubber mat and grab the envelope of cash, peeking up over the dashboard as I do so. Cash in hand I then stick it into my travel bag and zip it up. I get out of the van and, constantly scanning my arcs and doing my best to make it subtle, I walk towards the hotel to get some well-earned sleep. I'm intending to be up and about relatively early and I know for a fact I won't sleep too well in a shitty hotel—I don't even sleep well in good ones either, so doubtless a rough night lies ahead of me.

Dawn is breaking as I wake up. I look at the time and it's just after 07:00—that'll do me. Shit, shower and shave—I'm trying to soften my appearance and looking like a fat, unshaven skinhead won't fucking help. Prior to departing my room I get eyes on the cash again and double-check that everything is in order. As I do, I pull out a couple of Ladens for my upcoming travel expenses. Fuck knows what the train's gonna cost and although Neil says the parking for the car is paid, I'd best be ready for a bill if not. I've already spunked the majority of the €300 on ferry and hotel costs and I'm determined not to touch mine. I've got just over €450 plus the two Bin Ladens—that will be ample to get me to Fuengirola.

Again I'm fucking scanning my arcs, walking towards the van and again as usual it's clear. I get in, start up and fuck off. I'm still observing radio silence and the missus isn't expecting a call anytime soon, but I do miss chatting to my kids. As always that urge has to be suppressed so I can concentrate on getting the job done. I hate it—why can't I have a normal life and be there for them all the time? I feel like a part-time dad and not a very good one at that. I'm dominated by these subconscious thoughts, but I honestly believe that they give me a look of relative vacancy while I'm doing what I do, and that must have its uses. The train station is easy to find; even without the satnav it's easy enough, as is the car park which is literally across the road from the station. I park up and gather my goods, mindful of my pot tin under the seat, in fact, fuck it I'll roll a victory joint now and stash it in the tin—that'll be a right treat when I get onto the return journey.

I find the ticket machine and start throwing money into it. If I've read it right, it'll cost about €45 for the week—not too bad. I return to the van and put the ticket on the dash, then I get my shit together, double checking the van is empty and locking it up. Yet again I walk around the van and ensure all the doors are locked. I then stash the keys out of sight, on the back wheel.

Looking like a tramp with my bag and slug, I head over to the station to suss out the tickets and departures. It's quiet with just a few commuters—it's approaching eight in the morning and it's Friday, so who knows how busy it'll get. I walk in and have a look at the departures, but not making a lot of sense of them I opt to go straight to the ticket office and ask instead. A short time later, after speaking my worst French ever, I establish that I can pick up the high-speed train direct to Paris. It arrives in about half an hour and will have me there by late morning; all this for the princely sum of €78. A piece of piss, or at least I thought it was until I produced a Bin Laden, when I got that all-too-familiar look, the same one I got last month from the woman in the service station. She starts shaking her fucking head, but surprisingly she took the money and gave me the ticket, along with a fuck load of change—loose change. I guess that's a bit of payback.

Looking around the station, it's clear to see what side I should be standing on as there are only two platforms, and one looks like it heads for the sea. I join a group of commuters and dig in for the next 15 minutes, taking in my surroundings and pretty much measuring up every fucker standing on the platform; killing time; doing my best to suppress my intrusive thoughts. As I debate whether pushing some random person onto the track is a good idea or not, the train silently pulls into the station. Ooh it's electric! I've not been on one like this before, just the clatty old diesels back home. These are meant to be quick.

Only a couple of people get off and, being British, I start queuing but realise that this is fucking pointless over here, as everyone else steams towards the small door and bottlenecks themselves in. While this is happening I look into the carriage and see that there are plenty of seats available so, feeling chilled, I simply bide my time until the door is clear of angry, stressed-out commuters. I enter the train and a calm sense of silence and peace descends upon me. Walking past the luggage storage racks, I find a seat by the window and place my bags on the seat next to me. I sit back, take a deep breath and relax, preparing to be thrilled or not, as the case may be, by the speed of this beast.

Stretching my back up I peer over the top of the seats to suss who's on the carriage and for the most part it's relatively quiet, so I slowly slump back into my seat, and as I do the train starts to move. It's so quiet; even the tracks don't have that clackety-clack sound that I'm used to. As we slowly accelerate I can see the power lines are supported by gantries every 100 or so metres and these gantries are passing me by faster and faster as we leave the built-up area and head into the open French countryside. We keep accelerating until the train hits 200 mph—that's officially the fastest I've been on land. I'll add that to my achievements list.

I spend the journey reflecting and thinking about how nice life will be once I've paid the debt off, and consider that once that's done, I'll be getting out of the game and going straight. But these are just dreams at the moment—simple dreams to keep me pushing forward. The same kind of dreams you imagine when stuck in a fucking wet hole on operational duties, and I don't mean the female kind. I'm remembering the address that Neil gave me yesterday; I have a look in my pocket and thankfully it's still there. I'll taxi it from the station to the hotel and get the parking sorted. I'm bouncing down through

Andorra again so, time depending, I might plot up there again for the night.

It's just after 11:00 and we're slowing down. Paris is close and the next leg should be a short one—well I fucking hope so, as I don't wanna be hauling 80 grand through Paris. As we close in on the station the scenery transforms from rural to urban in a flash and as it changes, so does my state of mind. Different environments will always require a different tact. When in a rural area my obs are covering a wider area over a larger distance, whereas urban it's the total opposite. This is close-quarter stuff; pickpockets in this city are rife and if these fuckers knew what was in the bag, they'd be retiring on it.

The train smoothly pulls into the Gare du Nord and stops. The majority of passengers are already up and waiting, but I'll sit tight, as I don't want to get held up in a crowd. The doors open and the passengers all spill out onto the platform. As they do this I follow them—keeping a bit of distance and pushing through a few impatient fucks trying to board the train before I've cleared the door—fuck off! Successfully off the train I immediately head for the taxi rank; plenty to choose from so I just get into the first one I find and deploy my excellent French, asking him to take me to the Hotel d'Alsace. He says, "Oui, monsieur", and drives away from the station. I barely start taking in the sights of Paris when the driver pulls over and says, "Hotel d'Alsace monsieur, onze euros". What the fuck I could have walked! I was only in the car for about three minutes, for fuck's sake. I offload some of the change I was given at the train station and get out, checking the seats are clear as I do.

Nice hotel—I walk in and look for signs for the car park. There should be a multi-story somewhere, hopefully it's attached to the hotel and not fucking miles away. I approach the reception desk and ask if they can direct me to the car park; the receptionist indicates that the lift will take me to the lower first floor which then provides access to the car park on the opposite side of the road, via a footbridge. Ok happy days—off I go, trying not to become complacent with my load, but at the same time subconsciously forgetting about the stress allows my body language to look more relaxed and less drug dealer-like.

Ok so red Golf, third floor, off I go. Over the bridge, looking down at the busy Paris traffic below, soon to be one car busier. Fortunately the bridge exits on the third floor and it's not exactly massive. I wander along the row of cars looking for the Golf and it's easy to clock, as it's the only red car in a sea of darker colours. Stress levels rising as my hypervigilance kicks in. Again questions: Is the car marked? What has Trev been doing in it? Is it carrying anything that I don't know about? I walk past it once and have a precautionary recce and, once satisfied, I approach the car and go straight for the back wheel. Choice of two and I get the wrong one—perfectly normal for me. I do the same every time I open a packet of paracetamol; I always open the end with the instructions folded over the pills; 50/50 every time and I lose.

I go to the other wheel and momentarily the thought occurs to me that the keys might not be there. That would be a drama, but luckily I feel around and get my hands on them. Feeling relieved I pop the alarm, open the boot, secure my bags and close the lid, but having second thoughts I pop the boot, go into the bag and dig out the drug money. I'm stashing that in the car somewhere, as I still need to get this into Spain. While I'm there I dig out the satnav, then close the boot and get in the car. I have a look around and familiarise myself with the interior, looking for somewhere to stash the cash. Bollocks it's a well-made car so there aren't really any nooks and crannies to hide it, so I go back to the boot and have a look in there. Boot lining is looking good. I don't need much space, just enough. I pull away at the top over the wheel arch and manage to tuck the envelope in nicely—somewhat more easily than with the two keys of coke in the boot of the Vectra.

I pop Andorra la Vella into the satnav. Jesus, 860 km! That's a 10-hour drive with stops; it's only 11:45 now and I'm definitely not speeding, so my ETA will be around 22:00—I guess that's my overnight stay sorted. I drive out of the space and exit the car park, joining the traffic. These Parisian drivers are bonkers so I'll have to be mindful as I head out of the city. Surprisingly, the route out of Paris went well and I hit the A10 south. The route is long, relatively straight and mind-numbingly boring, but plenty of coffee stops en route.

The miles and hours while away, as I progress through the limited collection of CD's that I always carry. Plenty of Hed Kandi, which keeps me awake and reminds me of the days when I got caught up in all this mess. Fond memories with no stress—pills in clubs, very little cocaine and a lot of dancing. It's a long haul but I'm gradually reeling Andorra in; a few more hours and I'll be in the mountains. As the daylight begins to fade I can just make out the Pyrenees mountains in the distance, and as they draw closer the sun finally disappears, for yet another drive through the mountain roads in the dark. It's tiring and slow, but a refreshing break from the monotony of the motorways. Every corner I take I hope to see the glow of Andorra la Vella, and although the satnav says it's close I still can't see it. Suddenly it just fucking appears.

Finally the sight I've been waiting for, Andorra! I'm here, running a tad later than I'd hoped, but these mountain roads are slow going, especially if you get stuck behind a coach. I head straight for the same hotel as last time as it was cheap and did the job. I'm not particularly hungry as I've been picking at shit all day so a good sleep is all I need. I even manage to park up in the same place as last time. I get my bags and decide to leave the money where it is, as the space is well-lit and right outside the hotel, so it's unlikely that the car will be broken into. Even if it was, are they really gonna be rifling through the boot lining? I pray not.

Checking in was painless and with my bags in hand I beeline straight for my room. Last time I was here my head was battered, but this feels different, almost enjoyable. Hot shower and bed, I do however take some time out to call home and catch up with family life. Surprisingly, I actually feel somewhat attached to everything, whereas normally I'd just go through the motions, but this is different; it feels nice and natural, not as if I'm trying to force the emotions. As the obvious pressure to pay up reduces, my head is getting better, and although I'm still on the happy pills, I honestly feel like I might not need them for much longer. I can most definitely sense the stress of the debt is being reduced. Along with being considered an asset, working with Neil over here and helping Cliff shift his stuff with help from Hassan, my faculties and rational thinking are beginning to surface. And to think only earlier today I was thinking of walking away from it all—as if!

I wake up feeling good. I can hear the ski lifts in the distance operating and this tells me one thing—I've slept in too fucking long. It's gone 09:00 and for me that's way too late; I normally surface at around 07:00 but am usually stirring from 06:30. This is the time the door goes off if it's on top, so I tend to sleep light around this time. There's no breakfast included here, in fact I don't think they even have a restaurant. Gathering my kit, I check I've got everything and head on out of my room and down the stairs, handing my key to the receptionist as I exit the hotel. I clock the car quick time and seeing it still there and intact brings a sense of relief.

I pop my bags into the boot and double-check that the money is there and well stashed—it is. I get in and prepare for the final leg of this part of my journey. Fuengirola dialled in, here we go again; well over 1000 km; another full day's driving. I pull away and head for the first petrol station to fill up the car with cheaper, tax-free fuel. Once that's done, I hit the road that crosses the border and thankfully it looks unmanned. Passport in hand just in case, I gingerly drive towards the checkpoint and notice two guards sitting in the office. They both look at me as I pull up to the virtual border and immediately gesture at me to keep going. Happy days— I'm in Spain, cash successfully smuggled over, and I've kept the expenses to a minimum. If I'm going by the cost of the last deal, I'll need around €80,000, so I've actually got a few quid spare, and that's going into my pocket.

The drive out through the mountains was pure joy. I'm that close I can almost taste the cocaine. As I progress into Spain and due south, I whack on my burner and give Neil a shout to see where he is. He answers fairly quickly and we spend a few minutes updating each other. He's confirmed that my destination is still Fuengirola and he's already there but we won't be hanging around. We'll be leaving first thing to head straight back up to the Mad one. That's gonna be a quick turnaround, as I'm not going to be getting to the coast until about 23:00. Neil said to check into the same hotel as last time and he'll get me squared away with the expenses first thing. This is fucking mint! Not only have I saved a few quid on the way down, but he's also gonna return the wedge I've dished out.

There's a noticeable change in the temperature as I get further south. Then again it is spring but the difference to last month is noticeable—probably should have brought some shorts with me, but oh no, I bring fucking ski kit that I've got to haul around! I do keep forgetting how dry and empty Spain is compared to the UK. The only real sight that is worth seeing is these big fuck off silhouettes of bulls on the side of hills—apart from that it's fucking boring. It even makes the M42 seem interesting.

The hours and kilometres are racking up and I'm smashing it. Satnav is saying arrival at 22:00 but I'll be having a piss stop and a coffee soon, so 23:00 is more likely. Once again I'm driving around the back of the Sierra Nevada mountains and yet again I can't see a fucking thing—it's pitch black and with no ambient light, so all I can see is fucking traffic. Closing in on Fuengirola is such a nice feeling and again I'm comparing my sense of emotions from last time, and this definitely feels better. I like working with Neil and he's already said that Trev is on board again. Trev does give me the feeling that he wants it to kick off, as opposed to a peaceful resolution where we don't lose any money, drugs or lives.

Although I was plotted up here for a few days last month, I don't really know my way around the place. The easiest option is to head for the seafront and locate the hotel from there. I'm looking for the signs saying *Playa* or *Paseo Maritime*, which mean "beach" or "seafront"; not really sure if I'll see either or if the Spanish bother with stuff like that. While I'm busy figuring this out I see the seafront; keeping the Med on my left, the hotel will be on my right. I drive past the area where Neil took me to that club full of whores; I'm smiling as it reminds me of the days on the Hamburg Reeperbahn.

After the better part of an 11-hour drive, I find the hotel and park up in one of the spaces opposite. I take a deep breath and relax. Even though it's been relatively easy, this was still a mission to get the dosh here. Understandably I'm not quite done yet but all I have left to do is give this money to Neil tomorrow. I'm left feeling curious to see what my role will be after this, but that's tomorrow and another day. I gather my stuff, this time getting the money from the boot. Hearing the sea is nice and the evening air is almost warm, but late March I guess it would be. I walk across to the hotel and check-in for one night then, €180 lighter, I take the lift up to my room.

I fucking love hotel rooms—they allow me to exercise my lazy side—but as I enter my OCD immediately kicks in and I have to get all my shit in order before relaxing. First job is to check the money. My €450 has gone and I've broken into that Bin Laden I pulled out, from which €260 has gone including the hotel, so Neil owes me about €700. To be fair, even if he just reimbursed a monkey I'd be more than happy. I'm not gonna ask for it, as I like these things to be offered, and if they aren't I'll just make the adjustments with the money I have prior to handing it over. I double-check the drug money and there's still the 83 notes in there. Thinking ahead, I pull out another Laden to round it down to €41,000, which I'm presuming will be near the amount he needs for the deal tomorrow. Next job is to sort out my personal stuff, which includes a shit and a shower. I'd love to call home but I can't, not from here. Maybe if there's time I can do a public callbox tomorrow, but the impression I've been given is that we won't be hanging around. Neil said I'd be fully briefed in the morning, so that being the case I crack on and get my nut down.

Chapter 13

OVERSEAS OPERATIONS-1

T he time has come. I wake up with the feeling that today is gonna be the start of a new experience. Working closely with Neil and Trev does bring me a sense of relief—about how the job will be managed and how we'll deal with it, should it start going south. As I prep and get ready for a bit of a continental breakfast, I mull over the possibilities of what exactly today will bring. It might bring fuck all, otherwise known as "hurry up and wait", but if I'm honest with myself it doesn't really matter. I'm here and I'm eager to get started, but if I have to spend a few extra days basking in the Med then so be it—who am I to complain? Life's been pretty shit until now.

I don't have a start time as such; Neil simply implied that we'll be heading off first thing. I'm ready either way and my burner hasn't been switched off, but no missed calls or texts and it's approaching 08:00, so apart from a quick trip to the restaurant for brekky, I'm good to go. The breakfasts here aren't all that appealing but the taste is irrelevant; it's more a case of me being able to enjoy the experience without having the weight of the world on my shoulders. Walking into the restaurant, I give the waiter my room number and am ushered to a seat. I then go into full autopilot as I go through the motions of eating the various delights on offer, but I'm not really thinking about the food, as I need to focus on today's mission and getting my head into the game. Not knowing my role is a bit frustrating, but I would guess I'm on a need-to-know basis, so until I'm fully integrated into this firm I'll most likely be in the dark. I'll do most things, short of killing someone. That will only happen if I'm faced with a life-or-death situation, and how often do those occasions present themselves? Well, in this world more than you'd think and way more than I'd like to admit.

I'm cramming the last pathetic sausage into my gob when Neil calls—as if he's watching me and somehow knows I'm finishing off. I say, "Yes, mate?"; he responds with "Ok, we're pretty much good to go—how long do you need?". As I get up and head towards the lift I say, "Give me ten minutes and I'll be outside"; Neil says, "Good stuff, we'll brief you in a bit", then hangs up. I continue on up to my room where I'm more or less sorted; I get eyes on the dough one more time, gather my personal effects and start heading out of the hotel, over to the car.

The sun is out and it's fucking hot. Well, compared to the UK it is; it's gotta be over 20°. I knew I should have bought some shorts—I'll be sweating like a pedo in a fucking park at this rate. Walking over to the car and again getting a view of the Med makes me feel that at times, bullshit aside, the lifestyle here appears to be worthwhile. I quite like the idea of coming over here on a permanent basis; not sure if the missus would be up for it, but I'd love it. Operating out of the south of Spain is plausible, as her in-laws are already out here and they're raving about how nice it is.

I dump my stuff into the car boot and have a quick scan for
Neil, but no sign of him or Trev so I head onto the beach for a
bit of fresh air and to allow myself time to get focused. No
sooner than I set foot on the sand I hear a familiar sound: "Eh
la, where do you think you're off to?". I turn around to see Neil
and Trev standing by my car. Fuckers snuck up on me! I do a
swift about-turn and head towards them then, handshakes all
over and done with, we get down to the business end of why
we're all here. Neil says, "Ok so we're gonna take two cars up
to the Mad one (Madrid). Me and Trev will meet you when we
get closer to the city, but it's best we make our own way up and
stay separate for now". He then goes on to say, "The Prof is on
his way down through France as we speak and will be set to
catch up with us tomorrow midday—so far he says. I repeat
"So far", and Neil continues, "Today we'll be checking into a
hotel but we're not sure which one yet, as the pickup point
hasn't yet been confirmed. Pick up is set for tomorrow and this
will be your part of the deal". As he finishes this sentence he
looks at me for some kind of reaction; I say, "Cool, looking
forward to it". Neil looks at me and says, "Don't be so sure;
you don't know who you're meeting yet", to which I respond
with, "Mate, 'in for a penny, in for a pound'—simple". A big
smile spreads across Neil's face as he looks at Trev who, for a
change, smiles back. Neil asks, "Have you got the money?"; I
respond with a moderately sarcastic, "No, I spunked it all on
brass last night". They both smile and Neil says, "I'll grab it
off of you now mate, but do you have enough for expenses?".
I briefly weigh up what I have, not including the money I
brought with me as that doesn't technically count, and say,
"How much do you need for the deal?". Neil replies "I'll need

80 bags, la. What's left can go into the expenses kitty; it'll be worth you pulling a bag out anyway". I head back to the car, pop the boot and go into my bag, opening the envelope and yanking out two more Ladens; that should do the job, or I fucking hope so. Presumably Neil will be covering the costs of the hotels from his end. Neil closes in on me and as he does, I discreetly pass him the money, Trev scanning the area as I do.

Finally I'm temporarily free of the burden of carrying something that could bury me. I look over towards Neil who is securing the envelope in his pocket and say, "Do you have an address to head for, or shall I just head for Madrid?". Neil responds, "Hang on la, I'll have a think", then turns to Trev and says, "What do you think? That place with the garages attached?". Trev simply nods as if to agree. Neil looks at me and says, "Ok, so if you head towards Madrid, as you get closer you'll pick up signs for the M50; it's like an M25 but for Madrid. When you get to that there are plenty of service stations; pull into the first one you come across and we'll meet you there". Neil then says, "By then, we should have confirmation on the pickup time and location, so we can then decide on where to plot up for the night". I smile, nod and say, "Great, see you in a few hours". We head our separate ways and get into our respective cars, ready for yet another long drive.

Windows down, music on, sun reasonably warm and currently zero stress to manage. This is gonna be a sweet journey, with an ETA of approximately 15:00. Yet again this brings another sense of relief, as there's no way I'll be doing the deal today—a deal that sounds somewhat ominous. How will I be doing it? How much am I collecting? At least two keys for sure. I then reflect back to my brief encounter with Lofty, where I witnessed them all extracting box after box from the backs of speakers. I saw at least 20, plus whatever hadn't yet been unwrapped. This daunting reality takes over my entire thought process as I head north towards the Mad one.

I've already managed to fill my stomach and the car, and as I get closer to the capitol I'm eagerly looking out for these signs of the M50, hoping I get it right. From experience I don't wanna be overshooting my mark, as the traffic is absolute chaos in Madrid. The K's are getting less as I finally pick up a sign for the M50, and sure enough there's a service station immediately after. I slow down and pull into the rest area, only to see Neil and Trev chilling on a patch of yellow grass next to their car. I drive past them and pull into a space a little distance away.

I get out and walk towards them, having a fucking good stretch as I do. Neil shouts, "Hey la, how was your journey?"; I reply, "Yeah good, no issues". "Good" says Neil, "because we're on, the days have been brought forward". I feel my bowels shift and, trying my best to not give away the sudden urge to shit my pants, say "Happy days, where am I going?". Trev laughs and says, "Your fucking face!"; Neil then says, "Only joking la, pick up isn't yet confirmed". Mixed emotions; feeling a dick but a relieved one at that, I say, "Dickheads! My fucking arse dropped when you said that". Neil says, "Yeah, we could tell by your face". To think I thought I did a good job of hiding it! Neil then says, "You'll need to work on your poker face, son". "Fuck off!" I say, "My poker face is on point. I was sitting in a police station with two up my arse last month and didn't fold". Neil nods and says, "Right, follow us. There's a handy little hotel down the road. It's perfect as it has a private carport below the hotel room, so we can do the pickup and then the Prof can do his bit in relative safety".

This all sounds good and I mull over the plan, a plan which I am yet to be enlightened of, but I'm a cog again; as long as I know my job the rest will do theirs. I follow the lads out of the services and stick my mind into neutral as we convoy towards our next destination, which is a lot closer than I thought, as we are already pulling onto a small complex of what looks like adjoined coach houses. I must admit it looks perfect for what we need. We both pull into a space, then Neil gets out and gestures for me to remain put, as does Trev. I take this moment to assess the local area while in the car. It looks quiet with very little movement and seems perfect—almost too perfect. I don't know why but this place doesn't work for me. I continue this conversation with my gut feelings, trying to convince myself that Neil knows what he's doing, when Neil reappears from the hotel reception, brandishing what appear to be two sets of keys.

Neil beelines straight for the rooms and not for us. I can see Trev shifting, deciding whether or not he should de-bus. Well I fucking am, so I get out and head in the same direction as Neil, again having a good stretch as I do. Trev follows and slots in behind me. I like Trev but I'm struggling to connect with him; he seems far too serious and is always spoiling for a fight; he's definitely fucked in the head, probably PTSD. Poor fucker, that must be a nightmare to live with. In perfect sync we all close in on the rooms and they do look ideal for our needs; a nice, private garage underneath what looks like a small, self-contained flat.

We walk up a small flight of stairs and into one of the flats. Going in as if on some kind of CQB exercise, we check the place out systematically, one room at a time. "Clear!", I hear in my head as we do. The part I do like is the door at the back, which leads to another stairwell that drops down to the garage below. I head on down to recce it—fucking hell it's perfect! I can just imagine reversing the car in and loading or unloading it; it would also appear to be big enough for a van, presuming the Prof is in a van. I go back upstairs to rejoin the lads, but Trev isn't anywhere to be seen, so I'm guessing he's in the bathroom. Neil is on the phone with a big fuck off grin on his face—he looks at me and gives a thumbs up, pointing at the handset as he does. He's speaking in pidgin Spanish so he has to be talking to his suppliers.

Neil hangs up and says, "We're all good—tomorrow at about 14:00. I've got a meeting location, which we'll sort out in a bit. We need to go shopping first though". I hear the flush go and out walks Trev, sniffing as he does; I look over and say, "That's the best part of you gone"; Trev looks over and simply says, "Fuck off!". I laugh and say, "Charming, you have such a way with words". Neil says, "Right, let's fuck off and get kitted up". We all head out and as we do, Neil says, "Trev, we'll go in ours—you can drive", throwing the keys at him. I mean throwing them *at* him and not *to* him. I can sense some bad air here. Trev hasn't been right since this morning; he's always fucking miserable at the best of times, but he's definitely got the hump about something.

I assume my position in the back seat. The lads take up their respective seats up front, then Trev pulls out onto the main road—I'm guessing he knows where we're going. I take this chance to ask Neil what we're getting, and Neil says, "Yeah la, we need to get a few bits for packaging the stuff for transit; packing tape, vac packer, some repellent spray; it's worth getting some gloves as well. There's a large shop that sells fucking everything about 20 minutes away, so we can get it all in one place". I have a quick think and say, "Sounds like a proper dodgy list. Is it not a potential compromise buying it all in the same place? Or are we separating and buying a few bits each?". Neil looks at Trev and says, "Clued up for a Tanky, isn't he?". Trev shrugs his shoulders and keeps driving. Neil laughs out loud and says, "Trev isn't happy because he didn't think of that when he went shopping for it all last time; poor fucker had to haul it all around on his little lonesome". Well, that statement went down like a fucking brick! I can sense the atmosphere get even worse as Neil keeps laughing at Trev, and I mean he's right in his face. Trev is getting visibly pissed off and he looks like he's gonna fucking pop any minute. Think I'll back off from the sarcasm for now—I don't know him well enough to see how far he can be pushed, and I'm not ready to get involved with whatever domestic these two are going through.

One relatively short and somewhat uncomfortable drive later, we arrive at our destination, and from the face of it, it looks like a Spanish version of John Lewis. We all walk in and I'm blindly following, as Neil seems to know where he's going. Trev is bringing up the rear and he's still in a right piss. Neil looks at Trev and says, "Can you go grab the vac packer, la?", as he hands him some money. Trev snatches it from Neil's hand and heads off in a different direction. I look at Neil and before I even need to ask he says, "Yeah, I know, he's not happy. He's constantly borrowing money from me and I've told him he needs to sort his life out or he's off the firm". I know what it's like to be in the shit with money and say, "Sounds bad, is he ok?". Neil replies, "No la, his head's fucked from the Falklands"; I immediately say, "Fuck, that makes sense, I did think he wasn't right". We both continue on our way through the store with Neil picking up what appears to be random shit as we do.

We circle around and walk back towards the checkout section, where I clock Trev who's already queuing, still with a face like a smacked arse. We don't acknowledge each other while we go through the payment process, then Trev walks outside with us not too far behind. Trev still looks ready to kill someone, so I ask him about the vacuum packer he's bought. Oddly enough he answers saying, "They're good bits of kit; it'll keep the smells down and waterproof it just in case". I reply, "Nice one mate, I take it they're relatively straightforward to use?". Trev grins, saying "Yes, even for a fat tankie like yourself". I guess I was due that one after the crayon comments. Neil decides to drive this time and he's remaining quiet, so I use this opportunity to have a chat with Trev. I feel bad that he's suffering from his time in the forces and that we clearly lack the compassion to deal with it.

I've come to realise that Trev is fucked for a reason and, like me and probably Neil, we all got a bit lost when we left the forces.

We pull back into the hotel and Neil immediately shouts, "For fuck's sake!". "What's up?" I ask; he stops the car short of the entrance and says, "See that car over there?", as he gestures towards a a car with three lads standing next to it. I look over and Trev says, "Is that those fucking scousers?". Neil says, "Yeah", then he looks at me and goes on to say, "They're another firm—hot as fuck. We can't operate from here because if they're around it's too fucking risky". He drives slightly off plot, pulls over out of sight of this other firm and says, "Ok la, as they don't know who you are and your car has Spanish plates, if you can dive out here and grab your motor, 'cos we'll have to move the location to another hotel. I'll start driving towards Madrid, so call me when you're in the car". He then looks at Trev and says, "take these keys and get us checked in". I nod, checking I have my keys I get out and head over to my car. As agreed, Neil drives off. I approach my car and they are right fucking next to it—standing around, smoking and chatting. I can definitely hear scouse and lots of it, everywhere I go. They all clock me as I get closer and they immediately stop talking—thank fuck for that. They continue to eyeball me as I get into my car, looking at them all as I do.

As I start up and pull off I look in my rearview mirror and can see them all standing there, staring at me as I drive off. Fucking hell, Neil was right! They are on top; talk about bringing attention to yourselves. I give Neil a call, Trev answers and explains roughly where they're heading; this of course makes zero fucking sense as I don't even know where I am. From what I can gather though, is that I stay on this road and keep heading towards central Madrid, where there's a hotel they've used before. He said it's the only one in what looks like a new-build area, which not very helpful as the whole country looks like a fucking building site. I wonder if Neil had paid for the first hotel and if so how much we lost; presumably he won't be seeking a refund of any kind.

I see a hotel that fits Neil's description and drive into the car park, only to see Neil and Trev getting out of their car, both laughing for a change. Again I drive by, recce and park up, then get my phone, lock up and head over to join them. We all walk into a large, plush reception area. Fucking hell this is nice, there's marble fucking everywhere! Neil goes up to the desk and asks for one room. One room? I'm not sharing, fuck that. I look at Neil and say, "Are we all spooning then?". Neil says, "No la, we're just gonna haul up here for a few hours until I get the call. If we stay overnight then I'll grab another couple of rooms". We call for the lift and go straight to our room. The time is getting on a bit now and I'm hoping we can plot up here; it's definitely one of the nicest hotels I've been in.

We all walk into an equally luxurious room; white sheets, white granite and mirrors everywhere. I opt to go take a shit, as I haven't had the opportunity yet. While I'm sitting in absolute bliss taking the most luxurious dump of my life, I can hear the faint tone of a phone ringing, followed by the unmistakable sound of Neil talking. Next thing I hear is, "Hurry up la, we're fucking moving!". Again? That's mental, we've literally been here five minutes. I finish off and walk out to see them both ready to move, so I ask "What's the crack?". Neil says, "The pickup has been confirmed for tomorrow at 13:00, but the trouble is it's too far from here as you'll be using taxis, so we need to be closer. Plus the Prof has said he'll be on a quick turnaround to get himself back up to France so he's recommended a hotel that he's used before". Neil then says, "I'll give you the address in a moment".

179

We walk back out of the luxurious room then into the lift, and I'm now beginning to understand why cocaine costs so much when it hits the UK. All the money that goes on expenses—it's fucking ridiculous; already three hotels in as many hours! We exit the lift and Neil doesn't even bother to ask for a refund. We walk out and head back to the cars, Neil telling me the name of the hotel which I text into my phone. Getting into the car I immediately switch on the satnav and input the destination of the hotel. Looking up, I see that Neil has already left; I then slowly pull out, still in a semi-state of disbelief about the hotel situation. The next one is over 40 minutes away—looks like central Madrid. I am now getting curious about the pickup scheduled for tomorrow. Who am I meeting and how much am I getting?

It's now early evening, the sun is getting lower in the sky, and I'm closing in on the hotel— hopefully for a good night's sleep. Today's been non-stop; it would be a lot fucking easier if I knew what was going on, but I half get the feeling Neil doesn't know much more than I do, and Trev's only here in case things go tits up. I drive into yet another hotel car park and go through the motions, again. This place doesn't look as nice as the last one and definitely doesn't have a garage to take advantage of. What it does have is a fuck load of steps leading up to the reception door. I see Neil has his bag with him, as does Trev, so I shout out "We definitely digging in for the night?". Neil shouts back "Yes la, get your shit together", so I spin round and go back to get my belongings. I'm in need of a shower, some food and a good night's kip.

By the time I get up to the top of these fucking steps and into the reception, Neil has already sorted the rooms. He throws me a key and says, "Pop over to mine once you're settled, so we can go over the plan for tomorrow". I say, "No problem, cheers". I look at my key and the fob has 324 written on it; I look at Neil and say, "What room are you in mate?". He says, "Room 300, la. I don't wanna be anywhere near yours when you're loaded up tomorrow". Trying my best to hide my concerns, I say the usual, "Cool". But it's not fucking cool; I think I've bitten off a lot here and I've not even considered raising the question of payment, payment that must be considerably reduced, due to the excessive abuse of the expenses. I must look at the bigger picture; this is an experience, it's getting Cliff off my case and it's putting me in good stead with Si. I'm sure some form of payment will come, possibly in kind; maybe a nine of pure when we get back.

We exit the lift, me turning left, Neil and Trev turning right. "See you in a sec", I say. As I proceed down a relatively long corridor, I see my room is on the right. I walk in and I'm immediately disappointed with it; out of the three hotels this one is the shittiest. Clean but neither plush nor luxurious—I guess you could say it's practical. I throw my stuff on the bed then walk straight out again and back along the corridor to see Neil in order to get briefed on tomorrow's job. Neil's door isn't even closed properly so I just walk straight in, announcing myself as I do. Neil says, "Yes la, we made it, so here's the plan. You're meeting our contact tomorrow at around 13:00. You'll get a taxi there, pick up work and then taxi back". I say, "Sounds straightforward enough, what else?"; Neil then says, "After that you'll go up to your room and prep the kit for the Prof, the prep going as follows". He picks up the bag from the shop and empties everything out onto the bed, then says,

"Right, first I want you to vacuum seal the coke. Do them one at a time. Once it's sealed, I want you to tape it so that it's neat again, then pop it into another vacuum bag, spraying some of this in it". He picks up a spray bottle from the pile of shopping and shows me what it is; it has a picture of a dog and a lemon on it. Putting the bottle back on the bed, he says, "Then, seal it and pack again with tape".

Fucking hell that's a lot of work, but I guess its needed to secure the load. I say, "So how many are we picking up, and how long do I have before the Prof arrives?". Neil says, "The numbers are being confirmed but it'll be enough". "Enough"? That's not the kind of answer I'm looking for! Enough to get me 5 years, 10 or 20? Neil says, "The Prof will be here before you leave and will be ready when you are". I look at the kit on the bed and say, "Ok, sounds like a plan, I'll take this with me now so I'm all set". I then say, "Look, it's been a long day and tomorrow's getting closer. I'm gonna call it a night so I'm all set for tomorrow." Neil says, "Yes mate, go get some rest, but Trev and I are gonna get some food, are you in?" I reply, "Nah mate, I'm gonna chill with room service". Neil says, "Fair enough, see you tomorrow for breakfast". "Yes mate, looking forward to it", I reply, walking out with my bag full of shopping then heading back to my room, where I settle down for the night. The reality of tomorrow is creeping in and I'm still not completely sure what the fuck's going on.

Chapter 14

OVERSEAS OPERATIONS-2

Waking up, I'm always haunted by the same feelings. Even though I'm smashing the happy pills, I still have that overwhelming sense of dread when I awake, especially if it's a day like today. I've spent the last few days on the road; yeah a bit of money to worry about but the gravity of today's job is sinking in and it makes the pressure of carrying cash feel rather light in comparison. I did however have a nice chat with the missus and kids last night—I even said how nice it might be to live over here. She wasn't opposed to the idea but then again she didn't exactly leap for joy, and this is one of the reasons I married her. She's much more sensible than I am and she's been around me long enough to know that something else will likely come up before a move to Spain is a reality.

The morning hasn't even started and it feels like it's gonna be a long day. What a fucking ball ache, wrapping all that coke millions of times each, and how many will there be? Ten, twenty? The most I've ever touched is three or four and that's bashed, but this shit's fucking pure. While I mull over the quantity of coke I'll be handling, I'm trying to figure out what to wear. I've had a look outside and it's looking like another sunny day—no shit it's Spain, it's meant to be sunny and warm! Part of me is thinking that I might go get some summer kit; I've got all morning and I can't be arsed to hang around waiting for the off. Yesterday on my way here I did notice a nearby complex of shops; there must be somewhere there to buy some shorts and a more appropriate T-shirt.

The clock is ticking, so I decide to head down to get some fresh air but no Med this time, just the chaos of Madrid. I exit the hotel and the sun immediately hits me as it reflects off of the bright concrete floor. I am definitely getting some new clothes—fuck wearing jeans on a day like today! It's only just gone 09:00 but the warmth is like a British summer, and as I stand here basking in the sun I sense a presence. "Eh la"; I turn around and there he is— Neil, looking fresh and in shorts. That's it, I say, "Mate I'm gonna go get some shorts, any suggestions?". Neil says, "Yeah", and points over the road to a complex of shops that I hadn't yet noticed. He says, "There's a sports shop in there la, I was going to suggest this as you'll be sweating like a pig in what you're wearing today". I say, "Thank you for being so honest ya fucking nob, do you know what time they open?". Neil quickly says, "Now, mate— I'm just grabbing some brekky and I'll head over with you if you want". Sounds good to me, so I say, "Sure thing! Where's Trev? Is he joining us?". Neil says, "Fuck knows, he was smashed last night and he ended up arguing with a couple of lads down the road. This is why I want you on the firm. He's becoming a liability; I've only got him on board today because the money he'll earn will cover what he owes me". It's a cruel fucking world but a debt is a debt and if he owes then it needs to be paid. I know all about that. That's why I'm here in the first place.

We both sit down and pretend to enjoy our breakfast, but it's just as shit as the one in Fuengirola; shit scrambled eggs, shit sausages and shit bacon. This doesn't stop us from demonstrating how we've both clearly served by stuffing our faces in record time. We were trained well, but why do we eat so fast? I'll tell you why; during basic training your troop corporal says, "Right lads, fall out, go get some scran, and be back here for 13:00 in lightweight order". Bearing in mind this order is given at half twelve and within that time we need to march to the cookhouse, queue up, eat, march back, get changed, look good and rock up five minutes before the parade. That is why we eat quickly.

Neil and I spend the next couple of hours chilling and shopping for slightly more suitable attire for today's job. To be fair, I was thinking I'd buy some sports kit, but sports kit wrapped around my fat carcass won't really go that well, so I opt for a more conservative style of short trousers and light shirt. I now look like a fucking local, very beige. The time is approaching 11:00 and still no sign of Trev, but I get the feeling he's not needed today, as I know for a fact I'll be doing the pickup alone. Neil's had an update from the Prof and he's on time for arrival at about 13:00. We walk into the hotel reception and Neil walks over to the desk to grab a couple of things from a display case, then he joins me at the lift and says, "Ok, here's two cards for the hotels; this one here is for this place and the other is for where you're going to do the meeting". I take the cards from him and have a quick look; fortunately there is a picture of this hotel on one of them, so it's obvious which is which. I stick them in my pocket then Neil says, "When you get into the taxi, hand him the card and he'll take you there—the same on the return journey. Don't get involved in a convo with them, especially on the way back". Ok so this sounds like a plan; I then ask him, "Mate, how will I know who to look for?". He smiles and says, "When you get to the hotel, go and sit in the reception. Your contact will come in and you'll know him because he looks like Tony Montana". I look at Neil and say, "You're fucking joking, right?". Neil says, "No la, he's the image of him".

We head back up to our rooms and go our separate ways. I'm still deciding on whether meeting a Montana lookalike is a good or bad thing; I suppose if he looks the part, then at least the coke will be good. I go into the room and straight to the toilet for a quick nervous shit, then I double-check all the kit and slide it under the bed. Since I'll be doing the prep on the floor, at least then if I need to hide everything, I can just shove it back under the bed. While I debate on having another trip to the bathroom there's a knock at the door. My heart skips and I go into full alert, looking around the room to ensure that all the kit is out of sight. I open the door and it's Neil. "What's going on la, are you ready?"; I say, "Yes, mate, let's fucking do it". We exit the room and head down into the lift, Neil saying, "The meeting is set for 12:30 but he might be late, so just plot up. I've described you to him so there's no reason why you won't catch each other's eye".

Neil has already booked the taxi and as I exit he stays inside and says, "Radio silence from now on, bro". I look at him and say, "Sure no problem". As I check my pocket for money and the two business cards with the hotel info, I select the correct one and head down the steps to the small taxi layby. I look back and Neil has disappeared back into the building; I don't blame him, I'd do the same if I were in his position. A small taxi pulls up to the curb and I get in the back, say, "Hola" and pass him the card. He looks at it and says, "Ahh, comunidad

Colombiana". I say, "Si", but to be fair I haven't got a clue what he said—I'm just being polite. He pulls off and I sit in silence; as the journey continues, we appear to be going into central Madrid, or that's what it looks like—all I know is that it's getting busy, with little city cars and bikes everywhere. We pull into an area that looks quite different from the usual Spanish town; I can't quite put my finger on it but this feels different. The taxi pulls over and the driver points towards a large glass doorway. I see the name and realise we are here, so I pay the driver €20 (€8 more than needed) and get out, gesturing for him to keep the change.

I exit the car and the inner-city heat hits me hard. I casually walk into the hotel and into a small reception, which is literally a couple of sofas and tables opposite a reception counter. The receptionist smiles and I say in my best Spanish, "I'm meeting a friend". She looks at me and says "Ok". I take a seat facing the door, sit back and look out through the large glass windows into a busy street. I can't quite put my finger on it, but I like the feel of this place. As I sit here wondering and contemplating what I'm getting into, I look towards the door and in walks Tony fucking Montana. Oh my God, he's even got the glasses on and the clothes! Is he doing this on purpose, or is this how they dress? He smiles at me and says in what is clearly a Colombian accent, "You are Rich". I respond by shaking his hand and saying "Yes", thinking I'd best not refer to him as Tony. He looks me up and down and says, "Are you strong?". I say, "Yeah, fairly"; he laughs loudly as he walks out and says, "I hope so".

So I'm meeting more Colombians? Interesting. Tony and I walk out of the hotel and towards a ridiculously small car, a bit like the one Neil was driving when we first met. There's another guy sitting in the back, and Tony gestures for me to get in, so I walk around and get into the passenger side. I look over my shoulder and say, "Hola" to the other guy, who just smiles. Tony starts up the car and says, "This is my brother, he will wait with you while I go and collect your things. He doesn't speak much English". I look at Tony and say, "Sure, no problem". I don't even know where we're going; I'm doing this with pure blind faith that I'm not being kidnapped or handed over as some kind of ransom. Strangely enough I'm not at all worried. I'm quite enjoying this unique experience; what an amazing story to tell my grandkids one day! "Hey kids, guess what grandad used to do? He used to meet the Colombian cartels for cocaine." The in-laws would fucking love that one.

Tony and his brother start having a conversation, but with my limited Spanish I haven't got a fucking clue what they're talking about, so I zone out and take in the scenery as we slowly drive along a busy road. Either way it sounds as if they are planning something, because Tony's brother (who I've decided to christen "Manny Ray", as he was Tony's right-hand man in the film), looks as if he's preparing to move. I ready myself just in case, and as I do Tony says, "Ok Rich, if you go with my brother he will take you for a coffee, I have to prepare everything for you". Manny gets out, I smile, look at Tony and say, "No problem, see you soon", then I de-bus and join Manny, as he casually walks across a wide-open pavement towards what looks like a small café. We walk in and I am immediately impressed; there's comfortable seating on the left and a serving counter on the right, with two middle-aged, well-dressed baristas in trousers, shirts and ties, and wearing smart, white jackets. They look like catering jackets, but go well with the attire.

Manny looks at me and peers at the menu behind the baristas. I'm gonna guess he's probably thinking how to ask me what I want, so I look at the gentlemen behind the counter and say, "Café con leche, por favor". Manny looks at me, nods and orders the same; I take a seat and he joins me. The place isn't full but there are a few people in here. I look around and, trying to think of something to say to break the uncomfortable silence, look at him and say, "¿No hablas ingles?". He looks at me and says, "A little". Well, it's a start, because two men sitting in a café not talking is just fucking weird. The baristas announce that our drinks are ready, so I get up and get the coffees, thanking them in the process. I return, passing one to Manny, sit down and take a sip—fuck me that's good coffee! Manny sees my face and says, "Colombian"; I smile and say, "Si, muy bueno". I'm not joking, this has got to be the best coffee I've ever had—it's fucking incredible. If the coke's on par with this, then it'll be a good fucking day. As I savour the flavour, Manny and I attempt a conversation, but it's pretty pointless as collectively we have around 20 words that we both understand, so we run the risk of the conversation getting a bit repetitive.

I take the last sip from the cup and Manny says, "We go". Pointing to one of his ears then discreetly looking at the men sitting to our left, he says, "Too many ears". I'm with him on that one; fuck knows who they are, so we get up and walk out. I thank the baristas as I pass them. We walk back out onto the street and head along the rank of shops, cafés and restaurants. Manny would appear to know where he's going, so I walk next to him, point around the area and say, "¿Colombian?". He nods and says, "Si, this is my community". Once again I find myself smiling; I knew it felt different. I had no idea there would be a Colombian community in Spain, but then again, why wouldn't there be? I am now genuinely curious to know if these guys are linked to the cartels of South America—if so that would be so fucking cool. I'm curious to know if Cliff or Si are even aware of this.

Manny peels off to the right and enters yet another coffee shop, this time bigger, less artisan and more franchise; either way I choose to do the honours and head to the counter. I look at him and say, "¿Café con leche?"; he says "Si, gracias", then walks towards the window and grabs a table. I order the drinks and hang around for them, scanning the place as I do. Manny is on the phone, eagerly looking out of the window; he must be updating Tony with our whereabouts. The two coffees soon arrive, so I grab the tray and walk over to Manny, popping the tray on the table. Curious to see if this will be as good, and so totally immersed in the moment I'm forgetting that I'm due to pick up a load of yayo. I take a sip and close my eyes; I can almost taste Colombia. It's good—not quite as good as the last one, but still knocks the bollocks off anything in the UK.

The clock is ticking and Tony's been gone for a while now, must be nearly an hour. I'm all coffee'd out and would really like to get this show on the road. Manny shifts slightly as he looks out of the window and sure enough Tony has returned. There goes my arse—the nerves kick in and I'm back in the real world. I'm here to collect coke, not drink the best coffee of my fucking life. We exit the coffee shop and walk back to the car, where Tony gets out and says, "Sorry for the delay, I had to get a stronger case". What is that, some kind of fucking code? Looking perplexed, I say, "But we're all good, yeah?" to which Tony replies, "Fuck yeah". At this point, if I wasn't in so deep I'd have made him aware of the reference to Scarface. We all get back into the car and take up the same seats, Tony passing me a small piece of paper. I take a look at it and it has two shapes and two numbers drawn on it. Tony says, "Ok Rich, of this shape there are 12, and of the other there are 38". Sounding like an amateur I say, "Kilos, yes?"; Tony chuckles and says, "Yes, we don't do anything else". I immediately apologise and Tony says, "This is ok, I will drive you out of our community and drop you off, yes?". I say, "Yes please, near a taxi if possible". Tony nods and continues driving out of the area. Fifty kilos? Holy Mary, Mother of God! That's gotta be a million at wholesale and at least two or three street. This is a huge amount of coke.

Feeling the burden of responsibility returning, I try to visualise how big this fucking case is, and to be fair I'm struggling. Is it a holdall or a suitcase? Fifty boxes? It must be a case—or is it two cases? Fuck it, I'm overthinking it; if it's 50 keys of coke, who gives a fuck what it's in? We slowly drive out of the area, and this time I can feel that the air is different. Even though these guys are more than likely linked to the cartels, they're still human, and getting caught with this much coke will bury all of us. Several minutes pass and it feels as if we're out of the Colombian area, as the buildings and shops present in a slightly different way. Tony pulls over to the side of the road and says, "Rich, it was nice to meet you, please be careful with my cocaine". I look at him, trying to conceal the fact I'm shitting myself and say, "Yes, you too, and don't worry, it's safe with me". I look back at Manny then Tony and say goodbye.

I exit the car and walk around to the back, noticing that Tony and Manny are clearly anxious for me to fuck off. This is it! I pop the boot, lift the lid, and there it is—a dark blue ArmourLite suitcase, as big as the fucking boot. I reach in and grab the handle, but immediately realise that this is a two-hand job, so I seize the handle with both hands, heave the suitcase out of the boot and slowly lower it to the ground. Thankfully this beast has wheels and an extendable handle which I pull out; I then quickly look over the case. It does have a combination lock on it, but I'll be fucked if I'm gonna mess with that for now; if it's locked, Neil can sort that with Tony when I get back.

I drag the suitcase onto the path, and as I do so Tony pulls away, rapidly disappearing into the flow of traffic. I'm on my own in the middle of Madrid with a suitcase rammed to the hinge with 50 keys of coke. The next stage of my journey should prove interesting! Trying my best to blend in, I begin walking along the road, making out what looks like a taxi rank ahead. Feeling uber alert, I quicken my pace slightly. I don't fancy walking too much farther with this, but short of going too fast and running the risk of the case breaking and spilling a couple of mil's worth of the finest Colombian all over the Spanish pavement, a brisk yet conservative walk will suffice. I approach the taxi rank and head directly for the car at the front, park the case at the rear of the car and pop the boot. As I do this the driver gets out and I say, "No problem, I have this". Reaching into my pocket, I retrieve the other business card and hand it to the driver, who is looking a tad confused. As he takes it from me I heave the case up and drop it into the boot, the car visibly lowering with the sudden increase of weight in the rear. Hoping the driver hasn't noticed, I get into the back seat and take a moment to compose myself.

The driver pulls away and I'm hoping he's going to the hotel, but there's no telling; the paranoid part of me is thinking he knows what's in the case and is either gonna drop me at the cops', or drive straight back into the Colombian sector to have me robbed. This makes for a very uncomfortable journey, amplified by the fact that I haven't got a fucking clue where I am or how to get to where I'm going, so this journey will remain stressful until it plays out. The only way I can gauge if I'm close is by how much the bill will be, €12 being the magic number, unless the driver's gonna fleece me on a longer journey. Good luck there driver—if you knew what you were hauling, you'd get this journey done fucking sharpish.

The taxi meter clicks onto €11 and I'm eagerly trying to spot anything that looks familiar, then as the meter clocks up €12, I see the hotel; more so I recognise the steps outside. I dive into my pocket and pull out another €20, ready to sort the driver; I do not want him touching that case. I'm literally ready to bail, the car pulls up to stop and the hotel is on my right. I hand the driver the €20 and say, "Gracias", then hastily get out and go straight for the boot. Thankfully the driver sits tight while I pop the boot and once again lift up the case; I then drop it on the deck and deploy the handle to drag it with. Looking at these steps and feeling a bit like Rocky about to finally conquer the steps in that film, I start the mammoth task of dragging this thing into the hotel. Bang, bang, bang, every fucking step— with each bump I'm hoping that the structural integrity of the case will hold out, and looking around I wish I had eyes in the back of my head. I've never felt so exposed, and this part of the mission is going slow.

So far so good—the case is holding out. I breeze straight past the reception desk and towards the lift, which thankfully is on the ground floor. I push the button and the lift makes that common sound as the doors open. Looking over my shoulder, I check my rear as I walk into the lift. There are no cameras in here so I can momentarily relax, but it's the next bit I'm dreading—the repackaging. I reckon it'll take me a couple of hours at least, and the time now is approaching 13:45. The door slides open at the third floor and I exit the lift, taking a left towards my room. This time however it's not going to remain in a state of relative calm—it's about to take on the role of a repackaging factory! A few short seconds and I'm into the room.

I park the case up and take a moment to recompose myself. Looking out of the window to check for any activity, all appears to be quiet, but I'll err on the side of caution and go out for a bit of a recce around the hotel, prior to the next phase. The case isn't fitting under the bed as it is, so I park it inside the wardrobe. Not feeling too happy with leaving it unattended, I head back out of the room and give the hotel a fucking good recce. I check every floor, reception, bar, restaurant and outside, even the toilets. I head back up to my room feeling as happy as possible, walk in and lock the door. Noticing a "Do Not Disturb" sign hanging on the handle, I decide to hang that fucker on the door outside. Locking the door once again but not feeling too satisfied, I look around for something to prop against the door as an added layer of security. The chair looks pretty heavy, a cross between an armchair and a dining chair, so it gets dragged across the room and wedged against the door. That'll do.

Time to prep the coke. First I pull out all the kit from under the bed, the vacuum packer taking the main spot on the floor. All the other stuff is on the bed. There's not a lot of space to work in here; kneeling down with the vac packer in front of me, I open the vac bags and ready the spray. I put on the gloves, get up and walk over to the wardrobe, open the door and take out the case. On paper the room looks like there is loads of room to operate, but my mind is thinking where the fuck do I hide all this if the door goes? I lay the case on the floor to my rear, my train of thought being to remove one key at a time, prep it and then stack it under the bed.

The time has come. It's time to open the case and hope it's not full of breeze blocks or stones—imagine that! I look at the combo locks and they're still on 000 so, hoping that the code hasn't been set, I flick the first catch—"click". Yes, it opened! So without delay I pop the second one, which also opens. I slowly open the lid to reveal a lot of brown packing tape, and I can immediately see the two different shapes—not that different though. My immediate concern is that once repackaged, will the difference in shape be noticeable? I'll have to mark them up somehow, so I look around the room for a pen and luckily there is a complimentary one on the desk. I have a quick change of plan; I'll do the two different types in one hit. Ok so I guess I should count them first. Fucking hell, basics! As I do, I sift out the 12 that are a different shape and place the others back into the case. Feeling happy that there are 50, I then close it and pop it back into the wardrobe.

Ok—this is better and manageable. I pop the first one into a vac bag, seal it then tape it. Fucking gloves are catching on the tape, making for slow progress but are essential; I don't fancy my dabs all over the packaging. I then pop it into another bag, spray the lemon-fresh dog repellent in, hit the vac packer once more then tape it again. Once taped, I scrawl in a star with the pen and stack it under the bed. One down, 11 to go. Once into the flow it's not too bad; the only worrying part is that the vac packer is fucking noisy, so I'm getting quite para about the noise travelling.

Well that took me longer than scheduled—at least an hour. I wander over to the wardrobe, retrieve the case and swap the contents, placing the newly packed 12 in the case, parking it back in the wardrobe and restacking the other 38 under the bed, slightly to my rear. Here we go again, this time remembering to not mark the outside. Five done then 10, 20. I'm fucking flying—there's coke everywhere and my stacking has become slightly shit, because the repackaged ones don't stack as well, so they keep falling over. I start vacuuming the 21st one when suddenly I hear a loud knock at the door. I immediately freeze, silencing the machine as I do, then quietly push all the coke out of sight under the bed. The door knocks again, this time louder. I push the rest of the kit under the bed, and with a good shove everything is out of sight. The door knocks again, I approach and say, "Who is it?". In a faint voice I hear, "It's me, the Prof".

Fucking hell! My nerves settled, I move the chair out of the way then open the door. "You twat!" I say; the Prof laughs and says, "That's payback for the time you shit me up in Coquelles". I look at him and shrug; it's a fair point. He walks in and I lock the door behind him. Prof says, "How you getting on?"; I sigh and say, "Well, I was doing ok until I was disturbed, but yeah not bad mate, probably be done in about an hour". The Prof says, "Ok, that works for me, do you have any I can take now so I can start packing the van out?". I walk across the room and look out of the window; looking down at the steps I see the Prof's van parked up, ready and waiting. I say, "Fucking right I do mate, at least 30!". I walk over to the wardrobe, drag out the case, pop it open and proceed to reach around under the bed to retrieve the coke that's been repacked. While I do this the Prof writes down his number and says, "Give me a call when the rest is done and I'll pop the case back up". I just nod in agreement.

Successfully loaded up, Prof fucks off to do his bit. I'm now only carrying about 20 kilos of coke. I reset my packaging line and crack on with the rest; one by one I'm getting closer to the end. Seeing the finishing line ahead I do wonder what other involvement I might have regarding this particular shipment. As I wrap the last one, I get a definite rush as the relief sets in; that I've so far successfully completed one of the biggest ball aches of my life. I pick up my phone and give the Prof a call, informing him that the rest is ready and to get his arse up here ASAP. I'll only be truly relaxed when all the coke has gone. There's a knock at the door; once again I say, "Who is it?" and yet again I hear the Prof say, "It's me". I open the door and in he walks with the case in hand. As I'm still gloved up, I do him the honours and reload the case with the last 18 blocks. He walks out and cracks on with his bit, while I have a tidy up in the room, putting all the packaging kit back into the carrier bag it came in.

At last it's fucking done. I sit back and relax for a bit, then looking at the time decide I'd best update Neil with my progression. I call him and he answers, saying, "Guessing you're done la?". I reply, "Yes bud, all sorted, you around for a quick catch-up?". Neil says, "Yeah la, pop down". I hang up and leave the room, feeling well-relaxed and slowly slipping back into holiday mode. I approach room 300 and knock on the door; Neil answers, I walk in and take a seat. He looks at me and says, "Nice one mate! What did Tony say?". I look at Neil and say, "Thanks mate, he didn't say anything, only gave me a piece of paper indicating two different types. I've marked the 12 with a pen on the outside". Neil says, "Thanks, I suppose you want to know what's next?". Still looking at him I say, "Of course". Neil then says, "Ok, so once the Prof has finished packing the van, we're gonna plot up for the night. We'll be leaving early doors tomorrow—around 06:00, same route as last time—but do try and keep up". "Twat!", I say. Neil continues, "We'll escort him all the way, one car upfront checking the tolls and *péages*, the other at the rear, so far". "So far", I say. Neil continues, "We'll maintain radio silence unless we see something that could be a problem; we'll also all keep ourselves to ourselves tonight as we don't want to be connected in any way". I have a quick think and say, "Ok so that's all good but what's the plan when we get there? I'm presuming we're going to Coquelles?". Neil says, "Yes and hopefully our man for the channel will be ready, but we'll need to cross-load the kit from the Prof's van into the boxes that you brought over with you". I scratch my head and say, "Right, so once we're safe and sound in Coquelles, I'll go get the van but what about the car?". Neil says, "Leave the car there and Trev will get it;

the Prof will be heading for a particular multi-storey car park—one that a van will fit into. He'll handball all the coke back to you, but did it come in a decent bag?" I say, "Did it ever!". Neil carries on saying, "Well he'll put all the coke back in the bag that you gave him. You then reload it into the boxes and basically babysit it until Gunther arrives". "Gunther?" I say. Neil says, "Yeah, he's our Belgium courier, he goes over the water every week with his job and doesn't get pulled as he's so regular".

Chapter 15

OVERSEAS OPERATIONS-3

I wake up early, before the strong Spanish sunlight does it for me. Yet another relatively pleasant night, in that there were no dramas back home, plus Hassan who seems to just crack on, and I'm more than content in his abilities to do so. Family life is all good—well most of it anyway. All of these positive aspects put me in a much stronger position to do my job over here. The bills are paid, the debt is going down and Cliff's off my case, so I'm simply cracking on. I don't know if I even need these happy pills anymore; I'm tempted to bin them once I get to the end of my six months, something I'd never have thought possible less than a year ago.

I'm ready in a snap and already heading out of the hotel when my phone rings; I look at it and it's Neil. I look around before answering, checking he's not already clocked me. Can't see the lump anywhere so I answer and say, "Morning, mate"; Neil promptly replies saying, "We're on the road already mate, the Prof wanted to crack on so he left at 05:00, the silly prick". Feeling a bit of déjà vu kicking in, I say, "For fuck's sake mate, what's he fucking playing at?". Neil says, "Yeah, sorry la, his arse started twitching and he wanted to get on his way, so we're playing catch up now". I ask, "What time did you leave?", and Neil replies, "About ten minutes ago; the Prof won't go over the speed limit, so we should catch up with him fairly soon". Feeling under unnecessary pressure, I say, "Ok bud, I'll make haste but I'm not going mental". Neil says, "Not a problem. I'll call you when we're an hour short of the border. We should have caught up with the divvy by then".

I switch the phone off and head over to the car. My initial reaction is to feel pissed off, but when I consider that I'm clean and not currently breaking any laws, then what have I got to stress about? I'll do my best but I'm not hammering it. I'm in the car, destination dialed into the satnav and I'm off—nearly 1000 miles to do. Once I get out of the city limits I'll squeeze the accelerator a bit more and take it up to around 85mph, which is where I'll keep it. I'm not even that fussed about it; if I catch up, I'll catch up; other than that fuck it.

The border comes and goes, but no calls from Neil so I'll maintain radio silence for now. I've still got a good 13-hour drive and the time is already fast approaching midday. There's no fucking way we're gonna make this in a reasonable time for me to do the work tonight— fuck it, I'm calling Neil. I pick up my phone to call him and he quickly answers, "Yes mate". I reply, "How's it looking? My satnav is saying a silly time of arrival, are we plotting up for the night en route?". Neil goes quiet for a bit and says," Hang on la, I'll call the Prof and see where he is. I'll get him to find a place to settle for the night. I'll call you back in a bit". He hangs up and I crack on; this makes much more sense as I'll be fucked if I'm getting caught up cross loading all that in the middle of the fucking night. The phone rings and it's Neil; I answer it and he says, "Ok mate, yeah the Prof will plot up for the night once the clock hits 21:00. He agreed that he didn't fancy driving too late, so he'll let us know where he is, once he lands".

201

That's more like it! I've still got a trek ahead but at least it'll be broken down a little. The hours and kilometres wind away, and as I close in on Paris, the sun goes down then sets. I'm now driving in darkness, music on and loving it. The clock hits 20:00 and I'm closing in on Paris, or the outskirts of it anyway—the route takes me around the outside. I remember this road well, and I reduce my speed down to a legal, more acceptable level. The clock hits 21:00 then 21:30 and eventually my phone rings. It's Neil; I answer and say, "Please tell me he's found somewhere". Neil says, "Yes indeed, it's an F1 hotel—shit but cheap, I'll text you the address now". He hangs up and almost instantly my phone beeps as a message comes through. I take a look and stick the new destination into the satnav; thankfully it's not a million miles away, just under a half-hour's drive.

I have to be honest, I'm fucked. I'm definitely gonna sleep well tonight. Just a few minutes away and I call Neil to get the plan; he answers and says, "Ok, we're doubling up tonight mate; I'm in with Trev and you're sharing with Prof". I say, "Sure, I'll be there in a bit", then hang up. As I put the phone down I see the familiar logo for the hotelF1 complex; cheap and not-so-cheerful. I pull into the car park and see the Prof exiting the back of the van, struggling to carry the suitcase. I walk towards him and say, "You need a hand with that, miss?". He looks at me with what I would best describe as a sense of humour failure and says, "No, I can manage, can you get the door for me?". I walk with him and he passes me a keycard to open the door with. We approach the building and he says, "Room number 17". I get eyes on and walk ahead to get the door open, ready for him to haul the case inside. The case looks like it weighs more than he does.

We both enter the room and the Prof drops the case on the floor, saying, "Fucking pricks! Neil made me bring the coke in because he didn't want it left unattended". I look at the Prof and say, "I can understand why you're pissed off mate, but it's a lot of money to leave unattended overnight in a dark car park. I wouldn't fancy the Colombians breathing down my neck, fuck that!". The Prof, looking slightly less pissed off then says, "I suppose so; well we're sitting on this tonight then". I say, "Yep, but we ain't got too far to go now". Looking at the sleeping arrangements, I say, "Top or bottom?"; the Prof replies and says, "Bottom, please".

The time is cracking on and I just wanna hit the sack; shit, shower, teeth then bed. The Prof has already retired; the scruffy cunt didn't even shower. I climb onto the top bunk and settle down, mindful of the fuck-off BIG case of coke sitting in the corner. I fall asleep instantly, only to be woken by the Prof fucking whinging again. I say, "What's up mate?"; he's sitting on the edge of his bed with his head in his hands and says, "You're fucking snoring, it's driving me nuts, I can't stay in here". Trying my hardest not to laugh, I say, "Sorry mate, you should just say 'roll over', like my missus does—that normally shuts me up for a bit". He says, "No, fuck it. I'm sleeping in the van", and walks out, slamming the door behind him. I look at the case in the corner, say to myself "Guess I'll be babysitting the bugle tonight then", roll over and go back to sleep.

What seems like moments later, hearing the door open I spring out of bed, ready for whatever or whoever it is. The Prof, looking somewhat startled and tired, says, "I've come to grab the case". I look at him, rubbing my eyes and say, "What time is it, anyway?". The Prof says, "Just after 06:00", grabs the case and walks out. Fucking hell, he can't half hold a grudge! He's beginning to wind me up now. I fucking hope he isn't just gonna shoot off again. I call Neil, he answers and I say, "Are you ready to move as I think the Prof is?". Neil says, raising his voice, "WHAT? THE FUCKING, STUPID, DICKHEAD!". He hangs up and I hear another door go from outside. I then hear in a strong scouse accent, "OI, YOU FUCKING DICKHEAD, WHERE YA GOING?". Unable to resist the temptation of the show, I crack the door open a bit and have a sneaky look. I see Neil storming across the car park in his boxers, a towel draped over his shoulders, a fucking great gut hanging out—makes me look slim! I still don't fancy being in the Prof's shoes though. Then again, he should fucking realise what this is! He can't just swan off carrying all the coke. The guy hasn't got a fucking clue.

Neil walks back over to his room, pacing like a fucking silverback that's considering ripping limbs off, looking at me as he does. I smile and shake my head, as if to say, "What the fuck?". Well, I may as well get my shit together; I don't need a shower and there's nowhere to have brekky, so it's a five-minute job. My phone rings and it's Neil; I ask, "You settled down now mate?". Neil says, "Yeah la, thanks for the heads up, the idiot was about to fuck off without us again". I say, "Yeah no worries mate, he's a miserable fucker isn't he?"; Neil says, "He always is, but looking like such a geek makes him useful, plus he never gets pulled, but I'm seriously considering dropping him off the firm along with Trev". I go quiet for a while and say, "Might be worth dropping him, but will you find a replacement that fits the bill as well as he does?". Neil says, "Probably not; most of the people I know are dickheads, I'll have to have a think. Right, let's saddle up and hit the road, brother". We end the call and meet outside, Neil this time wearing clothes, Trev still looking pissed off and the Prof sitting in the van like a naughty fucking schoolboy.

We've got a relatively short drive in comparison, only around three to four hours, so we should piss this one, but this time we'll do it properly. From what Neil says, we'll have maybe one or two toll checkpoints to pass through, but he reckons they won't be an issue, as the ones in the Bordeaux region are the hottest, and the Prof steamed through those yesterday all on his lonesome. I take up the advance part; the Prof is in the middle with Neil, and Trev is bringing up the rear. The game plan being I get far enough ahead to recce the toll for any police checks, and if there are I call Neil and they all peel off the motorway before they hit the toll. This means that they will have to remain far enough to my rear to ensure there is an exit to come off at. Seems relatively straight forward, but with the way the Prof works he'll probably not fucking listen and do his own thing anyway.

The majority of the drive was uneventful and the first toll checkpoint was clear, but as I approach the next one I can see what looks like a police car. I join the short queue to pay at the booth and call Neil; he picks up and I say, "We got one; one car parked up, two rozzers sitting in it". Neil says, "Ok la we'll drop back, you pull up ahead, observe and report, we'll pull over and look at an alternative route". I progress through the checkpoint, checking out the police car as I do, driving by and pulling onto the side of the road. It's not a hard shoulder as such, nor is it a service area; it just seems like a place to pull over and maybe do some checks. I get out, go to my boot and rummage around for a bit, then I go to the front and pop the bonnet, continuously checking the police car's movement. They're just sitting talking, possibly on a break as they don't appear to be too fussed. I call Neil, "Mate they're doing fuck all, just sitting here, you coming through or taking a detour?", I ask. Neil says, "We'll come through la, the Prof will be first then us, if it looks like the Prof will get pulled create a diversion or something". I have a think and then say, "Yep, not a problem".

Thinking in advance, my thought process is rather than cause a diversion, why not keep them busy while he goes through the barriers? I keep an eye out for them, but still not quite sure what kind of tactic to use, I go back round to the car and drop the bonnet. As the bonnet drops I see the familiar sight of the Prof's van, he's two cars deep so I take the opportunity and run towards the police car. As I approach I try to apply a slightly distressed look on my face; fuck knows what it actually looks like but hopefully it'll get their attention. I can see in my peripherals that the Prof is the next to pay, so as I approach the car I lean forward and knock on the passenger's window. I manage to startle the two of them, so I already know that they weren't looking to pull anyone coming through. The police officer winds down the window and I say, "Pouvez-vous parler anglaise?"; the officer looks at me and says, "Oui, a little". I smile in relief and say, "Merci, I have a problem, my navigation is broken and I'm going to Calais, is this the correct road?". The police officer smiles, and as I see the Prof disappear up the motorway he says, "Yes sir, you continue his way, it is about two hours away". Feeling more relieved than he'll ever know, I say, "Merci, monsieur", and I fuck off sharpish.

I get back into my car, take a deep breath and relax. My phone rings and it's Neil, I say, "Yes mate, we all good?". Neil replies, "Yes son, good move, I saw you talking to the filth, thought you were shopping us for a moment". I say, "How dare you suggest such an outrageous thing!". He laughs and says, "Right, that should be the last toll to worry about. The Prof will let us know where he plots up, I know the place well so if you head back to get your van, I'll drop Trev in the general area to grab the car off you. If you're early then leave the key on the wheel or something". All agreed and sorted; another hour or so and I'll be there.

Hopefully Gunther will be with us today and I can get back home tonight; Hassan's doing a sterling job holding the fort, but we'll all be waiting on this to land before we can work.

Coquelles is moments away and I attempt to locate the train station car park. I find it with relative ease and as I draw closer I clock the van; feeling slightly cautious I apply the standard recce and have a little drive around it to see if there are any concerns. As well as this I park well away from it, the intention being to do a foot recce around the car park to see if there are any eyes on the van—this fucker will be full of coke in a few hours. Feeling content and not too fussed about getting a ticket for the parking, I'm happy that the car is in a good location, so I proceed to collect all my stuff, lock it and stick the key on the back wheel. Bags in hand I slowly head towards the van, taking a wide berth as I do. The car park isn't full by a long shot, so any cars I do see I check for occupants that might be suss. I can't see anyone and part of me thinks I'm probably overdoing it, but I'd rather it be that way than the opposite.

Again feeling cautious, I approach the van. This fucker has been parked up for nearly a week and in my mind that's definitely suspect; UK plates, hired van coupled with the duration of stay—this usually equals dodgy. However, there's not a lot I can do, so I go straight for the back wheel and reach around for the key. A huge sense of relief hits me as I make contact with my fingertips, carefully retrieving the keys, trying not to push them off over the back of the wheel and under the chassis. Keys in hand I unlock the doors, again relieved that the battery hasn't fucking died on me. I get in and pop my belongings on the passenger seat, the satnav gets stuck on the window and I start up. With the engine running I get out and go back to sort the boxes. The more I can do now, the less I'll have to worry about when I'm knee deep in coke.

Still scanning the car park, I open the back doors. Confronted by these two really subtle monstrosities that we have called boxes, I get in and can smell the fresh woody scent you get when in a timber yard on a hot day. Now, being mindful of the size of the case the coke is going to be in, I have a think about how this will work best. The lids are leaning against the bulkhead so they're not really a problem. I'm thinking that removing the false bottoms now would be a good idea, as that requires me to put the boxes on their sides so the bottom falls away. With absolutely fuck all room to manoeuvre, I somehow manage to get the box nearest the rear doors tipped over enough for the bottom to fall away and slide out.

Grabbing it, I slide it down the front next to the lids, then repeat the process for the second box. I then push them right up towards the front of the van, barely giving enough room for the case to be opened and emptied, but it'll do.

I head on out of the area and towards the town, still hoping that the Prof will be ready and Gunther is en route. It's only a few minutes to the town so I call the Prof, who answers and says, "Are you here?". I reply, saying, "I would be if I knew where "here" was!". The Prof replies, "Oh shit, yeah sorry, there's an underground car park opposite a hotel, I don't wanna say the name of it but it's easy to spot as it's the only car park here". Well that's understandably vague so I say, "Ok, I'll be with you soon, are you ready on your end?". He replies, "I will be in a few minutes, there is a space next to my van if it helps". Perfect! I say goodbye and head for this elusive car park.

No sooner than putting the phone down, I clock what looks like an access ramp leading down to an underground car park. It's opposite a hotel and albeit a small one, it's the only one that fits the description. The dead giveaway is Trev walking up the access ramp, still sporting a miserable look. He notices me and gestures with a discreet wave to head towards him. This was obviously my next move, seeing as I'm in the process of turning into the car park. I pull the van up next to Trev and drop the window; he says, "He's down on the right, about halfway along. Do me a favour and kick the side of the van to shit him up". I nod and say, "Sure, it'll be a pleasure". I drive on down into the car park, but I've got no intention of kicking the fucking van or doing anything else that might bring attention to what I'm doing.

I carefully drive along the rank of cars and vans; seeing as vans do fit there are a lot in here, probably all loaded right up with drugs. I spot the Prof's van and thankfully there's still a space next to his. I reverse in, mindful of access to the back doors, and park up giving what I hope is enough room to get in the back with the case. I get out and text the Prof, informing him that it was me pulling in next to him. Moments later the back door to his van opens and a very red and stressed-looking face appears, saying, "Thank fuck you texted me! Someone was booting the side of the van just now and I was shitting my pants". Fucking hell, so he didn't even know Trev was here! What the hell is he playing at? The guy is definitely a liability.

The Prof squeezes out of the back and places the case on the deck behind his van. He looks at me and says nothing. I walk over and pop my doors as he closes his, pick up the baton and manhandle it through the tight gap between the partially-opened doors. This isn't easy trying to push a case and its contents, which must weigh close to sixty keys, through a gap barely big enough to squeeze a child, but determination prevails and, followed with a swift kick, I climb in behind it. I gently close the doors, making sure I don't lock myself in. Here I am again—50 bricks of coke in a small, enclosed working space. The sooner I get this shit in those boxes, the happier I'll be. I wait a few moments, firstly to allow my eyes to adjust and secondly to take stock of my environment. It's quiet down here, I'm about to start making a fuck load of noise, and I've got absolutely nowhere to run. if I'm clocked I'm done, period.

I can't hear a thing and as my eyes adjust I can see enough to take a look at the boxes. Obviously 25 in each makes sense, but the sizes and shapes will determine how good a fit they'll be. I look at the case and pop the lid—there it is, again. I grab the first block, lean into the box and gently place it on the bottom. It fits nice and snug, and as they're fairly symmetrical they ought to all line up nicely. I continue the process, counting them as I do. I'm not saying I don't trust the Prof, but if I come up short Neil will be finding out, and I'm not taking the hit if some greedy fuck has light fingers. I easily lay 24 on the bottom in six rows of four, and they were the slightly bigger ones, so what should happen (and I say "should" as I'm operating on guess work and not precise measurements), is the rest should fit in the second box perfectly. I reach around the back and as quietly as possible grab the first of the false bottoms. This is the awkward bit; I try to manoeuvre it over the top of the box, then drop one end in and lower it down, but they are such a tight fit I need to hold it flat over the top and drop it in, so it slides down onto the top of the coke. It's almost a machine fit; I feel the displaced air rush out as the false bottom makes its way south.

Well that looks ok; it's dark but I can make out that it looks discreet enough to pass, and Neil should be providing me with these car parts to fill it up with, which will definitely do the job. I crack on with the second box, and this time I'm flying; the bricks are going in nicely and I can already tell that they'll fit easily. I lay the last one in, but there's a bit of room so I spread them out and make the load even, so the bottom sits flush. I grab the next bottom and position it over the top but as I do, a thought enters my mind—"I've just handled all this with no fucking gloves on; do I start again or say 'fuck it?'". I go for the latter, knowing I have a clean slate and my prints or DNA aren't on police record, so unless I get caught then I should be ok. The lid slides in and as it does there's a loud bang on the side of the van. I stop moving, silently listening; I then hear a familiar voice, "Hurry up you cunt". It's Trev and I'm presuming he's been on stag—that's why he was hanging around when I arrived.

I shuffle around the boxes and towards the back of the van, now feeling a bit like how the Prof did. I say, "I'm done mate, just tidying up, where are we going next?". Trev says, "Fuck knows, ask the fat one". I laugh and simply say, "I will, let me crack on and I'll see you in a bit". Trev wanders off and I go back inside, grab the two lids and pop them into the boxes sitting diagonally across the inside; pointless securing them yet if they need loading up. I finally take the case that has proven so useful, placing it at the front of the van by the bulkhead, now occupying the same place the lids and bottoms did. I exit the van and secure the doors, and rather than staying in the van, I walk towards the exit and call Neil. As I do, he answers and says, "You done la?"; "Yep all secure, what's the plan?", I ask. Neil says, "Come see me, I'm parked down the road". I hang up and head on out of the car park, take a left and wander along the road a bit. It's weird; between these high-risk parts of what I'm doing, there are these moments of apparent calm. It's like waking up from a nightmare and entering the real world for a bit, only to be plunged back in it, time and time again. It's difficult to determine which version of the world I actually live in—am I dreaming when it's calm, and awake when it's dangerous?

Thank fuck for hypervigilance and good observation skills! I see Neil parked up discreetly on the other side of the road; I can also see the Prof hanging around; Trev and Neil must be sitting in the car. The Prof sees me as I approach. I walk around to the driver's side and squat down, looking through the window. Neil says, "Right la, we're nearly done, the plan now is simple babysitting. There's a Holiday Inn just down the road; if you take the van there, park up round the side and I'll see you there in about half an hour. I'm gonna take Trev to get the car you dropped off. Prof's gonna fuck off as his job is done". I look at the Prof as he smiles and says a simple "goodbye" then fucks off. I say, "Right, do you have an address for this place and how long am I there for?". Neil says, "Yeah hang on la"; he looks through his text messages then shows me the message. I write it into my phone and then say, "So when's he due?". I hear Trev chuckle as Neil says, "Monday". "Monday, Monday", I say; Neil looks at me; I then say, "It is Thursday mate, so I'm sitting on this for five days? It's no problem, but I don't think my ex's will cover it though". Neil says, "That's ok, I've got another €500 or so you can have. Gunther won't come any sooner as he says it's the wrong shift pattern on". "That's fair enough mate, I'm happy as long as you are, I'll keep my eyes on the van and make sure everything is sorted Monday". Neil says, "Thanks bro", then he and Trev drive off back towards the car park where I dumped the Golf.

Yet again I venture back into my reality, heading back to the van ready to begin the mother of all babysitting jobs. Not too much pressure, looking after a couple of mils' worth of bag that's presumably on tick from the Cartels! I can't wait to see how this goes tits up. Noticing that the Prof's vehicle has gone,

I cautiously approach mine, walk around to the front and get in. It's always the start of a move that causes the most stress—once I'm on the road I'm happy as a pig in shit. I drive out of the garage not even thinking about payment—there weren't any barriers and I didn't see any machines, so fuck it! I head out onto the road then pull over to stick the address into the nav system. Ten minutes away—I can live with that, so long as there are vacancies at the hotel and I don't end up doing a merry fucking run around.

One relatively stress-free drive later, I'm pulling up to the hotel; it's quite small but looks ideal. There's a nice little car park running along the side of the hotel and looking around the area there's fuck all to do. This may sound shit but it does mean that I'll be sitting tight here, and not straying too far from the merch. What I do like is that there are trees and bushes bordering the car park, so I reverse into a space and back the doors up against a bush, blocking access to the rear of the van, therefore securing the coke that's in the back. I switch off, get out and walk around to the front of the building where the main entrance is located. I walk in and sidle up to the reception desk—and here we go with a bit of French! I say to the receptionist, "Avez-vous une chambre pour quatre nuits?"; the receptionist smiles and thankfully says, "Oui monsieur". Feeling a whole lot happier I then go through the process of paying and as part of the booking-in procedure I reluctantly have to leave my details. Fucking paper trails everywhere I go; sometimes it's almost impossible to not leave a scent somewhere. Laughable really—here I am worrying about a hotel reservation, but none of that compares to my dabs all over the yayo in the van that is currently hired out in my fucking name.

This is a result! My room is on the ground floor and I've got eyes on the van outside. Taking the responsibility of the coke away, I'm feeling relaxed. This is quite a nice way to wind down the last few days, which seem to have been non-stop. I've yet to retrieve my bags from the van, but seeing as Neil is coming back with these car parts, I may as well sit tight until he gets here. I grab the room service menu to have a look at what level of French cuisine I'll be enjoying over the weekend. Not too bad; there's a good choice and seeing as I've got a fuck ton of money I don't really give a monkey's how much it's gonna be. Plus I'm banking on Neil loading me up with some more expenses. I do feel a bit tight, but he hasn't even said what my payment is for this job, so based on that I'll cream the ex's, just in case the payment isn't forthcoming.

Fuck this waiting around lark, I'm going outside! I grab my room key and head outside; it's sunny and warm, not as warm as Spain but warm enough to enjoy. There are some tables and seats in a small communal area so I plot up and wait for the lads to arrive. A short wait later I see the familiar sight of Neil and Trev arriving, and for a change Trev is laughing. They pull into the car park and reverse the car in so it's next to the van. I walk around and greet them; Neil gets out and says, "Are you sorted la?"; I say, "Yes mate, all booked in until Monday". Neil says, "Yeah, you might want to extend that by a day as Gunther won't be here until late morning on Tuesday". No point in even questioning this so I simply say, "Well as long as he isn't too much longer, it's a long time to plot up in one place with this stuff". Neil agrees and reaches into his pocket, pulls out a wedge of money and hands it to me, saying, "There you go la, that should cover your ex's and a bit of a wage for you".

I'm not one for counting money handed to me by people that I'm supposed to trust. What a great look, standing in the middle of a car park counting money like a dickhead next to a van full of coke, plus I think it's disrespectful. So I pocket the dough and say, "Cheers, la". Trev smiles and Neil says in an exaggerated high pitch scouse accent, "Eh Trev, ark at im all scouse la". Trev looks like he's about to attempt to say something clever but instead opts for steely silence and just says fuck all. Neil pops the boot and asks me to pop the side open; I look at him and say, "What side?". Neil says, "This one here, you fucking weapon". I walk around to the van and fuck me sideways, there's a sliding door on the passenger side! I've never noticed it—oops! I say, "Oh yeah, I thought you meant the driver's side". Trev says, "No you didn't, you didn't know there was one here". I look at him and shake my head; there's no coming back on that one. I unlock the van and Neil slides the door open, I get in and take up a position in the doorway. Trev steps in between the two of us as Neil starts to unload the boot.

Brake discs, box after box, from boot to Trev to me, then into one of the boxes. I ask Neil, "Mate how many you got so I can divvy them up into both boxes?". Neil says, "Twenty mate, but Gunther will have a load of stuff in his van that'll also be going in, so don't worry too much about what goes where. I'm now thinking about the weight of these boxes that haven't yet been field tested. Can the bottoms take the weight of 25 kilos of coke, plus the weight of whatever goes in on top of it? I don't want to be the poor fucker carrying the box that breaks and spills coke all over the place. We continue to handball the brake discs into my van and subsequently into the boxes—a few minutes' work and we're done. Reminds me of ammo bashing—if you've served then you'll know.

Boxes sorted, vans locked and the load is ready for handover to Gunther. We walk away from the vehicles and discuss the plan that should come to fruition over the next few days. From the sound of it it'll be the same as last time, where the coke will end up in Windsor. The only difference this time is that I'll be loading the coke up just before it goes over. This way I'll have a fucking good idea of when it'll be arriving and can make better plans my end with Cliff, Si and Hassan. The lads understandably don't hang around, in fact they fuck off pretty sharpish—can't blame them to be fair. Besides, this money is burning a hole in my pocket and needs to be counted.

I float back to my room, lock the door and have a tally of my funds. Not looking too bad; I'll definitely be going home with more than I arrived with, plus looks like with expenses to one side, I've earned at least two grand, plus whatever Cliff is gonna pay me. But two grand is only good if I don't get caught, and it ain't over yet! I look out of the window and dig in for the next few days, eagerly waiting for my phone to go; Gunther should be making contact either Monday or worse case Tuesday morning. The alternative is barely worth thinking about, and that's me driving the fucking van across myself, but I can't see it—I'm way too hot for that.

The weekend passes uneventfully. I managed to remain fairly local and keep eyes on the van for the majority of the time. If anything it was fucking boring; you'd think sitting on all this coke would be exciting, but it's not. I switch off to the pressure and chill, eating crap and drinking. Tuesday arrives and still no phone call; the morning drags on with me constantly checking my phone for calls, even though I know nobody has called. But to me "radio silence" means zero comms unless absolutely necessary. My hotel situation is now fucked because I've checked out. I'm still plotted up in the same area, using the bar area for food and shit but this is now getting a bit tedious. It's now mid-afternoon and I'm considering booking myself back in, but I can't do it indefinitely. Feeling hesitant I consider my options on who to contact, Neil or Gunther; either way it's not an easy call to make, but Neil will need to know what's going on in any case. I call him, he answers and says, "Yes la, how was your weekend?". I reply, "Fucking boring, I'm still waiting for Fritz, any ideas?". Neil says, "For fuck's sake, he was meant to call you and update you! He's running a few hours late as he needed to hit the night shift instead, as his contact had a last-minute change of shift pattern. He reckons he'll be with you for about 19:00". I breathe a sigh of relief and say, "Ok that's not a problem, but his comms fucking stink. I'll grab some scoff and wait out then. Cheers!". I hang up and, looking at the time, I've got a good three or four hours to go, so I wander back into the hotel and chill, planning on a bit of food for my evening meal.

It's 18:30 and my phone rings. Yes, it's Gunther! I pick it up and say "Hello"; Gunther says, "Hello, I am outside". Shit! I say, "Ok see you in a minute". Gunther hangs up and for the last time I walk outside. The sun is setting and we now have the cover of darkness. As I approach the car park I see a work van, covered in what looks like German sign writing, clearly a delivery van. It reverses into a space next to mine, the same one that Neil was in. He gets out and says, "Hello, shall we load up?". "Yes, fucking please" I'm thinking, but I politely say, "Yes mate, I'd love to, the boxes are heavy mind". I slide the door open, quite handy really as his van has sliding doors on both sides; he conveniently slides his door open to reveal a relatively empty van, apart from a few small boxes and what looks like a load of dismantled engine parts.

Gunther has a look and says, "This is good yeah, the stuff is in the bottom?". I reply, "Yes mate, plus the brake discs on top". We weigh up our options and decide to lift the whole fucking box with contents intact; I manoeuvre the first box into place, ready to be slid or carried into Gunther's van. Luckily because the boxes are so fucking big, they comfortably straddle the two vans without the need for much lifting—more of a push and slide. With the first box in, Gunther looks inside and asks, "How many brakes?". I promptly reply, "Twenty; ten in each". Gunther then says, "Next box please; I will need to rearrange some things but this is good". I slide the second box over, feeling somewhat calm that the area is safe and we are out of sight doing this, because this must look dodgy as fuck.

With both boxes safely boarded, Gunther goes to the front of his van, pulls out what looks like a sales receipt book and proceeds to write in it. What's he doing, fucking invoicing me? I look at what he's writing and he's adding the brakes to what looks like his delivery inventory, and what must be a bogus delivery address. Ahh, I like it! He looks at me, winks and says, "This will keep them happy". He then says, "It was nice to meet you, I will take it from here". I reply saying, "Yes likewise, see you on the other side". I walk away from the area, allowing Gunther time and space to sort his load out. At last, I've done it! I can physically feel the weightlifting from my shoulders. The mere thought of all that coke being on my watch is enough to send my brain into a complete meltdown, but I reflect on the journey it's taken with me alone, successfully collected and transported all this way, and this leg of the journey isn't anywhere near the end, as the other part is gonna continue over the water back in England.

I relax in the communal area, still reflecting on the last few days, the what-ifs and whys, subconsciously waiting to see Gunther drive away. Even though I'm in chill mode I'm still mega observant. This technically isn't over; I want to see him drive off and disappear from sight before I feel happy to move on. I hear the sound of a van start up; presumably it's Gunther. A few more moments pass and I see his van pull out of the car park, driving off towards what must be the port. Now I can relax—no need to call Neil, all I need to do is get on the boat and fuck off home.

Chapter 16

ZOLTAN THE ...

I don't know where the time has gone. It's fast approaching 20:00, and all that waiting around and faffing about has written off most of the day—it's already dark when I drive into Calais ferry port. I drive into the car park for the ticket office, which is surprisingly busy, but luckily I'm able to find a space, so I park up and head on in to get my ticket. I go into the office and join the back of a short queue, taking this time to ensure that the money I have on me is sorted and that I don't accidentally produce a Bin Laden by mistake. The queue slowly shortens and from what I can hear from the people ahead of me, the ferries are full; not good news but apparently the later sailing has got plenty of room, so nothing to worry about.

After listening to the girl behind the counter repeatedly deliver the same script to all of the previous customers, I'm more or less ready to accept the fact that I'll have a bit of a wait, so when I finally approach the desk I'm just relieved to be getting served—the time of my crossing is irrelevant. I smile and ask for a ticket for myself and a van for the next crossing to Dover, only to be given the same script saying that the next two ferries are fully booked but there is space on the 23:15 crossing. This will do me nicely as all I care about is getting back on British soil. I pay the fee and head back out to the van, carrying all the paperwork with me.

So I've got basically two and a bit hours before we start loading, which I can handle quite comfortably. Fucking hell I've been sitting on 50 keys of coke for five days, so this will be pure joy. I get into the van and display the relevant information in the windscreen, then drive around to a holding area where I can plot up and chill until around 22:00. I drive round and join the queue of waiting HGVs and cars, pull up to the back, switch off and decide to have an hour's kip. I drift in and out of consciousness as I hear vehicles coming and going. Feeling as if I'm gonna miss the boat, I wake myself up and have a look around. I check the time and it's gone 21:00 already.

Looking in my wing mirrors I see a figure walking around. Looks like a guy, dressed in black; is he security? I have a momentary panic and remember that I'm clean as a whistle, apart from a few grand of drug money that can be easily explained, so I just observe his movements. He's knocking on all the doors of the lorries and cars, looking like he's fucking lost someone. Well, whatever he's looking for, he's about to ask me. He walks away from the car behind me, and as he does so the vehicles in front start up and begin to move. I start up and prepare to move also, but as I do he gets to my window and knocks on it. I look out at him; he doesn't look too stressed or menacing and definitely not security.

I wind down the window and say, "Hello, can I help you?". In broken English, the man says, "Do you have space for?". I'm thinking if I had the boxes in the back I'd stuff him in one of those, but deciding that that may be a little cruel, I respond by saying, "Do you have a ticket?". He replies, "No but I get one, I cannot go as foot passenger on boat so need car". I'm not sure if I can smell bullshit or not but realistically what have I got to lose if he gets a ticket? Where's the harm in me driving him on and off the boat? I say, "Sure you can come with me, but you need to get a ticket first". A massive smile spreads across his face and he says, "Thank you, I get now".

He fucks off over to another office that I didn't know existed; I can see into it as the whole frontage is one big fucking window. He goes in and sits down; there are two desks and he is sitting at the one nearest the window, and while he presumably is getting his ticket I'm sitting here thinking about my decision-making process. What part of me thinks it's a good idea to pick up what looks like an illegal immigrant? But then who am I to judge? I've just sent a case full of coke over the same stretch of water. Conscious of the traffic moving, I pull out of the queue and allow the vehicles behind me to crack on. I pull up outside the office where I look in and see a staff member holding a piece of paper up into the air; it's hard to see what it is, but they are giving it a good going over. Several moments later the man gives my new passenger the item back and hands him some additional paperwork, probably a ticket of some sort. He gets up and leaves the ticket office, walking towards me. I gesture at him to get in, which he does and, smiling like a Cheshire cat, he looks at me and says, "Thank you, my name Zoltan". I hold out my hand and say, "Nice to meet you Zoltan". Zoltan says, "I have travelling for long time, I have lift from Romania". I look at him and say, "Fuck me mate, that's a trek, I'm gonna call you 'Zoltan the Traveller'", which went completely over his head and he just smiled.

When I ask him what the hold-up was in the office, he produces a small document and says, "My ID much old". I look at it and realise it's not just old, it's written off. We carry on talking as I rejoin the steady stream of traffic, looking at the time we'll be boarding soon. I'm happy to take Zoltan with me but I can't be arsed to have a deep and meaningful conversation with him. Not being rude but I have to constantly bullshit him about what I've been doing here, but then again I guess it's good practice if I get a tug by customs. In a relatively short time I have learnt that Zoltan has had a hell of a difficult life coming from Romania, so I rechristen him "Zoltan the Brave", which still went right over his fucking head.

At last we've crawled our way to the boarding lanes and it's fucking rammed; not many cars but plenty of commercial vehicles, and no sooner than I switch off they all start up. I look across at Zoltan who is still smiling and I prepare to move. The van in front pulls away and I move with it, Zoltan's smile seeming to increase as we do. I thought I was happy to be going to the UK, but he looks like he's about to cum his pants! I had no idea how much this could mean to someone—he's like a kid at Christmas. I say, "I take it you haven't been to England before?"; he looks at me still smiling and says, "No, I have friends are there for long time, they say I work with them". As we proceed along the lane and onto the boarding ramps I look at him and say, "That's good", and I'm about to continue and ask him something else but my inner self says to me "Don't you fucking dare". Too late! I then say, "Oh? Where in England?". Zoltan says, "Birmingham".

This is my biggest problem; I can't stop myself from accommodating people who need help, even if it's a stupid decision. Finding it hard to believe what I'm about to say, I then come out with, "Birmingham? I can take you some of the way, where I live is on that route". Already regretting what I just said, Zoltan looks almost emotional and says, "Thank you, you are kind". What the fuck am I doing? I don't know who he is or anything about him. Either way, I'm committed, in the same way I was when hauling the coke, but it is what it is. We slowly drive onto the boat and park up, then I say to Zoltan, "I will see you back here when we arrive"; he looks at me and says, "Ok". Glad he did because I wasn't really giving him an option. He seems like a nice guy but I'm not here to make friends, because at the rate this is progressing he'll be in the spare bedroom and running drugs by Wednesday.

We go our separate ways and I just spend the next hour or so chilling out, looking for some useless tat to buy the missus and kids. Failing miserably I eventually return to the car empty-handed, but Zoltan is nowhere to be seen. I get in and feel the ferry shudder as it starts docking with Dover. The drivers and passengers are slowly returning to their respective vehicles and still no sign of Zoltan. Is this gonna be a no-show? Doesn't really matter as I'm going anyway and it's in his best interest to be here before I go, otherwise he's gonna have to get his thumb out again. The ferry bumps to a halt and, looking around, I see every other fucker is set to go.

The doors begin to drop and as if from nowhere here he is, sporting a combined look of panic and relief. He gets in and says, "Sorry, I fell to sleep". I smile and laugh saying, "Not to worry, you are now known as 'Zoltan the Late'". This time he gets it and laughs; probably not a real laugh as these names are for my own personal entertainment and there's no way he'll get it, but fuck it. We drive off the boat and down the ramps—touchdown. I look at him and say, "Welcome to England!".

Zoltan, looking elated, says, "Thank you, I wait long time for this". "I fucking bet you have", I think to myself. I say to him jokingly, "We have customs now, do you have any drugs on you?". He looks at me and, feeling as if I've opened a can of worms, he says, "No, I will not do that". I respond saying, "That's good, because I've got tons in the back". Zoltan looks at me with an expression of concern and says, "Have?", clearly too concerned to add the rest of the question. I then laugh and say, "No mate, I'm joking". Zoltan relaxes back into his chair and smiles. Fucking hell, that scared the shit out of him! We should call him "Zoltan the Scared".

We approach the customs shed, thinking that I'm clean, but am I? I've got a fat joint, a bit of drug money and a potential illegal on board—this could get interesting. We close in on the checkpoint and I wind down my window, ready to have a conversation if needs be. My passport is at hand, just in case. We creep closer and closer, Zultan still smiling. I'm trying to see if any of the previous cars have been pulled into the search shed which is on the left. We're next! The customs officer has a look at us as we approach and waves us through. Instant relief—my joint is safe. I drive out of Dover and towards the M20 as quickly as possible; up the hill and off we go.

I reach under my seat and fumble around a bit; there it is. I pull out the joint that has been sitting there for ages, but before I light it up I stick some music on. It takes me a few moments to find some lively music but when I do, I light the wick at the end of my joint—I can't be arsed to rip it off—and have a big fuck off puff, Zoltan looking on as I do. I have a few more and say, "Would you like some?". He reaches over and says, "Thank you"; I say, "Be careful, it is strong!". Zoltan says, "It is ok, I smoke all time". I'm thinking, "We'll see". Zoltan takes several short sharp puffs and hands it back. Is that it? Cool, more for me. I continue to enjoy it as Zoltan starts giggling. I say, "Are you ok?"; he says, "Too strong". "Zoltan the Stoned" sits back and falls asleep, to be renamed "Zoltan the Sleepy".

I periodically have a smoke for the duration of my journey while Zoltan gets what must be some much-needed sleep. I only wake him as we close in on Chippenham, because this is where I'll be dropping him off at the services. I'm so close to home now; I'll be in my bed in less than an hour. Zoltan wakes himself up and prepares to be dropped off. I drive up along the slip road and into the services. I clock a police car outside and, being cautious, I drive past and pull up out of sight. I look at Zoltan and say, "We're here"; he says, "Birmingham"; I say, "No mate, Birmingham isn't on my way". He says again, "Birmingham"; I say again, "You can say Birmingham as much as you like, it's not going to get any closer". I pull out my emergency road map and show him on the map where we are, where I live and where he's going. He looks at me and says, "Ok, I understand". I pull out a piece of paper and write down the general directions and roads he'll need to get there; I go over it with him and he appears to comprehend.

He gets out and holds his hand out—we shake hands and he thanks me. I say, "Watch out for the filth round the corner, they might have you". I drive away, leaving Zoltan looking confused. I kind of hope he makes it to his destination, but he's no longer my problem. I hit the M4 west and crack on home; at last this journey has come to an end, all I need to do now is wait for the heads-up to collect the coke from Neil.

Chapter 17

THE MONEY

Things are good—*really* good. Hassan is absolutely smashing his role as a runner and the feedback is generally good. Some say he's a bit fucking moody but what the fuck, we're shifting drugs and being PC isn't a fucking priority. He's a huge asset and I hope he sticks around, as I can only sense things getting better. Without Hassan I'd be facing a hell of a juggling act, what with my thing, Cliff's things and now Neil's thing; plus I need to fit in family time amongst it all. Hassan is now comfortably covering the majority of Cliff's and mine; there's maybe a couple I still need to do myself, but generally he's got it boxed off. The anomaly is Neil's thing, as this takes me out of the equation for days at a time and fuck knows where it'll be.

It's been a little over a month and we've all gotten busy shifting the 50 boxes—Cliff and Si did theirs in only one week, so I was sent back to reload. The stuff was still in the same fucking boxes sitting in a shifty-looking garage, and I wasn't too keen on being there to collect it, as it was way too exposed, especially as it was with Muggy and for some reason I can't take to him. Either way Neil never seems to be around so I have to work with his firm but he does pay fairly well. The money is coming in from all angles; for the last run Cliff dropped my bill by £2,000 instead of £1,500 and I've managed to feed him two more, getting my bill down to £16,000. I've paid back

£64,000 in less than a year—that's fucking good going! The strangest thing is that right now I feel like I'm in a much better position than when it all went tits up. My next logical move would be to get a safehouse sorted, but not just yet; it's better to load people up and let them hold their own kit.

The general feeling is that we're getting close to another run. I've been told to prep for next week and that Si will be coming over himself; not sure why but he said he has friends that live reasonably local to Fuengirola so he's gonna take a chance to chill; fair do's and why the fuck not? We've been getting on well and I can definitely tell that we're gonna build something in the future. Cliff has gone quiet for some reason; I still have comms with his boys but Cliff's become somewhat elusive; he does this from time to time so I don't tend to read into it. I'm trying to use this time productively to reconnect with my family, but it's hard when I live a constant lie. I'm still going through the motions and throwing a bit of money at the situation, hoping it'll make things better. It seems to be working, the only issue being I'm rarely around to enjoy the moment, as I'm on the road most of the time.

Thursday brings the usual busyness and Hassan is hard at it, or as much as he can be because the coke has more or less run dry. There's a couple of nines left to get rid of and for once Boe has been useful as my new warehouse person; I've made good use of his uselessness by loading him up and collecting it the following week to give to someone else. He thinks he's getting a good deal on extra coke but the reality is he's basically providing free storage. Hassan has him well-managed though—Hassan just growls and people do as they're fucking told. With all of these things boxed off it's quite a welcome feeling when Neil gets in touch and asks me to take a trip to Liverpool to round up the last remaining dosh. His contact won't be ready until about 17:00 and Neil is plotted up somewhere in Windsor, so he wants me to drop the dosh down there ready for the exchange. He's also got a plan for the next trip over and wants to brief me when I get there.

I decide to hit the road at about 14:00, which gives me enough time to get to Liverpool by 17:00. He's asked me to head for a retail outlet just off the M56, Fuck knows— Liverpool is Liverpool as far as I know. The journey is long and fucking boring; Birmingham, Stoke, then Manny and Liverpool—I hate the M6. All that aside, I arrive promptly at 17:00 and make contact with the guy I'm collecting from. Neil has said he's spot on and it'll be between 50 and 60 bags. I'm in the unmarked car and I've cunningly dropped the back seats down and filled it with household junk from the garage. Looks like I'm moving house and not money. I would prefer not to have my bill topped up again by getting caught collecting dosh.

When you're involved in drugs, you'd think that collecting money would be the easy part, but the problem I've found is that sometimes the money comes in a bigger package than the one the drugs came in, and then it becomes fucking stressful.

Neil's contact answers the phone and says, "Yes mate, are you here?". I reply, "Yeah, near the cinema". The phone goes quiet for a moment and he then says, "I'm gonna be a couple of hours yet as there's more coming from up north". Up north? What the fuck is he on about? We *are* up north! I say, "Yeah, Ok mate I'll get out of the area, give me a shout when you're ten minutes out", then hang up. Since now I've got to kill time for a couple of hours, I drive over to the cinema to see what films are playing. There's plenty on, but regrettably nothing that will allow me time to sit back and enjoy without cutting my timings a little fine. Best option is to get out of the area and plot up for a bit of sleep. Catnapping is something I got used to when I was in RECCE Tp when I was serving; we had a system whereby even grabbing a couple of minutes could keep you going for another hour, especially when you're hanging out of your arse. We also used to adopt a method of, if you can stand still then do it, if you can take a knee, take one, if you can sit then fucking sit and if you can lie down, get on the deck and rest your body. All these little drills help recharge your batteries and keep you relatively sharp.

There's no shortage of locations to park up in and to be fair, seeing as I'm not holding anything, then it doesn't really matter. A busy layby full of HGVs is perfect; I park up, recline my seat and get my nut down. I'm literally drifting off with that nice, fuzzy feeling when my phone goes. I look and it's Si; I answer and he says, "You busy brother?". I reply, "Yes bud, up in Scouseville at the moment, what's up?". Si says, "Nothing much, Cliff's gone dark at the moment so won't be on this one. I've got paperwork to add to the filing you're doing for our mate". I say, "Yeah, I did wonder about Cliff, he's been a bit elusive and his boys aren't saying anything. When do you want those papers grabbing?". Si says, "Not sure, when are you doing the exchange?". I have a bit of a think and say, "The impression I have is that it'll be tomorrow at some point; I'm going down tonight but I'll likely be doing the M6 then the M1. Can one of your lads meet me down there? Failing that, I might be able to grab it in the morning and go back down". I can sense

Si is debating something as he's taking time to respond, he then says, "Tell you what, I get the feeling that Neil is taking a lot over. I can get mine done separately, so I might bring it over myself and give it to you when I land instead". That's a slight change of direction but I can understand why so I say, "Ok mate, if you're sure, I don't mind diverting but it'll be getting late, probably around 22:30". Si says, "No it's ok, I'll manage it from this end, besides once it's changed it'll be easy enough to hide". I can't argue with that, so we say our goodbyes and I get my nut down again.

I fucking love drifting in and out of consciousness; time seems to slowly float by, but it does pass. I naturally begin to liven up before 19:00, hoping that Neil's guy is gonna be on time and I'm not kept hanging around all fucking night. I get out of the car and have a good fucking stretch; feeling the blood flow back into my legs wakes me up and the groggy feeling slowly disappears. Clock watching isn't going to help so I throw caution to the wind and drive back to the meeting place, where there are a fuck load of retail outlets and fast food restaurants to take advantage of. No wonder I'm such a fat pig—all I seem to consume is fast food and alcohol, Maccy D's or KFC or, more to the point, dry or greasy. I go for a dry, stale Maccy D's; at least I'll remain fairly clean. Might feel like I've eaten a load of cardboard but it'll keep the hunger at bay for a short while.

I plough through the meal in the standard sub-five minute time. It's starting to get dark so I hope this money arrives soon, and as usual my thoughts have managed to manifest the reality. My phone rings and it's Neil's contact; I pick up and say, "Yes mate, are you ready?". He says, "I am, sorry for the delay, it needed sorting because the fucking pricks were light. I've told Neil and he says to get it handed over, so I'll be there in a bit. Can you do me a favour? Come out of that complex, turn right then the next left. It's a residential street but nice and quiet. I'll be there in five". He hangs up and I drive off to quickly assess the pickup location.

As instructed, I turn right then left. First impressions are that it's good; houses on my right, with trees and bushes on my left, not much street lighting and there's enough darkness to give cover. The only problem I have is what the fuck is he driving and what does he look like? Having an indication helps, but spotting a dealer is easy enough; how many other vehicles will be coming down a dead-end residential road, apart from the people who live there? I drive to the bottom end, do a quick u-ey and casually drive back up towards the entrance. I then reverse back down part of the way and tuck my car into a space— lights and engine off—observe.

I see a set of headlights pull into sight and a dark car slowly drives along the road. I look at it as it passes by and the driver fits the image that I imagined—he looks just like me. I bail out of the car and start walking down the path in the same direction as him. My phone rings and he says, "I'm here". I say "I know, look behind you", as I emerge from the pavement and onto the road, directly behind him. He drops his window, leans out and says, "Fucking hell la, you'll get yourself shot sneaking up on people up here". I laugh and say with a cheeky, sarcastic smile, "You'll need to be more observant then, mate!". With no comeback he hands a carrier bag out of the window and says, "There's 58 there". I take it and say, "Cheers, bud, have a good one". We shake hands and both get the fuck out of dodge as soon as possible.

I get back onto the motorway as quickly as humanly possible and head south. I input Windsor into the satnav; fucking hell nearly four hours, it's gonna be a late one. I call Neil and inform him that I'm all good and will be with him for around 23:00. He's happy with that and says he'll update me with this exact location once he goes to ground. He's got his firm rounding up money all over the shop, so no doubt it's chaos down there at the moment. The money is well buried in the back, in amongst my junk—I can only hope I don't get pulled. I didn't bring a joint as the temptation to have a sneaky puff would be too great and would definitely be smelled by the filth if they decide to pull me. Fuck me, in the summer you can smell if someone's smoking a joint in a car in front of you, even two or three cars in front!

The stuff stinks, that's why it's called skunk.

I'm about an hour away and Neil has finally gone to ground. He's given me the location and as to be expected he's in another hotel somewhere in Windsor, so it'll probably be a nice one. Carrying drug money or drugs for that matter is a weird one, and I know I've said this before but the only dodgy parts are point A and B; the bit in-between should be easy and stress-free. As long as you're playing the game, don't have a marker on you, don't get involved in an accident or haven't been grassed up then you ought to be fine. Saying that, there's an awful lot that can go wrong, and carrying illegal goods will definitely make dealing with these things somewhat complicated.

I'm close now and as I carefully navigate through Windsor I call Neil to let him know I'm imminent. He tells me the room he's in and requests that I drop call him as I approach the room. Happy with these instructions, I crack on and locate the hotel. I enter the hotel premises and park up; it looks reasonably quiet and not being sure what car Neil is in, I opt to park up somewhere dark and discreet—standard drills. I grab the carrier bag which is stuffed with money and have a look to see if I have anything in the back that I can put it in. Fortunately I do have a small rucksack full of one of the kid's clothes; I have no idea why I grabbed it, but I'm fucking glad I did. It's more than likely old clothes that have been added to an ever-increasing pile of unwanted stuff accumulating in the garage.

An almost perfect fit! Clothes now liberally scattered around the back of the car and the money bagged and safe for transit to the hotel room, I de-bus and walk over to the main entrance. It's late, quiet and I'm looking for Room 8 on the ground floor. I don't want to be interacting with staff, so regardless of anyone being present I steam on through the posh reception and towards what I hope is the correct way to Room 8. With a choice of two directions and a 50/50 chance of getting it wrong, I make a U-turn and walk the other fucking way, going down the other corridor and having to pass the receptionist as I do. I consciously lower the bag and sheepishly say, "Wrong corridor"; I'm not wanting an answer or an explanation, I just felt like saying it, to prevent them from asking what the fuck am I doing wandering around their hotel in the middle of the night.

Room 8 in sight and with Neil's number set to dial, I drop call him and stand at the door, waiting for him to answer. The corridor is deserted and quiet; I listen for movement in the room, and I can hear the faint sound of a voice then footsteps. The door opens partially and I'm greeted by Neil's Colombian bird Antonia. I wasn't aware she'd come over; she smiles and in that accent asks me to come in. I walk in and close the door behind me, turn around and I'm about to say hello to Neil, but I feel my eyes and attention drawn to the biggest pile of fucking money I've ever seen—it's everywhere! All over the bed, floor and sides. Neil is busy flicking through a wedge and he says, "What's happening la? Don't be fucking shy, get amongst it, this lot needs sorting by the morning". Still feeling a bit mesmerised by the sheer volume of money, I say, "Fucking hell mate, is it all in then?", as I place my bag onto the bed to join what looks like other bags that have yet to be opened. Neil says, "Is it fuck, this is only half but Tony wants it brought over anyway". I say, "Ah ok mate, I'll crack on with the one I brought with me". Neil looks at me and says, "Yeah good luck with that one la!". Not really understanding why he says that, I open the bag, remove the carrier and find an isolated space on the bed to pour it onto.

I have to push a few bags to one side in order to accommodate the money I've collected; it's not been counted by us yet and will need to be checked properly. Mixing up bags of money before they've been properly looked at won't help to identify who's light. I tip the money out of the bag and immediately know why Neil said what he said, it's a fucking mess! Not only that, it appears to have notes that I don't recognise. I grab one and look at it— what the fuck is Clydesdale Bank? I look at Neil and say, "Mate what the fuck's this?". Neil laughs and says "It's Scottish and they have three different notes, so you'll have different designs of £20's, £10's, etc, and the real fucker is that the exchange wants them packaged not only by denomination, but different banks as well, so crack on la!". He just sits there giggling to himself while counting through what now seems like an easy pile of English money.

I can feel myself shimfing like fuck, but fortunately it's not all Scottish so I crack on, separating the notes into denominations and different banks, straightening them out as I do. I'd have thought at this level the money would be arriving in style, but this shit looks like Murray's been sorting it. There's a fucking huge pile of elastic bands on the bed, which are being used to bundle the money into 1000's and then 5000 blocks. It's slow and meticulous work, but progress is inevitable. We all count in silence—as time goes by, the money slowly goes from chaos to order and the pile of elastic bands slowly gets smaller. It's now 02:50 and we've counted our way through what looks like at least £500,000—possibly more. There's a couple of small bags left to do and Neil looks at me, saying, "Ok so the plan is ....."; fucking hell yeah, he's got a plan! Neil continues, "Antonia is going to fly back tomorrow and I'll be bringing over the ex and the kids for the Easter break. You'll bring over the money and one of my ex's mates— you can pose as a couple". I look at him and say, "Presumably your ex's mate is a female?". Neil says, "Yeah la, unless you'd prefer a man". I say, "Depends on your ex's mate; what's she like?". Neil replies bluntly, saying, "She's fucking nuts". Great! So let me get this right. I'm gonna be carrying what looks like half a mil, once changed into euros more like three quarters and I'll be accompanied by some psycho bitch I've never met? "Perfect", I say; "Cheers, can't fucking wait".

We tidy up the last few grand and pack it neatly into a suitcase. Neil says, "Luckily we didn't have too much Scottish, they give us less for it as it's a fucking ball ache, we usually get around 1.4 but they pay closer to 1.2 for the jock money". That's a bit harsh but I can understand why. Neil says, "So we'll be heading over on Saturday; the kids break up today so we'll be hitting the road Saturday morning. Are you ok to take your car over to Calais? We've got another renter waiting to be collected, so you can dump yours and swap". I say, "Yeah sure thing, as long as the location is secure". Neil says, "Yes mate it's perfect, we use it all the time, we've left cars there for days, no charge and no drama". Ok well fuck it, that's the plan. I say, "Well if you don't mind I'll get on the road and head home so I can spend tomorrow with the family and get all my shit in order". Neil looks around the room as if to try and find some more work and says, "Yeah, we're pretty much sorted here, so yeah I'll bell you tomorrow with Saturday's timings. The money will be sorted so we can discuss that when we catch up". Neil looking more than happy with his plan, I bid them farewell and fuck off out the door, faced with yet another fucking drive, and I am shattered.

Chapter 18

PSYCHO BITCHES

S aturday arrives sooner than I would have liked. Friday I was mostly zoned out—suffering from a lack of sleep. I didn't hit the sack until about 05:00, so I was written off most of the day. I did my best to keep everyone happy, even though it took some time to explain why the fuck I was rolling in at five o'clock in the morning. Saturdays are usually a lazy day for the missus so she's not even up when I leave, and yet again I have successfully laid down some smoke for my next trip overseas. In fact, she now welcomes it, because when I got home last time, I dropped a bag of sand in her hand and said I'd received a cash bonus from the person I was looking after. This made her day, and all of a sudden my prolonged absence didn't seem so bad.

Hassan hasn't got anything to do. With Cliff going dark and most of my customers still being cautious about returning to work with me, I have to make the most of what I've got. However there are a couple of old ones resurfacing, not to work with but some subtle comms to test the waters. I can't blame them too much as I was in a desperate place back then and I was juggling like fuck with everyone's money, causing untold headaches. I'd have dropped me out, so why shouldn't they?

Once again I leave the house for a third trip overseas. Neil has now dropped Trev out of the firm and he was reconsidering if the Prof was gonna be used again. He did promise me that I wouldn't be taking the Prof's place as I didn't have the right profile, and this was a decision that I couldn't agree with quickly enough. I'm to meet him in Slough this time. He's sorted the dosh and wants to spend time introducing me to my new girlfriend, who I'm mildly nervous about meeting. I'm not being unfaithful as it's just an act, but what if she's really tidy and gets carried away with the role of being my girlfriend? "Hang on a minute", I say to myself, "take a look in the fucking mirror mate, you don't have any hair and you're a fat twat". Based on this observation, I doubt she'll even want to go near me.

Feeling somewhat deflated that I no longer have the same appeal as I did a few years back, I load up the car and head for this shithole called Slough. Neil has said to aim for the town centre where we can all catch up and have a bit of lunch, then we'll get on our way for the evening crossing. Slough—I don't know what it is about this city. I've only ever been there once and that was on a surveillance job back in 1996. We had to plot up on an office outlet to look for our target and it fucking sucked. The target wasn't even there, so we were given duff information. We were then told to go to Heathrow where the client had been informed that the target was arriving on a flight from Germany. We were to follow him from the airport and get an address. They must have been fucking high! Follow a car from Heathrow? Not a fucking chance! Either the target didn't arrive, or if he did he possibly grabbed a connecting flight, so the day was a complete washout, and the client didn't want to pay as we didn't get a result. I fucking hate Slough.

Hate it or not, I'm here and looking for a parking space. Neil is already here and says he's waiting for his tribe to appear. After a bit of driving around in circles I locate a space and park up the unmarked. I'm not sure if I've interpreted if the space is free or not, so I decide that it is and I leave the car there. It's fucking Saturday and if a Hitler Youth traffic warden wants to stick a ticket on it then fucking crack on—Neil can foot the bill. I walk in what I believe is the correct direction to meet Neil and all I can see is misery. Most places have some kind of redeeming quality but not this place. My misery soon ends when I locate Neil sitting outside of what looks like a café or a bar so I take a seat next to him. We casually chat and I ascertain that his missus is running late, and still has to catch up with Andrea, who is gonna be my missus for the next few days. I ask him, "Mate so seriously, what's she like?". Neil looks at me and says, "I told you she's fucking nuts, but just keep her off the ale and she should be ok". This isn't helping so I say, "So what's the plan with the dosh?". Neil says, "The ex will carry it over in her bag". I'm attempting to visualise how many envelopes full of Bin Ladens we might have, but too taxing so instead I ask, "How many envelopes, mate?". Neil directly replies, "Seven and they are stuffed; we got just under three-quarters of a mil. The fuckers gave us a shit rate on the Scottish." I ask, "So they are the same size envelopes, not fucking A4 or anything daft like that?". Neil says, "No la, normal ones, we've done this plenty of times". I hesitate and say, "So if your ex is carrying the dough, why the fuck do I get landed with the nutter?". Neil laughs and says, "La she has her uses, trust me she's a good replacement for Trev". I look at Neil and, debating if I can take him seriously or not, I say, "Are you fucking kidding me, so she's our new enforcer, how big is she?".

"Oi, oi!", I hear to my rear. I look around to see a gaggle of kids and women arriving. I say slowly to myself, "Fucking hell, please God no, don't let this be them!". Neil gets up and says loudly, "Yes girls how are ya?". He gives them all a massive hug and what are clearly his kids are all over him. I remain seated, refusing to be a part of this fucking circus. Neil sits back down next to me and they all join us. I look across at what must be Neil's ex. She's what I would describe as normal looking; a bit of a biker chick if I had to say anything. "Hi there", I say. She smiles and in what must be a Slough accent says, "Hello love I'm Jan, nice to meet you". She seems pleasant enough. Neil is busy being a dad, so I look across at Andrea who is fucking tiny and stocky. She's already picked up the menu and gone straight to the back, looking at the booze. I say, "Hello Andrea, apparently you're my new missus?". She places the menu back down on the table, leans forward, looks me dead in the eye and says, "Oh yeah? You think you can handle me?". I look at Neil and before I open my mouth he says, "Told you la". I look at Andrea and say, "Probably not but I like a challenge". She smiles and picks up the menu, turns and looks inside what I now realise is a restaurant and shouts "Oi, waiter!". Jesus fucking Christ! I've got to drive across Europe with this and I can't tell if this is a sober or pissed-up version of her.

A waiter soon arrives and Andrea proceeds to order herself a lager. Neil immediately says, "Keep it to a minimum kid, you're meant to be working". His missus then says, "Fuck off, we're on our holidays" and also orders a drink. Neil looks at them both and says, "Look you pair of cunts, I told you you're working. If you fuck this up I'll be handing you both over to the firm, and you can explain to them exactly why we don't have their fucking money". Clearly hearing everything and unsure of what to do, the waiter stands there like a statue, so I say "Mate, I'll have a Coke please". I look at the kids and Neil and say, "Anyone else?". The kids all opt in, as does Neil. I confirm with "Five Cokes then please, bud". The waiter walks off and Neil proceeds to keep firing a few fucks into the girls, who are already on the verge of being out of control.

The waiter soon arrives with a tray full of Cokes and places them on the table. Andrea takes the opportunity and says, "Where's my fucking lager, son?". The waiter, not sure if she's taking the piss, looks at me for guidance and I in turn look at Neil, who says, "Two halves of lager please". The waiter scurries off to get the drinks and the girls, looking disappointed, quietly sit back. Neil reiterates to them, "Look please just keep a lid on it until we get over the water. This is gonna be hard enough as it is without you two pissing about. They both then settle down and seem to accept that maybe they're being slightly off key. The waiter arrives and hands the girls their drinks, which they both take without showing any signs of gratitude.

As far as I'm concerned these are bad signs. Standard practice is, when engaging in illegal activities, not to at any cost antagonise, upset or engage in any form of unnecessary confrontation with anyone, especially the general public. This will always shine an unwanted light on you and your activities, thus increasing the risk of getting pulled and consequently nicked. Be on the best of behaviour, smile and be polite—it's not fucking rocket science. I look at Neil and he can tell I'm not happy but it's his gig, so I'll just do my bit. If I feel these people are gonna compromise us then I'm gonna pull him and let him know.

I spent the next couple of hours trying to get to know Andrea and I'm fucking struggling. She's all right but too loud and energetic for this. Probably great on the piss but fucking awful providing cover as a couple, but I reserve the right to change my mind. Who knows? She might step up when needed. The other thought that crossed my mind was that seeing as Jan's carrying the dough and we're going over empty, Andrea would make a cracking diversion. I can actually picture her starting a fully-blown domestic in the car to get the customs to focus on us rather than the dosh or drugs. My concern is this fucking nutter would likely do it anyway.

Looking at the time it's already getting on and I could do with heading off, as we've got a bit of a drive to go and fuck knows what the plan is on the other side. I look over to Neil and say, "What time are we heading off, mate?". Looking at his watch he says, "I'm waiting for Lofty to bring us the money; he's been sorting a few more bits out to give us enough for expenses". Realising that we hadn't addressed that yet, I then say, "Fuck yeah, I'd not thought of that!". I just wasn't gonna be using my emergency grand, and seeing as Si was taking his own over I didn't have access to a ton of their money. Neil decides to call Lofty for an update and the conversation starts calmly, but soon kicks off when Neil is calling him a useless this and a useless that. It would seem apparent that Lofty has been sitting on his arse all day and forgot to pop the money over to us. Neil says, "Right, let's all fuck off". The girls finish off what must be their third drink and the kids all gather their random bits that have been scattered across the table. We all saddle up and fuck off.

Neil says, "Andrea you jump into the other car from now and do as you're fucking told. Remember you're working and if you fuck about then you won't get paid". He then looks at his tribe and says, "You lot with me". He looks at me and says, "I'll see you at the port ticket office. I'll sort you out with some expenses when we get there". I say, "Yeah that's all good, I'll see you in a couple". For a short while we walk together without much being said but eventually we divide, so Andrea and I are finally left alone. I say, "The car's just round here; hopefully it hasn't been given a fucking ticket". She looks at me and says, "Don't be surprised if the wardens round here are fucking on it". We walk around the corner and I look at the car but I can't see the windscreen yet as we're approaching from the rear. I'm looking for that annoying yellow bag stuck to the windscreen, but fortunately the car is clean and ticket-free.

We get in and make ourselves comfortable for the journey ahead. She's definitely calmed down and seems somewhat sedate in comparison. I say, "You've gone quiet. How many times have you done this for Neil?". She looks at me and says, I haven't, not over there anyway. I've helped with a few bits over here but this is a lot bigger. How about you?". I take the opportunity to explain my situation and I go off on my whole fucking life story in the process. She seems to be interested so I crack on. The conversation is good and as a result, the journey flies by. We're closing in on Dover and should be at the ticket office soon. I'm curious if Neil has managed to yet again defy physics and get there before me without actually visibly passing me, but then again I never know what car he's in.

Once again, here I am at Dover port and once again it's dark. I do oddly feel a lot better with Andrea sitting next to me. She's not necessarily what I would call a looker but she does have this pocket rocket kind of appeal, and she's only wearing a vest. Naturally I haven't taken notice of this, but maybe the customs guys will. Could that backfire though, as they might pull us just to check her out? Or is that just my mind working? I call Neil to get a LocStat and he informs me that he is just fuelling up and he'll be with us in a few minutes. I update Andrea and we sit back and chill. She's ok actually; it would appear that most of it is bravado, and she might just play up when Neil or his ex are around.

I get out of the car ready to greet Neil—my gut is telling me he'll be here soon but I'm wrong. I'm standing around like a fucking tool for what feels like ages. Andrea is the clever one, sitting in the car in the warm listening to music, and we've both realised that we've got similar tastes; we're both into house music. It's bloody cold as well—can't wait to get back over to Spain where it's now noticeably warmer. Fuck this! I get back into the car where it's warm, look at the clock and it's already past 20:00. We're gonna be fucked again; it's going to be too late for driving so we'll have to get digs. Then the penny dropped. How far does this posing as a couple go? Same room or what? I panic slightly. I'm a married man and have never so much as looked at another woman—ok I've looked but never touched. The thought of sharing a room with her sends me into a bout of anxiety. I then once again remind myself to take a look in the mirror; it's not happening, fat boy.

A set of headlights light up the car park and in rolls Neil, who finds a convenient spot but manages to take up two spaces in the process. I walk over and as he gets out. As I'm studying the car's logo on the front end, he looks at me and says, "What?". I sarcastically say, "Sorry mate, I was looking for the BMW badge". Neil looks back and, seeing how shit his parking is, laughs and simply shrugs it off. We both walk into the office to get our ferry tickets then Andrea gets out of mine and walks over to chat with Jan. Neil pulls a neat bundle of cash out of his pocket and pays for the whole lot. He then hands me my tickets, paperwork and boarding passes. I grab them and check them over. He's gone for a one-way trip as opposed to a designated return date, which makes me wonder how long this trip will be. It looks like we're on the next crossing, which could be about an hour or so away.

Neil hands me a wedge of cash as we walk out of the office and rejoin the girls, who have regrettably turned up their volume again. I'm not sure whether they're just a lethal combo or if one of them is a bad influence on the other. From my perspective Andrea is seemingly sound, or is it my calming influence? We all get into our respective cars and I'm immediately presented with the strong smell of alcohol. Andrea's drinking from a bottle of Coke; she looks at me and says, "I'm on my holiday now, mate", as she necks the drink. I look at her and say, "Not fucking yet you're not, what's in there, vodka?". She looks at me with a coy smile and says, "Maybe". I shake my head, but to be fair I shouldn't be too fussed as I've got fuck all on me. I look across at Neil and he's pulling out so I follow him. I can see the silhouette of his kids leaping around in the back like it's a fucking bouncy castle.

We close in on the passport and customs checkpoint. I eagerly watch to see if Neil is gonna get the green light and I see his kids still going fucking nuts in the back. He gets waved through and cracks on, as I do. That was nice! Zero stress for a change, but can't say the same for Neil in his car as it looks like a madhouse from here. We pull up into our chosen lane and switch off; it's 45 minutes or so before we board which I can handle. I chill for a bit and start to feel a bit sleepy, but instead of getting some shut-eye I decide to go for a coffee instead. I look across to a small service area and there's a Costa; not seen many of these around and it looks quite new. I look at Andrea and ask if she fancies a coffee. She says, "Nah but I'll see what else they have".

We both get out and as we do Andrea runs across to see Jan, who also gets out with the kids and joins us. I ask Neil if he wants anything and he says, "It's ok la she'll sort it". I nod and walk over to the coffee shop with them; the kids have calmed a bit but Neil's ex is clearly pissed. She must have been hammering the vodka or whatever it is stashed in the Coke bottles. She's not staggering but she's definitely on her way. As we enter the shop, I clock that she has her bag with her and I keep a firm eye on it—if that money is in there then I'm not taking any chances. We head towards the cash desk where the kids are grabbing all sorts of shite and sticking it on the counter. I'm first in the queue and order a latte; one of the girls behind the counter gets busy while the other asks Jan for her order. Andrea is just standing around.

Once Jan has completed her drinks order, she starts looking at the items on display on the counter. I don't think anything of it until I see her unzip her bag and open it up. I discreetly peer into it and see the envelopes full of euros inside. She then proceeds to take one of the items on display and slip it into her bag. I immediately grab her arm and say in a stern yet calm voice, "What the fuck are you doing? Are you fucking stupid? Put it back or fucking pay for it". She reluctantly takes the item and replaces it on the shelf. I look at her and shake my head, but she just fobs it off and, in a slightly slurred voice says, "Boring twat". I choose to not respond; probably best not to make a scene here for now. Once I'm happy that she's not gonna thieve anything else, I walk out and pull Neil aside for a private chat.

"Mate your ex is in there with all that dough and she's fucking thieving. I had to pull her. If she got caught, we'd risk losing everything for the sake of a fucking lollypop". Neil's face changes and I can see the anger brewing. He says, "Thanks la. The stupid bitch! I'm changing the plan. Are you able to take the money over? We've cleared customs so it'll be a piece of piss". I respond, "Yeah mate, get it over here now so I can tuck it away". Neil storms off to rip into Jan and fucking tell her he'll tear her a new one. The kids have shut up, Andrea has skulked back into my car and as for Neil's ex, she's been well and truly told. I get into my car and say fuck all. Jan walks towards me, I open the window and she proceeds to throw the envelopes at me, saying, "You fucking grass". I look at her and say, "Fuck off and sober up, you're a fucking liability". The last envelope bounces off Andrea's head and she turns and shouts, "Oi dickhead!". Jan says nothing and walks away.

I look at Andrea and as I gather the envelopes up I say, "Are you ok?"; she replies, "Yeah, but she's hard work, mate. I always regret things when we get together. She knows I'm useless on the ale, but she's a fucking nightmare". I look at her and softly say, "Look this isn't your doing, now let's see where we can stash this money". Even though we shouldn't be getting checked again, it's a lot of money to have sitting around. I don't wanna be carting it around the boat and I'm not risking leaving it in the car without it being stashed properly. I look up at the roof lining and consider if this can be detached in any way to tuck the envelopes in. They're full, but looking at it they should go relatively unnoticed if I spread them out.

The port isn't overly busy and with no sign of any uniforms around I start to pull away the roof lining from the front end, where the sun visors are located. A gentle tug and it partially comes away—perfect. I look at Andrea and smile, she grins and hands me the first envelope. I gently push it up and then back onto the top of the roof lining, it's now tucked away, between the lining and the car's roof. Andrea passes me another and I do the same, pushing the first one slightly further back which is nice because when I look up it's hard to see if there is anything stashed. We continue to tuck the envelopes away whilst periodically checking outside for any staff. I do my best to even them out so when the last one is tucked away, I've pulled away the whole front end of the lining. Now it's time to tuck it back up, and after some effort of trying to sort it whilst not looking obvious, I decide I'm happy with it. I get out of the car for a stretch and I casually walk around to the front to have a look at my work.

It's shit—I can see the lining hanging down on the driver's side so I get back in and try again. Andrea gets out to have a look so I can get direct feedback and when she gives me the thumbs up I relax and smile. She gets back in and I thank her. She's proving herself to be an asset—this shouldn't be too bad after all, I'll keep her away from the booze and all should be good. Now my eye is drawn to some movement in Neil's car. He's getting out of the madhouse and walks towards me, indicating for me to get out, which I do. "What's up mate?", I ask. Neil says, "Is that stashed? Looked like a right fucking hash job". I laugh and say, "Yeah it'll be safer there than in your bird's bag". He says, "You're not wrong there, bro. I don't know why I bother. The only reason I'm bringing her is that the kids are off for Easter and I wanted them to stay in the apartment with me. Otherwise, she drives me fucking nuts".

Neil then says, "So the plan for the other side is we have a Spanish renter parked up. I was using it last week to move some money, so when we get off the boat, follow me there. I'll give you the keys, drop your motor off and take the renter, as I can return it when we get down the bottom". Fucking hell, how many cars does he have parked up on hire? I say, "No problem, as long as the parking space is good I'm happy to ditch mine and crack on". Neil says "Yeah it's all good; once you've swapped give me the dough and I'll take it down to sort out Tony. There's no rush as he might not be around until Monday, but head for Madrid and we'll see how it goes". So I've basically got a day and a half to travel across France and down to Madrid; a long one but at least this time I have company.

The vehicles around us start up and we both get back into our car. I brief my co-pilot on the plan and we go over it a bit while I wait for the off. Andrea seems clued up enough to actually be helpful, so having a sense of confidence I feel relatively calm as we proceed onto the ferry. It's become a case of going through the motions and understanding the various stages of where it could go tits up, and this stage is one of those where I can relax, even if the roof lining is a bit warped. We finally board and head up to the upper decks; it's clear to me that Jan is going to go straight to the fucking bar and she'll likely convince Andrea to join her. I'm presuming it'll be down to both Neil and me to manage them so they don't get arseholed. Fucking hell the crossing is an hour; how much damage can be done in that time?

The answer is "a lot". Within 20 minutes Andrea is necking the drinks faster than I can drive past the police near Paris. Jan is fucking wasted and the kids are nowhere to be seen—probably running riot on the decks. It looks like Neil has given up—he's just sitting back with his head in his hands. The majority of the passengers are quite sedate and then there's us—what a contrast! But maybe there's logic in this move. Who in their right mind would run around with an obscene amount of money surrounded by these lunatics? So maybe this is what Neil wants, but looking at him would suggest otherwise.

I look at him and ask, "Is it always like this, mate?". I can see he's a beaten man when he looks at me, saying, "I told you la, they're fucking nuts. Antonia even seems quiet compared to these loons and she's a hot-blooded Colombian". I struggle to find something to say that will add to the conversation but fail, so I end up saying nothing and just sit back, waiting for the journey to end. Which it does eventually; the tannoy goes and the familiar pre-recorded messages are played over in a loop. We begin to rally the troops; I take Andrea and Neil does his best to manage Jan and the kids. Andrea was right about one thing—she is shit with drink. She's a true Jekyll and Hyde. I'm hoping that she's ok in the car but better still falls asleep; if she does I'm gonna crack on and drive as far as possible.

The lower car decks are loud and echo everything, especially Andrea and Jan's less-than-private conversation. Jan shouts out to Andrea, "Are you gonna fuck your new boyfriend in the hotel then?". This sends a sense of dread through my bones, and not because I'm shy—it's because I'm happily married and I wouldn't ever consciously put myself in this position. Andrea looks at me and responds to Jan, "Nah he's not my type". Feeling relieved and offended at the same time, I look across at Neil who is now smiling. I then look at Jan who just flicks me the bird and slides into the passenger seat of Neil's car.

I get into the car and Andrea looks at me, saying, "You are my type but I know you're married". My ego has now been restored. I look at her and say, "What, so you're into balding fat blokes are you?". She laughs it off but doesn't answer. Neil is in front of me as we all pull away and move off the boat. I'm mindful that I might get pulled from the French customs, or I might get a pull from Andrea; both concern me and right now I'd settle with customs pulling me, as that seems to be the less traumatic. Neil's car now looks a lot calmer than it did a couple of hours ago. They pass through the French side of the port easily, and there's no reason why we shouldn't too, because all the checks were done in the UK. However, this is a fuck ton of dosh and I need to do my best to make sure it's safe, and taking responsibility for it over Neil's stupid fucking ex had to be done. This money belongs to what must be the cartels or at least a very close connection, so losing it through stupidity is not a good idea.

We've all successfully cleared the port. I take up the rear and follow Neil to where the car is parked. Andrea is quite sedate which is good. It's almost a guarantee that she'll fall asleep when we hit the road. It's a good 15 or 20-minute drive through some winding roads. This would normally be ok but I can hear the money shifting from side to side as we drive along. I would slow down, but Neil is driving like a fucking nutter and I don't wanna be losing him. Eventually I see him pull over into a layby and park up. I pull in behind to see what must be the car. The Spanish plates give it away. I switch off and ask Andrea to get her shit together while I sort the money out.

I clearly haven't thought this through. How the fuck am I going to retrieve these envelopes once they've been pushed back under the lining? I gently pull down the lining and, trying not to cause any damage, I reach in. I can just about feel one of the envelopes. It's dark and quiet and I don't fucking like it. I manage to manipulate the envelope with my fingertips to a point where I can slip my hand under it and literally carry it out inch by inch on the back of my hand. Success! One down, six to go. Unable to feel the others, I decide to press up on the lining to see where they are. It's too fucking thick to get any real feedback, so feeling slightly pressured I just rip the lining down as hard as I can, opening it right up, an absolute nightmare. All the wiring from the interior light is connected and is restricting me from pulling the lining down all the way. Decision time. Do I destroy the lighting or rip the lining?

I go all gorilla, ripping the lining a bit more and reaching in over the passenger side where I locate three more envelopes. Two more have slid over to the driver's side. I only discovered this after I reluctantly ripped the wires out of the interior light. Stressed to fuck, I can only find six envelopes. What a fucking mess! Now second-guessing how many envelopes I had, I get out and walk across to Neil. I hand him the envelopes and say, "There were seven, yeah?". He looks at me and says, "Yeah, don't tell me you've lost one. There's like over 100 bags in each one". Remaining calm but clearly stressed, I say, "No mate they've just shifted around, give me a minute". I walk back to the car and can hear Neil shouting at Jan. I just about pick him up saying, "This is your fault, you fucking pisshead!". At least he's not blaming me. Andrea sits in the passenger seat of the renter, while I crack on and systematically destroy the interior of my car.

Feeling around in the dark with no torch or interior light to use, reminds me of being on exercise in the army. Operating in the pitch dark, I take a breath and relax; if I move slowly I'll be quicker. With a sense of calm and common sense, I know that the load has shifted from side to side, not rear or forwards, so the last one must be down the side somewhere. I pull the lining down from the passenger side even more, where a new cavity has been revealed—the one that leads down to the seat belt along the door pillar. The plastic trim is in two pieces so the top one gets ripped away with relative ease. All this time I'm mindful of what I'm doing and how fucking dodgy this looks. With my eyes slightly adjusting to the darkness, I look down into the remaining part of the trim where the seat belt roller is located. It's hard to tell but I think I can see it. I carefully reach down behind the trim, fingertips stretched out, scratching the skin off as I force my hand to wedge it open enough to get a feel. Yes, I've got something; this has to be it, it feels like paper and definitely has the correct dimensions. I reach in even further; this is about as awkward as it can be but

I finally manage to grip what I hope is the envelope and slowly pull it out.

Success! I've got it. How the fuck did it get down there? I couldn't have done that if I tried. I quickly get it handed over to Neil, and looking relieved he says, "You took your time". I reply by saying, "You're welcome, my car's fucked now". Jan laughs and I walk off in a right fucking strop. I join Andrea who is now doing a good impression of a nodding donkey. Feeling wide awake I decide to do as planned and crack on until I can't drive anymore. There's no need to convoy it so I stick Madrid into the satnav and get on the fucking road. I won't be going via Andorra on this occasion, so that will save a lot of time. It's still a good 14 or 15 hours, mind. But the car's clean—at least I hope it is.

The night drags on and I keep on going. Andrea is sleeping solid which is ok with me. She only wakes up slightly when I wind down the windows for some fresh air or pull into the services for coffee and fuel. I do enjoy driving through the night. I can give it a bit more and don't even mind if I get pulled, because the €90 fine is easily covered but fortunately that didn't happen. I spend the journey reflecting on where my life has been and where it might be going. A little bit of anxiety creeps in when I consider that I'll likely be meeting the Colombians again this week, but I'm also torn as next weekend is Easter and I'd like to be home for that. The journey continues past Paris and down towards the Bordeaux region. I can hear Neil's strong scouse accent in my head saying, "Yeah you gotta be careful in Bordeaux, this is where you get pulled on the return route". I can't be arsed with a hotel and the awkwardness that it will bring, so with Andrea still fast asleep I pull into a rest place, switch off and get some shut-eye for a few hours. I switch the engine on and off periodically to keep some warmth in the car, which keeps me semi-awake but it's enough.

The sun is rising and this wakes me up naturally, but can't say the same for Andrea who's catching flies still. I get out, go for a piss and freshen up, feeling surprisingly good considering I've been on the road nearly all night. There's plenty of movement around and I'm quite liking the idea of a strong espresso from the vending machine inside. Not knowing what Andrea prefers, I take the liberty of ordering her a coffee, and if she doesn't want it, I'll have it. Walking back I see she's not only awake but has got out of the car and is stretching to wake herself up. Much to the delight of the French truck drivers she's still sporting a skimpy little vest, despite the cold.

I offer her the coffee and say, "Fucking hell you can sleep for England!". She nods and says, "Yeah, you know what I was quite comfy there, thanks for the coffee". We chat for a while before she also heads off to the washrooms to freshen up. She returns with an armful of junk food and drinks. I say, "Good fucking skills, I see you've got us *croissants* and *pains au chocolat*". Looking at me in a confused state she says, "Eh?". I point at the items and say, "Those things there, fucking *croissants* and *pain au chocolat*". She shrugs and says, "Oh that", then gets into the car.

We've still got about seven hours to go so we crack on towards the border, wondering if Neil is ahead or not. I can't imagine what level his sanity would have gotten to if he's driven through the night, but hopefully Jan and the kids would have zonked out like Andrea. The border was busy, but then again I've never crossed it in this direction. The last time was last month but it is the Easter holidays, so maybe that would make a difference, but who knows and who cares? It is nice to hit Spanish soil though; it actually feels like I'm in a foreign country. France does a bit but Spain definitely does. It's dry and slightly barren, whereas France is green and lush like England. Still with about seven hours to go, I'm due to hit Madrid in the early evening.

Lunchtime comes and goes. Andrea and I chat random shit as we get closer to the Mad one (Madrid). With a little over a couple of hours to go, I call Neil to get a sitrep. He answers, "Yes mate, how are you getting on? Has she sucked you off yet?". Feeling slightly unsure if that was an option, I reservedly say, "No mate, how's tricks on your end?". He says, "Well put it this way, I haven't killed anyone yet. I'm looking for a hotel to check into". I butt in and say, "Hang on, how the fuck are you so far ahead? Did you not stop at all?". Neil says, "No la, my friend Charlie kept me company". This explains a lot—fuck that I'd rather sleep! Can't imagine being fully charged on nosebag and driving with that fucking nutjob Jan. Neil says, "I'll let you know where we are when we plot up."

We continue with our journey, which is beginning to feel never-ending but fortunately it's not. As the sun goes down we arrive at our destination and have been directed towards the Real Madrid football stadium. Now I'm not a football person so this means fuck all to me, but what does have an impact on me is the fucking road works. The whole area is one big building site, throwing my satnav into a total meltdown, but I'm doing my best to not lose my shit even though I keep going around in circles. After an age, I eventually pick up a road that leads me away from this fucking place. Real Madrid can kiss my arse. Eighteen minutes out and I've lost the best part of an hour. Andrea is just looking out of the window, taking in the sights.

I call Neil and say, "Right mate, I'm a few minutes away where are ya?"; he replies with "Ok you'll pick up a busy high street and our hotel is on the left. You'll see my car outside. It's fully booked so you can both check into the hotel on the opposite side of the road". I was about to say something when Neil says, "Yes, get separate rooms". I say, "You read my mind". He gives me the address and I stick it into the map. Two minutes, result. Andrea perks up, knowing that we'll be there soon. I get the feeling she'll be going on the piss with Jan. I clock Neil's car and look across the road to see what must be the hotel that we're staying in. I find a space and with a sense of relief switch off and get out, Andrea joining me.

Andrea is scanning the street for bars and clubs. I'm doing the same for threats and police. We both have a very different perspective, but you know what? She was ok. We check into what looks like a middle-of-the-road hotel, neither posh nor shit. Fucking pricey though. I ask for two single rooms and when the receptionist says the price, Andrea and I look at each other and both on the same wavelength say, "Ok singles it is". To sacrifice my integrity at this stage would be disastrous. I'm not even suggesting that anything could remotely happen but I couldn't put myself in that position just to save a couple of quid.

We walk away from the reception and both rooms are on the first floor, so we take the stairs, which for some decorative reason are bordered by rugged rocks on top of a bricked wall—very urban. We locate our rooms and start to go our separate ways, but as we do Andrea asks, "What's your plan tonight?". I say, "Fuck all, I just want to call the wife and speak with the kids. How about you?". Andrea smiles and says, "I'm on my holiday now mate, so I'll be on the piss with Jan within the hour". Now why does this not surprise me? I say, "Well, enjoy. I don't know how long we're here, so have a good one". We both go into our rooms; I kick back ready to relax for the night and I guess Andrea will be prepping for a night out in Madrid.

I give Neil a quick call for updates. He answers and says, "You made it then bro? How was she?". I say, "Actually mate, she was good as gold, no dramas. Do we have a plan in place yet?". Neil is quiet for a moment then says, "Yeah, but it isn't ideal. I've got a meeting with Tony tomorrow at lunchtime. I'm a bit light with the dough so he's not gonna work again until we've cleared the account". Feeling a bit uneasy, I say, "You don't have to say mate, but how light are we?". Neil says, "No it's ok la, you're part of the firm now. Only about 100 bags on this one, but there's a bit left over from the one before". Drug debts are commonplace and natural, but I don't know how it works over here. Neil doesn't seem to fuss and is spending money like it's water so I'll take it as it is—not my problem.

I wake up to hear some chaos outside on the high street—fucking shouting and singing everywhere. Fuck knows what time it is so I try and get myself back to sleep, only to be disturbed further by the sound of clattering about on the stairs and shouting. It's Andrea returning from her night out. I turn over and hope she doesn't knock on my door; I can hear her stagger past and hearing her fire fucks out on full auto I can't help but laugh. Sounds like she's struggling to get in her room, but after a while the fucks subside and I hear her door open and close, then I drift back to sleep.

That was a good night's kip. I wake feeling revived and alive, then shower, shave, shit and teeth. I need to indulge in one of the finest shit breakfasts that Spain has to offer. I walk out of the room and down the stairs, frowning at the oddly-designed stone walls as I do. I take a seat in the restaurant and relax, enjoying a coffee. Again reflecting and thinking about the last coffee I enjoyed over here, which was with Tony's brother Manny just before collecting the coke. It's now come full circle and we're handing over the dosh. What a trip! I get up and walk over to the sparsely laid out hot food and continental breakfast counter. I begin to fill my plate with those pathetic sausages when I catch Andrea in my eye as she enters the room. What a fucking mess! Her face is scratched to fuck with cuts and new scabs everywhere. I look at her and say, "What the fuck have you been sticking your face into?". Sounding completely unphased by her appearance she says, "I fell up the stairs last night and face-planted those stupid fucking rocks". Trying my hardest not to piss myself with laughter I say, "I take it you were hammered". With what I would describe as a combined look of distress and confusion she says, "Was? I still am, babe". She grabs a coffee and slumps down into the chair next to me. On closer examination I can see lumps of skin hanging off of her chin and her lips are swollen. No wonder she couldn't get into her room last night—she was written off.

We spend the next hour chatting. I'm trying not to focus on this loose skin on her chin, but my eyes are drawn to it, so much so that Andrea says, "Look, I know I'm a fucking mess but can you please stop staring at me?". I smile and say, "I'm trying but you must at least have a proper cleanup. I'd have yanked that fucking skin off ages ago". She feels around her chin and locates the offending item, gives it a sharp tug and rips the fucker clean away. As a trickle of blood starts to roll down her chin, she says, "Happy now?". I say, "Happier". I hand her a napkin to catch the blood before it lands on the table or her clothes.

Well, that made breakfast an interesting experience. I walk back up to my room, now scanning the rocks for the rest of Andrea's face. I enter and, mindful that we'll have to be checking out soon, call Neil for yet another update. He answers and says, "Fucking hell la my ex is ruined, I'm glad she was in her room with the kids". I say, "Is she in one piece? Andrea's fucked mate, she headbutted the stairs and was peeling parts of her face off during breakfast". Neil bursts out laughing and says, "Yeah she can't drink for shit. I'm on my way to see Manny now to drop this off. You can crack on down to Fuengirola and plot up. Are you ok to take Andrea with you?". I reply, "Yes of course mate, she'll probably sleep all the way anyway". He says, "Cheers la. I won't be too far behind you, how are your expenses lasting?". I have a flick through and say, "Just under a bag mate". He says, "Cool, that'll be enough. Check into that same hotel, go for two days for now, then we'll see where it goes from there".

I pack what's left of my stuff and walk out of my room. I head for Andrea's and politely knock. She answers the door. I'm now confronted with a pocket rocket in underwear with bits of tissue stuck all over her face. Clearly she's been sorting her face out, or shaving it; either way it looks well traumatised. She says, "What mate?". Trying not to look at her body, which despite the face is in fucking good order, I say, "We'll head off when you're ready". Andrea beckons me in and says, "Ok, I'll be ready in a bit". I decide to lie and say, "I'll go pack my shit and see you downstairs by the car. I could do with some fresh air before we fuck off". She looks over her shoulder, smiles and says, "Suit yourself, mate". Feeling like a frigid virgin, I tuck my tail between my legs and go downstairs, wondering what might have happened if I'd gone into her room.

Feeling torn about my sensible decision I head on out to the car, again scanning the rocks for bits of skin. The fresh air hits me and I take some time to chill. I look around to see if there is any sign of damage linked to the chaos from last night, but there's nothing. After loading the boot up, I get into the car. Andrea soon joins me and almost falls inside. Time for yet another long ass drive. Fuengirola, here we come! We've been literally driving for minutes and she's already asleep—I doubt she'll be waking up any time soon. She's guaranteed at least another five hours' kip, so I crack on towards my final destination.

We arrive at Fuengirola in the late afternoon, the journey being more or less a repeat of Saturday night. Andrea only woke up when I stopped and soon went back to sleep. This is my third time here and it's beginning to feel like I half belong. I drive straight to the hotel and park up in the same spot by the sea wall. Andrea gets out and runs straight off towards the beach. It was like letting a dog off the lead—she was gone. You'd think she'd never seen the Med before, but maybe she hasn't. I look across at the hotel and wait before I check-in, wanting to see where Neil is first. I find myself overthinking what might happen if I end up in a hotel room with Andrea. After these three days, I'm beginning to fancy her.

My phone rings and thankfully it's Neil; "Yes mate", I say. He says, "Are you there?". I reply, "I am indeed mate, what about you?". I can hear the commotion in the background. Neil says, "Just unloading the car now. Tell Andrea to call Jan so they can arrange to meet up. She's no longer your missus". Feeling both relieved and gutted I say, "Cool, I'm gonna check in and relax, my head is spinning from all the driving". I walk down onto the beach. Andrea is there with her shoes and socks off, leggings pulled up to her knees, standing in the sea relaxing. I stand just behind her and, trying to avoid the gentle waves, I say, "Neil has said for you to call Jan. She's gonna meet you and get you over to the apartment". Andrea turns and walks towards me, and I see the scabs on her face have darkened considerably since this morning. She says, "Ok mush, it's been nice travelling with you. You're quite good-looking for a fat cunt". I smile, laughing at my own expense and say, "Thank you, and you've been great company for a psycho bitch".

Chapter 19

CHANNEL HOPPING

I'm not sure how long I'm supposed to be plotted up for. I only checked in for one night and Neil hasn't given me any clue of a solid plan, so once again I have no doubt it'll be a case of "hurry up and wait". The only thing I can think of is to give Si a shout and let him know I've landed. He'll likely want to hand over his dough and if Neil is still light then Si's money might make the difference. Either way I'm not sitting around doing fuck all. Guaranteed Neil and his lot are partying but if I owed the Colombians money I'm pretty fucking sure partying wouldn't be a priority. I get the impression that Jan will milk Neil for every penny he has and I dare say that Antonia is not cheap either. It's the equivalent of forking out money to run a beautiful high-performance car whilst simultaneously maintaining a fucking banger.

The weather is starting to show signs that I'm in the Med, but for once I'd rather be at home. Easter is approaching and I'd like to be there to enjoy the bank holiday with the wife and kids. I do have a few days to decide though, so I resolve to get out into the sun and enjoy the weather, whilst making dodgy calls to the likes of Si and Neil. For a change there are people on the beach, which normally is deserted. Feeling like a proper expat I take up a position on the sand and get stuck into a load of calls.

As the sun climbs up higher the beach begins to fill. It's not packed but much busier than usual. I've spoken with Neil and Si, even calling Hassan to see how he was doing. Hassan has shut down as the goods are gone and the money is in and paid— legend! Si is at his mate's gaff and chilling out. He has a meeting with Neil later to talk business so I'm not needed. Neil has said he's waiting and will know more in a couple of days, so we should chill out until Wednesday and we can decide what to do from then.

Tuesday passes without any comms at all. I find myself calling home more than I should as I miss my family but unlike Neil, I wouldn't involve the wife and kids in what I'm doing, even if it meant a free holiday for them. Wednesday comes around and I could do with some kind of decision being made. I like it here; it's nice, warm and sunny but I feel a right sad case wandering around on my own. If I wasn't such a lump, I'd have been running or training, but I am, so it ain't happening. I've spoken to Si a couple more times and he's successfully handed over his money to Neil, so he's gonna plot up here for Easter break. I've already told him if we don't get a green light I'm gonna fuck off home for Easter, which he is more than happy for me to do. I mean it's costing over €100 a night plus expenses to keep me here. I can get an easyJet flight back home for less and come back the next day if need be.

I call Neil and he answers but does sound stressed, saying, "What is it? I'm in a rush". I say, "Look bud, if we don't have a green light by tonight shall I fly back home and plot up there? It's costing a fucking fortune staying over here". Neil replies, "Yeah la, you can shoot off now if you like. We won't be going again until next week, and the ex is doing my fucking nut in.

Spend Easter with your family and I'll get you back over here for when we go again". Feeling relieved I say, "Nice one bro, I'm gonna fuck off. I'll keep the comms down, is there anything that needs doing back over there?". Neil says, "Not yet but there will be next week and to be fair, I'd prefer you to do it as the others are a fucking mess".

I call the wife and explain that the security job has been postponed so I'll be flying back. The fact that the car is stuck in Calais is a slight fucking problem though. Wife happy, bag packed, looks like it's a taxi to Malaga airport which I'm pretty sure flies to Bristol. Travelling light makes this part a piece of piss and once again I'm crossing customs drug-free. I've got a couple of quid left, but nothing that will raise any alarms. I ask the receptionist to order me a cab as I check out of the hotel, remembering to leave the car keys at the reception for Neil to collect later. With the taxi due I walk outside to enjoy once again the fresh Mediterranean Sea air.

Arriving in the UK is such a nice feeling; for some reason I just wasn't feeling the energy on this trip over to Spain. Yeah it was highly entertaining with Andrea's antics but Neil's ex? Well she's just a fucking disaster waiting to happen. The flight over was pleasant but the departure was fucking horrible—too many bodies in one area. I'm now enjoying the taxi ride in from the airport, with a cracking view of the city. I arrive home in good time and for once the kids are awake. This time I came bearing gifts—sweets and toys for the kids and perfume for the wife. Everyone is happy, so I settle down for the night and order in the mother of all takeaways, so we can feast and I can get even fatter.

Easter passes without any issues or calls. Hassan has gone out collecting money. I'm calling Cliff's lot to see what the crack is since Cliff is still fucking missing. Apparently he's gone back over to his bolt hole in the States, something to do with a new connection for supply. So for now I'm simply treading water; I do, however, want to get my car back. I'm gonna have to call Neil to see what's going on anyway. He answers and I say, "Are you surviving, mate?". Neil replies saying, "Barely bro, she's done my head in so I've fucked her off. I told her she can fuck off back to that shithole Slough if she keeps playing up. She doesn't care so I booted her out of the apartment. The kids are with me and Antonia and Jan are in a shitty hotel with Andrea". Trying to sound empathetic but completely fucking it up I say, "Good because she's a dickhead. Sorry, I know she's the mother of your kids but shit bro, she's hard work!". Neil goes on to say, "Yeah I know, anyway how's things over there?". I reply, "Yeah good but quiet. Are there any updates from your end? I could do with some work and I need to see if it's worth getting my motor back from France". Neil says, "Nothing yet bro, but if you want a job, I do have an idea how we can kill two birds with one stone".

No doubt this will be a risky proposal so I say, "Yep what is it and when do I start?". Neil says, "Fucking hell la you don't care do you? It's easy. We need to drop a renter over to Calais, so if you fancy it then you can leave it where yours is and do a straight swap". Fucking perfect, so I say, "Spot on, I'll have a bit of that, what's the payment?". Neil says, "A monkey plus expenses". I couldn't agree quickly enough. Neil lays out the details and I get all excited about a quick road trip.

The renter needs dropping whenever so I opt for now. It's still morning and I reckon I could have the car hired and be on the road within an hour. I don't need any luggage, just my doss bag, so I'll just fuck off once I've grabbed some money and my passport, not forgetting to get my car keys in the process. Imagine that, all the way to France only to have forgotten the car keys, what a bellend! I don't bother telling the missus the plan; I just saddle up and fuck off, the only stop is at Windsor to see Lofty to grab the dosh. So with a brief drive by Windsor I'm on time to get the crossing at about 20:00. I could get the cars swapped within an hour and be home just after midnight. But who the fuck am I kidding? Once I hit the M25 the traffic grinds to a halt—for fuck's sake this is a disaster. I'm moving but my scheduled plan to hit Dover by 20:00 is slowly disappearing. I don't need to stop as the fuel is good. I simply have to accept that this might be either a very late crossing or a two-day mission, but for now, I'm parked.

After fucking ages the traffic starts to flow. My ETA for Dover has changed and even though I'll get there tonight the likelihood of me getting a return journey isn't looking too good. I didn't bring any smellies or toothbrush, so I might have to look into that if I get stuck over there, French hotels being the way they are. I mean those cheap French hotels don't have any complimentary toiletries—smelly fuckers! I eventually get onto the M20 and pick up signs for Dover. Considering I don't have any drugs or money on me I feel fucking stress-free, but once my timings slip my head falls off and I stress like fuck. I shouldn't because common sense tells me that it's ok to be late, but that's usually shared by people that haven't been bounced round the fucking square because they're not five minutes early.

All things said and done, I've made it. I've got my ticket and I'm in the queue waiting for the ferry. Yeah it has gone 22:00 so I'll likely have to plot up over there; I did decide to tell the missus and to be fair to her she's cool with it. I think if this was happening a few months ago when I was proper fucked, it would have been a very different outcome. So all in all, apart from the traffic, I've had zero headaches, and even customs was a joy, as is the crossing. I actually had a bit of a purpose on this one. I needed to purchase some toiletries and a quality deodorant, which was piss easy and by the time I'd done that and had a light snack, the boat was slamming the anchors on, ready to hit France.

"Roll on, roll off", that's the motto and this was exactly the case. The weirdest thing is though, when I was working this process in stages, each stage brought with it a roller coaster of stress followed by euphoria. This time it was head in neutral, thumb up arse and go. Adopting this state of mind while carrying is a skill in itself. I do know that although I can maintain calm on the exterior, the interior is going bonkers, but to have that sense of equilibrium on both the inside and out, now that's something. Actually it's just more of a matter of not giving a fuck!

It's midnight, I'm tired and I can't be arsed to do the swap now, so I head for one of the two hotels I know of. I'm feeling drawn to the Holiday Inn that I stayed in last time, unless of course, I pass anything else en route, which I do not. I soon see the familiar sight of the Holiday Inn and drive into the car park, remembering my last visit; the two vans side by side, us handballing stuff from van to van. Remaining hopeful that a room is available, I park up, walk into the reception and wait patiently for the receptionist to arrive. It's getting late but there must be someone in. I call out to get someone's attention and after a while a door to a back room office opens and out walks a slightly disgruntled receptionist who was clearly fast asleep.

Once relieved of €92, I walk directly to my room to get my head down for the night. All I want now is sleep; maybe a quick drink would be nice but I didn't plan ahead so fuck it. I get my head down intending to get an early crossing tomorrow, but as I fall asleep I begin to wonder if my car is still there; after all, it was abandoned, or at least that's what it felt like. I fucking wrecked it to find that last envelope! Well, I'll just have to wait and see.

I wake early, the sun just appearing through the edges of the blackout blinds. Feeling well rested, fresh and glad I didn't have a drink I get up, and just for a change I have a nice, long, relaxing shower. Breakfast is being served soon so I'll be stuffing my face with a continental, then I'll be homeward bound.

Breakfast was shit, but what else am I expecting? It filled a hole, and I've got bugger all baggage, not even a change of clothes, so I gas myself with deodorant to get rid of any lingering odours and fuck off back to the car. One thing that has occurred to me, which is where the fuck is the car? It was dark and from what I can remember relatively secluded. Shit, I genuinely cannot remember—why the hell didn't I consider this before? I'm gonna have to rack my brain on this one. I drive back towards Calais port so I can potentially remind myself of the route that I took, bearing in mind I did have a pissed-up psycho bird sitting next to me, which was slightly distracting. I approach the port and just before heading in I spin around and pull over at the next convenient spot.

I cast my mind back, remembering it was dark and we followed the main road for a bit. I don't recall seeing anything that particularly stood out, but I drive anyway, slow and steady, hoping to see something that jogs my memory. I know the drive was about 20 minutes and it was on some secluded road off the beaten track. I'm confident it was a right turn, soon after we got out of the port. The fortunate thing is that the countryside is quite open, so being able to see the car from a distance is a possibility. It's not long before I see a right hand turn, and even though I can't say if it's the one or not, I decide to hack a hard right and give it a go. This road goes on a bit and logic says, "How did Neil find it in the first place?". Surely it was instinctive.

I keep driving and it is winding a lot and even though I can't visually relate to it, it feels right. After a few more minutes—bingo there's the unmarked, in a layby exactly where I left it. I drive past and have a look around, then come back and pull in with the fronts of the cars facing each other. The first thing I notice is the state of it—it's fucking wrecked. The roof lining is pretty much off and the door pillar trims are nowhere to be seen; it's mostly cosmetic but still needs to be refitted before I head off.

I empty the renter and pop all of my bits on the passenger seat. Taking a look at the fucking state of the interior, I begin to slowly push everything back to where it belongs, and that's just the best I can do. I have no tools so it should be a simple case of relocating the clips, but I wish it were so easy. I've got the stress sweats already. I've managed to get the roof lining back up but it's fucked; in my haste I've bent it and it now has a crease along the middle, which is fucking annoying. I clip the door pillar trims back into place and have a good look at my feeble effort to fix everything, then I get out and give it an inspection from the exterior. To be fair I can't see any sign of damage, which is the important part.

Before heading off I hide the rental car keys on the back wheel for whoever is picking it up. It will probably be me but I think that leaving the keys there is a better idea than having a car over in France with no keys. Leaving the car behind, the drive back to Calais is short and sweet. I'm also feeling somewhat smug about finding the car so easily. It's still early and the port is thriving; the Easter holidays are still going strong so presumably this trip will be full of families. This will likely mean kids running riot everywhere, just like I used to. With the ticket purchased I go through the motions; passport, tickets, customs then joining a queue of cars in a designated lane.

It's all getting a bit routine for me now; I did a lot of crossings when based over in Germany but not as many in such a short space of time. Also, the dodgiest things I took over with me back then were stolen pyrotechnics and jerry cans full of red fuel, nicked from the RECCE Tp tanks. We didn't really give a fuck. The lads used to love the thunder flashes, blowing shit up for fun and shooting mini flares out of the car window when doing a mock drive-by shooting—good times! Whilst I reminisce about my military antics, it dawns on me that I left my fucking slug in the boot of the rented car. I've had that thing for years and I hope to God it's still there when I get the car back. Don't care about the car, but that doss bag is priceless to me.

The cars all start up and I follow the line of traffic onto the boat; same old shit, on and off. Once on board I find a seat to sit back and relax. My mind is on the business at home. Hassan is doing well but I have taken my eye off the ball slightly and I'm gonna have a look at my options, especially since some of my old customers are beginning to show interest in working again. I've gotten used to the way it works; people come and they go and it's not a personal thing, it's just how these greedy fuckers survive in this world. I'm as guilty as the next man for taking a tactical retreat just to assess the situation. When I land I'm gonna call Hassan and set up a breakfast meeting in our usual place, maybe see how he's getting on and if he's happy to ride it out for the long run.

The boat pulls into Dover and I find myself on autopilot heading back to the car. No real concerns, unless I do get pulled and they end up finding something that was already in the car before my purchase, which is quite likely considering who I bought it from! I close in on the familiar sight of the customs shed (I call it a shed but in fact it's a building—but to me it looks like a shed). It's busy as well. The cars are moving slowly and as I pull up next to the guy he looks at me then he looks inside the search bay, which is just off to my left. He looks at me again and walks up to the window. I wind it down and say, "Good morning". The customs officer looks into the car and says, "Morning sir, what was the purpose of your visit to

France?". I have to assume he knows everything, so I say, "I had to collect my car, it broke down and I had to take over a replacement part". Utter bullshit mind you. He looks inside the car again and says, "Ok, all fixed now?". I say, "Botched but should get me home"; he then says, "And home is where?". I say, "Bristol". He then steps back and says, "Ok, safe journey sir". Fucking hell, that was tense, even without anything on board.

I clear the building and pick up the road that heads out of Dover then ultimately home. The drive back is slow and the start-stop of traffic is making it arduous, but it was also highly productive. Hassan and I will be linking up tomorrow to chat about work. Cliff's firm isn't supplying as it seems he's dependent on Neil coming through and as much as I like and respect Si, I don't want to be in a position owing him money, so out of a sense of self-preservation, I can't work with him. I do have another option though and in the past he's been both a good supplier and customer, plus he's discreet in how he conducts himself. I can feel a meeting coming up with Blob.

I've known Blob for a few years now. We were inadvertently introduced to each other by a firm which I'll refer to as the "Gruesome Twosome". We both felt that the way they worked was fucking nuts so to avoid the risk of upsetting them, we started working together directly, up until the point where the Russian and I went our separate ways. It had appeared to be going well but Blob went dark on me so we just drifted. However we always had a way of tracking each other down if need be and for some reason, there are certain people you always end up crossing paths with again, sooner or later.

275

During the journey, I make several attempts to contact Neil but he's not answering, which isn't like him at all. I couldn't raise Lofty either, leaving me with no choice other than to contact that annoying git Muggy. For some reason this time Muggy was quite pleasant. I let him know the car was dropped off in the same place and to keep me in the loop as it's been hired in my name. Muggy said that the car could be picked up in a couple of days if they don't get hold of Neil in time. Feeling relatively ok with this I say, "Ok not a problem, don't suppose there's any work left? I'm pretty sure we're out". Muggy replies, "There is but it's been adjusted at this end. There's a corner if you want it; it'll cost seven". Knowing exactly how much the original cost is, I ask how much it's been adjusted. Muggy changes his tone and says, "If you don't want it then fuck off". I say, "All right, pick up your toys you miserable fuck! The fact that you won't be open tells me it's gonna be shit, so you can fucking keep it". Muggy then decides to go off on one, screaming down the phone, shouting, "You gobby cunt, I'll be coming down your house and smashing you up, show some respect you prick". I haven't got time for this so I say, "No, so fuck off", and put the phone down on him.

Feeling a sense of rage inside I continue my journey, now playing over several scenarios on how I'd like to fuck Muggy up. I hate these feelings and can't stand living with them. I need to shut this down now otherwise it'll consume me so I try to call both Neil and Lofty. Eventually Lofty answers and says, "Yes la, what's up?". I take a deep breath, compose myself and say, "Mate, that doughnut Muggy has been losing his shit threatening me. I won't work with him if he's like this". Lofty acknowledges this and says, "Yeah, you'll have to forgive him.

Neil has been giving him a right hard time of it. We still need to raise a bit and Muggy has been left carrying the can". I think back and reflect, knowing that some people react differently when under stress—clearly Muggy chucks his toys out of the pram. I say, "Yeah no stress mate, I was saying that I've dumped the hire car over there, in the same place that mine was left. It's on hire in my name and I just need an idea of when to collect it". Lofty says, "I'll try and get hold of Neil as he said he was popping up to France and was gonna need a car for a couple of days. He had a few meetings to go to, so was gonna use that one. I'll find out how long, or at least when you can collect it, and get back to you". I thank him for at least keeping me in the loop. I'm not too happy about a car in my name being used for all sorts of fuck-knows-what, but that's just how it is.

When I eventually arrive home I get there to an empty house. It's not a surprise as the missus will often take the kids to visit her family during the holidays, so this gives me a bit of breathing space to crack on without having to bullshit every minute of the day. Hassan and I have arranged to meet up for food tomorrow. I need to grab some cash off him and it would be good to catch up and go over my plans for the future. I've made contact with Blob and he's up for a meeting later in the week. He's apparently working with a London firm via a contact called Lawless, who has a good, consistent supply. This could be good as he's already offered credit and he wanted to run something by me face-to-face. This usually means good business is coming his way or better still, my way.

When Hassan and I catch up, it's a chance for us to reflect. It's occasions like these when I appreciate and value our friendship; it's also times like these that make me consider the gravity of what he is taking on on my behalf, but he's happy to remind me he's a big boy and can make his own mind up about what he does. This does have the effect of easing my conscience slightly, but not enough for me to forget how I might feel if he was to ever get caught while on my watch. Hassan is more than happy to remain on board and he's even happier for his workload to increase, although he does already handle a lot. That being said it usually only takes a couple of days out of his week and with good runners being hard to find, we agree that between us we can manage most things that come our way.

A couple more days pass, and I've even spoken to Terry and enquired about the pill situation. I haven't bothered lately as the money has been diabolical. He can still get them but was honest enough to say that they're still shit compared to what we could get 10 years ago. Jay has been quiet; I've not had access to the pure from Neil to supply him, and seeing as it was a conflict of interest with Si (as Neil is Si's connection), he'd want a slice and that would likely make it a no-go. But I'll definitely be seeing what Blob is offering. This could bring Jay and his cash back into the equation. Jay's money always came in handy to boost my buying power; yeah he'll always take pills as will Wedge, but I need to be offloading coke as well. A trip for pills alone ain't worth it.

The week grinds by and as the weekend creeps up I eventually get a call from an unidentified number. I cautiously answer with a "hello" and am greeted by a familiar scouse accent. It's Neil, and he says, "How's it going, mate?". I reply, "Yeah not too bad, did you get the car ok?". He says, "I did, but I'm hitting brick walls over here, you can collect the car as it's not being used. I've stuck it in the car park near the train station, you know, the one where you dumped the van last month". I say, "Yeah no problem. I'll collect it tomorrow as it's getting on a bit now". Neil says, "Sure, the keys are on the back wheel. I have a few meetings here. I'm well light with Tony's money and he said he wanted to catch up soon to discuss another load, so that sounds encouraging". I do feel slightly anxious at the thought of having to do that pickup again. I just say, "Ok bud, well good luck, let me know when you need me and I'll pop on over". Neil says, "Thanks la", and hangs up.

He doesn't sound himself—he seems very subdued and almost, dare I say, worried. I'd have thought that the profits made on 50 boxes would be plentiful, but then he is paying a lot out on expenses. I'm sensing a lack of coke on the horizon, so I call Hassan and update him with the plan. We need to move fast as we don't have any coke. Si has come back and is happy to sit tight until Neil comes through, having handed over his dosh. Cliff is still missing and I need a backup source so this meeting with Blob could come at a perfect time. With my lot still at the outlaws', I chill out for the night and get prepped for an early start tomorrow to go retrieve the car. I rented it for a week so I can at least enjoy it for the weekend. Hassan has offered to drop me at Dover port so I'll be going over as a foot passenger; again I'll be travelling light.

Hassan isn't known for being an early riser so we arrange for him to collect me at 10:00. This in Hassan's book is still early so when he turns up at mine five minutes before the parade, I'm fucking shocked. I jump into the passenger side and we head off. Hassan and I can hold a convo forever and that's exactly what we do; three-and-a-half hours of talking utter shite, but I also use this time as a passenger to make a ton of calls to most of my customers. It's important to keep everyone happy and hanging in there, and I have become ever-so-slightly detached from them while focusing on this work with Neil. Hassan has really held the fort but it's more than that. I need them to know I'm still here and available to discuss business. They need to do the growing for me.

Hassan swiftly drives into the port of Dover ticket office, where we say our goodbyes then he fucks off back home. I go in to grab a ticket as a foot passenger, only to be told the 14:35 crossing is full but they can get me onto the next one, which crosses at 16:05. That'll have to do, so I pay the fee and wander out then off towards the waiting area. I've not got on as a foot passenger before so I'm expecting to be sitting in a shitty departure-style lounge forever, drinking overpriced coffee and eating shite for the next few hours.

Finding myself people watching again, I've got myself backed up against the wall, with my eyes on all exits.

While I sit there considering how slowly the time is going, my phone rings and it's Neil. I answer and say, "What's up, mate". He says, "La, I've got a meeting with Tony tomorrow morning, so I'll let you know what the plan is. He said he has some good news linked with his source. I think we're gonna be good. I still owe a few bags but he seems ok and knows he'll get it on the next run". I reservedly say, "That's quality mate, so when do you think we'll be going again?". Neil says, "Soon, I hope! Oh, by the way, once you've got the car back to the UK, can you catch up with Lofty? When were you thinking of getting it?". I respond, "Mate your head must be battered, I'm at the port now. I sail in a couple of hours, so as long as I don't hit any more delays. I'll be back tonight". Neil, sounding surprised, says, "Oh, fucking hell la, I'll let him know". I reply, "Yes please mate, as I don't want to be faffing around too late". Neil says, "No problem, I'll send you his new one so you can speak with him and update him with your movements". I say, "Sounds good to me". We end the call and I start going into a bit of deep thought about a few things that are beginning to concern me.

I spend the remaining time procrastinating about this channel hop I'm about to do. Everything says to me that the car has been loaded up. Dropping it over for just a few days, then going to see someone on my way back? It has to be fucking loaded up and it's in my name. I'm literally fucked with this one. Everything points straight to me, and every part of me doesn't want to do this, but I've never backed out of a deal or an arrangement. I text Neil to remind him to send Lofty's new number so I can attempt a bit of reverse psychology; maybe I can get Lofty to shed some light on it.

The tannoy goes and an announcement is made for all passengers to proceed to the boarding gates. While following a fairly busy queue my phone beeps and I receive the text I've been waiting for from Neil. I open it and save the new number, deleting the old one in the process. I immediately text Lofty asking him to call me ASAP regarding tonight. I'm trying to get these calls done before we leave English waters as I don't have enough credit to accept or even make calls from overseas. As I'm due for a new burner, I'll be fucked if I can be arsed to top it up.

I move straight to the upper decks to get a comfortable seat. The stress levels are a tad high so I'm not particularly hungry. My phone rings and it's Lofty. I answer by saying, "I'm just leaving the UK now. I should be able to turn around sharpish and get back over within a couple of hours. Reckon I could be with you for about 23:00." Lofty replies, "Yeah la, take your time, I'm in no rush". I decide to go all out and just ask, "So what's so urgent that I need to see you tonight?". Sounding like a typical scouser he says, "Ah nothing major la, we just had to have a chat about things off comms". This isn't helping so I say, "Mate, is the car clean? I don't care if it isn't, I just need to know what I'm dealing with". Lofty, now sounding even more cagey, says, "Yeah la, of course it is". This has not instilled me with any confidence whatsoever, so I say, "Well let's fucking hope so". I say goodbye and put the phone down.

I was planning on a quick nap but there's no chance now. I'm way too stressed so I start fidgeting and wishing my life was different, looking at everyone else sitting here; fucking smiling, drinking, they're happy. I've got a strong feeling I've been thrown to the lions. It's times like this I'd simply get pissed but how can I? I've got to do this fucking bullshit. I spend the rest of the journey whinging to myself. It has the desired effect of making me feel a little bit better.

The boat hits the continent and I rush for the doors. I want to get off this boat and into a taxi ASAP. Once disembarked I scan for some kind of taxi rank. I don't even know what I'm looking for but eventually I find one. I get in and ask for the train station near Coquelles, hoping to fuck it's the right one. Fortunately I remembered to pocket a load of euros from my previous trip so money isn't a major issue. The driver heads off in what I hope is the correct direction. It's not dark yet so I'm trying to read any signage to at least give me an indication of what direction we're going in. It's not long before I notice a few things I recognise, but that's the problem with doing this when I'm running drugs. I'm not looking at the scenery, I'm looking out for threats, so everything seems to be new.

Eventually we arrive and thankfully it's the right place. I pay the driver and walk towards the car park. From here I can see the whole lot, so I decide that rather than rush in like a fucking idiot, I'll spend some time looking around. I can always pretend I've forgotten where I parked the car and carefully recce the whole site, which I do, clocking my car in the process. Feeling slightly better that the car park hasn't got a ton of police plotted up, I finally approach the hire car. There are no visible signs of tampering, so the exterior looks sweet. I drop my carcass onto the deck and look underneath the car—once again it's clear.

Now then, do I start messing with the interior? If it's visibly ok then I shouldn't start pulling the trim away. I pop the boot, hoping not to see another ArmourLite suitcase inside. All I see is my slug, looking lonely. Ok, feeling better again. Now for the interior; I have a quick look around the car park and, once I'm satisfied that all is clear, open the rear passenger doors and look under the front seats then pop up the back seat—again clear. I pat down the roof lining. From experience, I know for a fact that it's hard to hide anything lumpy up there—clear also. The door cards look good. I close all the doors and pull the bonnet catch. I go around to the front and have a good look around the engine bay. It's beginning to get dark but I can see that there's nothing concealed there. I know this because Del, one of my previous suppliers, was always keen on loading up areas of the engine bay. He did get caught eventually though, so maybe not the best location.

The clock's ticking and I've spent fucking aeons ensuring that this car is clean. I can't see anything that concerns me, but that doesn't mean it isn't there. So yet again throwing caution to the wind I get in, start up and fuck off back towards Calais. I don't know where the time has gone. I seriously need to reevaluate my internal clock as it would appear I'm way off in my estimations. I'll be on the last ferry at this rate and I know I'll be ticking all their fucking boxes for a puller. My mind is blank, genuinely not knowing how I should feel about stuff. I think this whole idea of working over here was appealing at first but I now think that was more down to me being in a desperate situation. Besides, my business is doing well now and Hassan's really helped me to pull it out of that hole. Think I'll do one more run with Neil and then I'll pull the plug. Neil hasn't been himself and the instability within his firm is beginning to show. Then of course if he's willing to use his family as a cover for moving money (who by the way were the worst people I can imagine) I think he's taking unnecessarily high risks with other people's lives and assets. For me, these factors set alarm bells ringing.

It's past 22:00 when I finally hit the lanes for boarding and as usual I reckon there'll be a short wait before the boat lands. Plenty of time for my nerves to elevate and end up in a right fucking mess. It's the not knowing that's bothering me. I'm 99% sure the car is clean but that 1% is still there. The reason it's there is because this whole arrangement tells me there's something in this motor. Neil and I had been discussing various methods of concealing coke and moving it, and one of them was to break it down into powder and vacuum seal it into a flat bag. This could then be slid under carpets or roof linings and because of this, I'm genuinely concerned. Even if you broke down one kilo, once flattened out, you wouldn't know it was there.

The traffic starts moving and I prepare to board, maybe for the last time, because of the way I'm feeling now, I'm out. I feel like I'm being taken advantage of. I mean I could be totally wrong and this could all be in my head, but right now I'm worried. The excitement has gone, the adrenalin has gone, and this now feels like a chore. Once it gets that way I know it's time for a change. With Neil's firm I'll always be staff, never earn a real wage, and these risks now outweigh the reward.

Once parked up on the car decks, the mixed smell of fuel and hydraulics throws me back to sitting in the turret of my tank. It's a unique combo of smells, none of them pleasant but what I would do to be back in a Chally right now. I used to have recurring nightmares about being back in, but now I'd do anything to turn back the clock. The only problem is I can't see myself passing a BFT any more; I'd be straight on the fat boys' Saturday morning remedial PT.

The return journey was just like the outward one, just with slightly higher stress levels. I can't even be arsed to find a seat, so I mope around like a stroppy teenager. The only event that held any interest was a trip to the toilet for a nervous shit. I'm finding every minute of this journey agonising, so to kill a little time I text Lofty with an update. He immediately replies, simply saying, "Hope to see you soon!". "Hope", he says?

What the hell is that all about? The paranoia is now kicking in and becoming a problem so I choose not to aggravate the situation and put the phone away. This is of course another issue, having a burner while going through customs; it's not the first time but this time I feel it's yet another box ticked.

The boat starts to shake like a shitting dog as it gradually moors up to the dock. For the first time, I'm not looking forward to it. Part of me even considered jumping over the edge then swimming and hitching back home. Just dumping the car on the boat, and if it wasn't in my name I'd have seriously considered it. I wander back to the car and again have a quick look over it but nothing too heavy, I just want to be as sure as I can. The doors begin to drop and as they hit the deck, the vehicles all start up. I join them and prepare for what I fucking pray is a simple and straightforward process. I mean only a few weeks back I had Zultan the Illegal sitting next to me, a joint under my seat and a fair bit of cash but I wasn't fussed. This time I've probably got fuck all and I'm shitting myself.

I follow the line of traffic off the boat then down the ramp and can see the customs shed in the distance. I initiate box breathing to bring my heart rate down, because I can feel it now and they'll see it in my body language. As the cars and vans move closer my nerves and anxiety begin to settle. Counting to four while exercising controlled breathing is working; my nerves settle and the anxiety is reduced. I'm now just a few cars away and the customs officers are waving them through rather quickly. It looks good—I could be on the M20 soon enough. I continue box breathing as I pull up to the checkpoint. The customs guy looks at me and walks away. My nerves are settled, he waves me forward and off I go, but suddenly he then puts his hand up to stop me and directs me into the shed. Fucking box breathing my arse, my nerves and anxiety have just hit the fuckin' roof.

Well, this is it, I've finally been pulled. I slowly drive into a spacious and well-lit search bay where the staff direct me to a spot above what looks like a sunken car ramp. The guy that pulled me walks up and I can immediately sense an attitude. He says, "Where have you been sir?". Pretty fucking obvious to me where I've been! My nerves having just been replaced with fight mode, I reply, "France". He looks at me and then says, "Ok, can you exit the vehicle for a quick body search? We will be searching your vehicle". I look at the smug cunt and say, "Fill your boots, mate". I adopt the position and stand with my feet apart and arms outstretched. He says, "Oh, I can see you know the position! I presume you get stopped a lot". I say, "No mate, I'm ex-mob and have conducted plenty of searches myself". This fell on deaf ears—obviously, his missus has been nailed by a squaddie.

Knowing I'm clean, the body search doesn't concern me. I look over at the customs staff all gathering to prepare to search the car. There are four of them plus the guy searching me, who finishes and then asks me to step away and wait over by a long bench. I walk towards it as the customs staff ready themselves to dive into the car. Trying to look casual, but without looking like I'm trying to look casual, is actually fucking hard going when you genuinely don't know what the outcome will be. So I casually lean against the bench which looks like it would be used to search items like suitcases and personal effects. I cross and uncross my arms, then I cross and uncross my feet, thinking body language, nothing to hide here.

There's a clock up on the wall and the time is 22:40—how long will this take, maybe an hour? Then having decided to sit on the bench, I put my hands behind me and push up, barely lifting my fat arse off the floor. After the third attempt I eventually get enough of a push to make it. I sit back and watch them slowly pull the car apart. The bonnet and boot are up and they have proper lighting, so anything out of place will be obvious. I'm beginning to doubt my own checks, but if there's something in the car and it's my time then I'll have to accept the consequences. I've had so many near misses that I know my time will come eventually.

An hour has passed and I'm getting fucking bored. They've gone to town on the exterior, emptied the boot and left my doss bag and phones on the bench next to me. The two phones must look bad, mind you. The car has now been elevated on the ramps, and if I didn't know any better it looks like they're giving it an MOT. The tools have come out and all I can do is look at my slug on the bench next to me. I ask one of the officers if I can text the missus, and he says, "Yeah, sure, no problem". I'm about to text Lofty with an update when "stroppy bollocks" says, "No! You can't make any calls while being searched". I look at him and say, "Fine, let me know when you're done". I grab my doss bag and pull it out of its stuff sack. It fucking stinks, but I'm getting in it. I lay it flat on the bench, climb up and get in, pulling the drawstring-draw at the top and closing it. I then roll onto my side and peek out of the tiny hole to watch them continue searching the car.

I'm not tired, but I wanted them to think that I wasn't fussed; whether it had the desired effect or not I don't know, but the next thing I see is the officer that searched me arriving with a suitcase. He opens it up and pulls out some equipment; now I'm curious so I open the bag slightly to get a better view and oh fuck, it's a fibre optic! He's shoving cameras into all the little nooks and crannies to save ripping the car apart anymore. Feeling genuinely intrigued I sit up, the doss bag partially falls and I'm now only half covered, curiously looking on.

Two things have happened and there's a shift in mood; these fuckers have been at it now for over three hours and I'm confident that the car is clean. The other thing is that stroppy bollocks isn't happy. I think he must have been convinced I was carrying. The staff begin to reassemble the car and one of the staff walks up to me and says, "Sorry for the delay sir, you're now free to go". I look over towards the stroppy fucker and say, "No problem mate, it's a shame that miserable cunt over there didn't tell me personally. What's wrong with his attitude?". The customs officer just says, "Have a safe onward journey, sir". I smile and walk back over to my car, but I can see some nuts and bolts on the floor, so looking at the guy with the attitude I say, "Excuse me, I do hope you've reassembled the car correctly. I'll be in touch if I have any mechanical issues". I get into the car and drive off, feeling smug as fuck. Looking in the rearview mirror as I exit the shed, I feel that somehow I've had a lucky escape.

Chapter 20

DON'T FUCK WITH THE CARTELS

L ast night was a right fucking ball ache. By the time I'd cleared customs, Lofty wasn't answering, so I just came home. I'm gonna drop off the hire car later today as it runs out tomorrow. I don't have a great deal to do, so I just text Lofty to see if he wants to meet up at some point. I know Neil is due for his meeting with Tony today so there may be some news to act upon. But Lofty doesn't reply and there's no way I'm texting that prick Muggy, so I crack on with my day. Feeling slightly motivated, I call Blob to see if he fancies a meeting at any point. He answers and says, "Yarse, I've been working hard and may have some work to put your way". I say, "Ok sounds interesting, I'm pretty busy mind you but I do have someone working with me, so if you're happy to trust my judgement regarding staffing, then we are good to go". I then add, "I've come a long way since last year mate, so don't expect to see that same desperate person I was back then". Blob says, "Glad to hear it, that's why I made contact". We chat for a bit but both understand that more can be achieved with a face-to-face.

The rest of the day goes with no comms from anyone. My money situation is slowly dropping and the family is due back later, so I do need to get something moving within the next few days. I leave Hassan alone to relax and enjoy some downtime. I've got a strong feeling that once I start working with Blob he'll be flat out; working with Cliff's firm, mine and potentially Blob's means a lot of running around. This may require another runner to support Hassan, but who? The Boy does spring to mind because out of all of Alfie's mob he showed the most promise, as long as he can stay away from the coke. Right now I can't afford to be paying for his habit.

I try to call Neil but his phone is off, so I call Lofty instead. He eventually answers, and I say, "Sorry about last night mate, I got fucking pulled by customs". Lofty, sounding concerned, says, "It's ok la, but have you spoken to Neil yet?". I say, "No bud, by the sounds of it his phone's off". Lofty replies, "Yeah we think there's been a problem. His missus has flown back with the kids, has packed her bags and has fucked off". This doesn't sound good. I say, "Any ideas?". Lofty goes quiet for a bit and says, "No, but we're shutting down until we know. Jan's saying fuck all and I can't raise Antonia—her phone's disconnected". I have a think and then say, "Well, I guess we'll go to ground for now. Is there any money outstanding that needs rounding up, just in case we get a call?". Lofty says, "No, it's all in and we're still over a 100 light". A hundred? Fucking hell! I didn't realise it was so much, so I tell Lofty, "Look mate, I'm shutting down and changing all my stuff over. It was me that met Tony and I don't fancy getting a visit from that lot. What's happened to Si's money? I can guarantee he'll be wanting that and mate, you don't want him to be on your case". Lofty just says, "I don't know mate, we'll have to find a way to get in touch when we know more". I close the call by saying, "Look, Neil has my contract number and he and Si have their own connection, so let's leave them to it and see what happens. You know, take it steady. Let's lay low for now".

None of this sounds good to me. Neil and Antonia's phone's are off, Jan has done a bunk, and he's maybe a 100 in the hole with the cartels. To top it off, it was me who met them. I wonder to myself, "Should I move just in case?". I had to do a panic move a few years back when a local firm was gonna kidnap the family, so I can't be fucked to put them through that again. Nope, I'm sitting tight, surely the debt sits with Neil and not his runners or staff. Then again for 100 bags, they'll have the resources to move mountains to find their money. I decide to take precautions, so I contact Hassan and let him know we'll be changing phones today and to go to ground for a few days.

The previous night.

Neil is sitting in his and Antonia's apartment stressing about money. He looks at his kids arguing, and they're doing his fucking head in. Jan has also been doing his head right in, constantly asking for money—money that he doesn't have. He sits back, looks up at the ceiling, puts his hands over his face and shouts, "PLEASE JUST SHUT UP!". He calls Jan who answers, giving her zero breathing space and says, "Right you bitch, come and collect the kids and get on the next flight out of here. I don't give a fuck how you do it, just fuck off". He cuts her off, takes a deep breath to relax and makes a phone call. He talks for a short while but isn't really feeling it; it's just another task that needs to be taken care of, so consequently the conversation doesn't last long. All he really wants is some peace and quiet. He gets up and goes into the spare room where the kids have been sleeping. It's a fucking disaster zone, so Neil quickly shovels everything into bags and cases. The kids have gone from arguing to crying and are screaming at him, trying to pull their stuff back out of the bags as he tries to put it in. He totally loses his shit and shouts at them, demanding they sit down, shut up and wait for their mother to pick them up. They quickly comply, knowing that when Dad is like this, it's best to shut up and do as he says.

Neil's anger is increasing with every item he stuffs into a bag but it's not anger with his kids, it's anger with himself. He knows he's fucked up and this is anger fuelled with a sense of shame and regret. With his kids sitting quietly on the sofa, he finally crams the last few items into a bag, then puts it with the others by the door. Being hit with an overwhelming sense of guilt, he looks at his kids, walks over to them and kneels down in front of them, opens his arms and gives them a big hug, saying, "Look you lot, Dad is having a few problems at the minute so you've got to go home now, plus you're starting back to school next week and you can't be late for that, can you?". The kids are all crying, with snot and tears everywhere. The doorbell goes and Neil answers it by buzzing the downstairs lock. He can hear Jan and Andrea coming up the stairs, they're loud so obviously pissed. Neil jars the door open, feeling relatively calm as they walk in. He attempts to explain what his plan is but as soon as he opens his mouth, Jan goes off on one, screaming at him and calling him a useless bastard and a shit dad, while Andrea secures the kids' bags and makes a hasty exit. Neil says, "Fine, get the kids and fuck off back to Slough, you useless fucking bitch. All you've done is piss my money up the fucking wall. I paid your fucking 70 grand gambling debt and this is what I get? Look at the shit you've put me in, you ungrateful cunt". Jan viciously laughs at him, grabs the kids and fucks off towards the door. Neil, in a complete rage, picks up a phone off the side and launches it full fucking pelt towards Jan as she leaves the flat. He doesn't want to hit her with it, he just wants to prove a fucking point. She slams the door shut as the phone hits the back of the door and smashes into a million pieces. Neil looks around the room for something else to sling and, seeing as nothing presents itself as throwable, he calms down enough to feel satisfied that the point is proven. The feeling is short-lived when he is consumed with immediate regret as he realises he's smashed up Antonia's phone and not his.

As he sits down, he can hear the faint sound of Jan and the kids getting into a taxi and hopefully heading for Malaga airport. He breathes slowly and deeply, feeling the rage reducing. He needs to get himself sorted for this meeting with Tony tomorrow. His phone beeps from a text message; he looks at it and sends a reply. He's feeling fucked. It's getting on a bit now and normally he'd go out and hit a club but he's not in the mood. Antonia's not due back for a few hours as she's with friends doing some kind of Colombian community thing.

An hour passes and Neil has not moved. He's sitting quietly, contemplating what tomorrow will bring. He hears the downstairs door go, and the faint sound of footsteps on the stairs getting louder. It sounds like Antonia's back, with some of her sexy Colombian friends. Neil gets up and walks towards the door to greet his beautiful girlfriend—such a difference to that bitch of an ex. He extends his arm to open the door and is immediately hit square in the face as it is booted open. Neil stumbles back as several men charge in with bats. He screams a war cry as he runs towards the men only to be swiftly greeted with the fat end of a bat square on the jaw. He goes down like a sack of shit, lights out. Neil is a big fella but he ain't winning this one.

Neil drifts in and out of consciousness as he is dragged by the men down the stairs with his head hitting almost every stair en route. He's then carted outside and bundled into a large car. The men all dive into the car; driver, front passenger and one on either side of Neil. They then go through the motions of securing his hands with zip ties, also covering his eyes and sealing his mouth with gaffer tape. Neil can barely breathe, let alone talk, but he knows what's happening. This is Tony's firm; they're talking in Spanish—this is definitely the Colombians. Neil remains quiet, remembering his military training that has taught him how to behave as a hostage. He's listening but not really getting too much; his ears are fucking ringing from being whacked and they're talking too quickly to translate the conversation.

Neil is sure that this is the end. The Cartels haven't taken him to prove a point to Neil, they've taken him to prove a point to everyone else—that's how it works.

The journey is long and gruelling. Neil is thinking about his kids and Antonia, but not his ex; this is her fucking fault. He had some ridiculous loyalty to help her out after she got into so much gambling debt. He knew that the bank was gonna take the house and he couldn't have the kids homeless, but now the kids will be fatherless. The journey continues and Neil begins to accept his fate. He's feeling calm and a little tearful, in fact, with the stress he's been under during the last few weeks, whatever happens next will be received like a man. He isn't going to plead, cry or offer up any excuses; it is what it is, so fuck it.

The car slows down and the doors open. He is pulled out, this time not being dragged and successfully managing to stay on his feet. The men escort him away from the car where Neil can hear the sea and more voices quietly talking. He is escorted even further away from the car. He can feel sand underfoot, which makes walking slightly difficult; the adrenaline is pumping so he can't feel any pain on his chin. He can hear the engine of a boat, as the sand below his feet changes to water.

The Colombians are surrounding Neil. He's been led to the stern of a small yacht where they push him towards a small ladder and once they have him in position one of the men grabs his left foot and shouts, "Levanta el pie". He repeats it as he lifts Neil's foot towards the first step, while simultaneously two men standing on the boat reach forward and grab his arms, whilst at the same time two more push him upwards. Collectively they manage to get him onto the boat. One of the men in the water returns to the car and drives off, while the others join Neil and the rest of the gang on the boat.

Neil is fucking soaked and the pain is now kicking in. He can't stand as his balance is fucked so he collapses onto the deck. He rolls to one side until he hits part of the bulkhead. He manoeuvres himself around so that he's sitting down, knees raised with his hands looped in front of them, still secured but feeling slightly less exposed.

The yacht's engines go from a calm idling speed to a slightly-less-calm cruising rate. The vibration of the engine resonates through the floor and Neil's body. It's some time before a few more men come up from the lower deck and join the rest on the upper deck; one of the men walks over to Neil and has a look at him. Neil isn't aware of the presence as the man steps back and nods to the others. One of the men disappears below deck and throws on some lights, illuminating the stern deck nicely.

The light hits Neil and although he can't see anything he can sense that something is due to happen. He can feel the boat accelerate even more, the voices are getting louder and he hears what he thinks could be Tony. Neil feels a sharp stinging sensation on his face and the tape is quickly ripped off. His eyes quickly adjust and he can see Tony and several other cartel members standing in front of him. One of them is holding a Stanley knife with blood dripping from the end. Neil reaches up to touch the side of his face, his hands still secured, and he can feel the blood running down. He can't believe they removed the tape with a fucking blade.

Tony walks over to Neil and says, "I like you and you've been good business but you owe too much money. You were given one last chance not to be late but you blew it and we can't allow this. My boss has given instructions and you have to go. I am sorry it has come to this". While Tony is reading Neil his last rights, two men walk over to the opposite end of the deck where two 50-gallon drums are standing. The tops have been removed and are lying separately on the deck. They proceed to awkwardly roll one of the barrels into the middle of the deck and stand it upright. Neil's heart sinks—he knows what's coming. Neil is a big fellow but he knows he's going into the drum. Tony looks at Neil and says, "Where is your friend? The one that I met, we want him as well". Neil looks at Tony and says nothing. Tony then says, "I'm sorry, I wish we didn't have to do this. The blood makes a terrible mess of the deck and I don't like having to clean it up". As he finishes speaking, one of the men appears from below deck with a chainsaw. He pulls the cord and it screams to life, revving it gently as he approaches Neil.

Neil screams in terror as two other cartel members slide a large block of wood under his legs, raising them from the deck. They then kneel down and hold his legs tight while the man brandishing the saw revs it up and sets about his legs; in order for him to fit in the drum they need to come off. Neil starts fighting wildly but the cartels have him pinned; the saw begins to cut into one of his legs, and his jeans rip open as blood gushes out, soaking the deck. Tony shakes his head in disappointment as the blood goes everywhere. Neil quickly goes into shock as his left leg is easily removed from above the knee. The Colombian takes it and throws it into the upright drum. The saw is then set upon his remaining leg. Neil is now lying totally still; he's alive but barely and the pain is excruciating. The right leg comes away but the cartel gang member loses grip and it slides across the deck like a fat tuna that's just been landed. The blood is pissing out of the two stumps. His right leg is thrown into the drum to make up the pair.

The men stop for a moment, clearly discussing the best way to get him into the barrel; they walk over to him, two grabbing him from behind and two more grabbing his legs, trying to avoid the soggy ends. Neil is considerably lighter without his lower limbs and is easily dropped into the drum on top of his legs. He's barely alive but still moving. One of the men goes back below deck as the other one slings the chainsaw over the side, and another begins to hose off the deck, washing away blood, skin and bits of bone. The man returns with a small welding plant, the power cable leading back down below deck.

Neil, feeling the pain in what's left of his legs, manages to open his eyes and looks up out of the barrel. He can hear the muffled voices of Tony and his firm. Neil knows he's gonna die and he's mentally accepted his fate. He looks up at the clear Med sky which he can just about see beyond the bright deck lighting. It's the last time he'll ever see it. The lid is carefully placed back on top, blocking all daylight. He is then hit by another light source as the welder gets to work; sparks and molten metal are landing on his blood-soaked body, burning what skin he has exposed, but he doesn't care. As the welder moves around the top, all Neil can see is a glowing orange circle as the welder gradually moves around and seals the top, which fades as the metal slowly cools down. The welding stops and it's getting hard to breathe now. Neil breathes slowly—the instinct to survive is still strong.

The Colombians look at each other, two of them inspecting the welds. There are a couple of holes but they are required to fill the drum with water, otherwise, the fucking thing will float back to shore, causing no end of dramas. The men touch the welds to see if they've cooled sufficiently, which they have so they immediately and violently push the drum onto its side, manoeuvering it and guiding it towards the aft. It starts to roll on its own towards the deck's edge.

Neil is violently thrown around in the drum as it rolls forward. There is a momentary silence as it falls a couple of feet into the sea. Neil can feel that the drum is now floating but as it tries to right itself the sea water begins to trickle in through the gaps in the welds. Neil can faintly hear the boat accelerate away, leaving him there alone in silence and darkness. The drum shifts and he is now face down, his severed legs moving slightly as a mixture of blood and seawater migrate towards Neil's head. The sea is now flooding in a lot quicker as the buoyancy changes and the drum flips a 180. Neil's head is now upwards again, and all the blood, water and his legs hit the bottom of the drum. The pressure increases, making the water flood in a lot quicker. Neil closes his eyes to avoid the stinging salt water but the pain in his thighs is fading. Before he slips out of consciousness, his final thoughts are of the love he has for his kids and the life he has led. A life which ultimately caused him to be entombed in a 50-gallon drum, rapidly sinking to the bottom of the Med, soon to join the rest of the failed drug dealers who dared to fuck with the cartels.

TO BE CONTINUED...

GLOSSARY

A and E	*Accident and Emergency*
About Turn	*Military drill command, for turn 180 degrees on the spot*
Aires	*French Motorway Services*
Ammo Bashing	*Moving large quantities of ammunition ready for ranges or war*
ANPR	*Automatic Number Plate Recognition*
Arcs	*Military term for an area covered for laying down fire or observation.*
B Road	*A Minor Road*
Bag	*Coke, usually a small personal amount*
Bag/Bags,"a bag of sand"	*Grand/s money*
Balance the books	*To take the edge off of being under the influence*

301

Bangs out	*Sells*
Bashed	*Cocaine that has been adulterated or mixed to reduce purity and increase volume*
Bass	*Pure Amphetamine*
Beak	*Slang for cocaine*
BFT	*Basic Fitness Test, Military*
Blender, Car	*Non-descript vehicle that blends in*
Blender, A	*Fits into a crowd and is very unassuming*
Bog roll	*Toilet roll*
Bollocking	*A good telling off*
Bollocks	*Testicles*
Bootneck	*Royal Marine Commando*

Boozer	*Pub*
Bought	*To believed*
Bovvy	*Bovington Barracks*
Box Breathing	*A method of beathing used to reduce heart rate and anxiety, commonly used by Special Forces*
Breakfast	*Early morning joint*
Brew	*Hot drink*
Brim it	*To Fill Vessel to the Brim*
Bugle	*Nose*
Burner	*A mobile phone used for illegal activities that can be disposed of*
Car parts	*Drugs*
Casing	*Watching*

Catching Flies	*Sleeping with your mouth open*
Charlie	*Cocaine*
Class A's	*Class A drugs such as Cocaine/ Ecstasy*
Clean up	*To get rid of or move any drugs or money from the warehouse*
Cloner	*A car that has had a set of false plates fitted to mimic the identity of a similar car*
Comms	*Communication*
Convo	*Conversation*
Cop shop	*Small police station*
Copper	*Policeman/Policewoman*
Cossy	*Ford RS Cosworth*
CQB	*Close Quarter Battle*

Dabs	*Finger Prints*
Dead Letter	*Items off loaded at a prearranged area, such as a layby or field*
Debus	*Military slang for get out of a vehicle*
Different kettle of fish	*To be in a different league*
Dig him/her out	*To catch someone out for lying*
Divvy	*Idiot*
DOB	*Date Of Birth*
Dough	*Money*
Doss Bag	*Army Sleeping Bag*
Drop call	*Let a mobile ring once without being answered*
Dry	*Drug and money free*

El no hablo ingles	*He doesn't speak English*
ETA	*Estimated Time of Arrival or Completion*
Ex's	*Expenses*
Expensive parts	*Cocaine*
Fags	*Cigarettes*
Fally	*Fallingbostel*
Filth, the	*The police*
First Parade	*Military gathering for morning inspection and body count*
Fiver	*Five pound note*
Fullscrew	*Corporal*
Getting on it	*Getting drunk/drugged up*

Going down	*Sent to prison*
Goods	*Drugs*
Got the hump	*Angry/ annoyed with something*
Gurner/s	*Ecstasy*
Hammered	*Very much under the influence of some kind of substance*
Handle on it	*Under control*
Hanging out the back of	*Having sex*
Happy pills	*Anti-depressants*
Hardware	*Guns*
Hedkandi	*Dance music compilation*
High power	*Good quality*

Hinge, to the	*To take something to the maximum*
HMRC	*His/Her Majesty's Revenue & Customs*
Hot	*Potentially under police observation*
Hot as fuck	*Very blatant in criminality potentially risking exposure to the authorities*
HQ	*Headquarters*
Hundred pound wraps	*Where you have a hundred pounds in notes, fold the last note and slip it over the top of the others*
Immediate Notice	*Be ready to move now*
James Whales	*Scales, digital*
Juice	*Steroids*
K's	*Kilometres*
Key/s	*Kilo/s*

Kip	*Sleep*
La	*Scouse for "Lad"*
Lady of the night	*Prostitute*
Laters	*Goodbye*
Lay down some smoke	*To create a diversion or lie*
lay on/laying	*To get drugs on credit*
Licence conditions	*A set of rules that the probation service imposes on someone released from prison*
Light weight order	*Military dress, for fatigues*
Loaded up	*Carrying drugs/money*
LocStat	*Military term for Location Status*
Mad one, the	*Madrid*

Mag to Grid	*Get Rid*
MIA	*Missing In Action*
MOD 90	*Army ID card*
Modified	*Cocaine that has been adulterated or mixed to reduce purity and increase volume*
Monkey, A	*500 GBP*
Mood Hoover	*A person that will kill a positive atmosphere within seconds of entering a room/ Depressing attitude*
NAAFI	*Forces shop/bar*
Natter, to have	*Talk/conversation*
Nicked	*Arrested*
Nifty	*50 GBP*
Nine	*Nine ounces of drugs AKA Nine bar*

Nose bag	*Sniff coke directly from the bag*
Nut down, to get your	*Go to sleep*
Nuts and bolts	*Ecstasy*
Nutted Off	*Sectioned under the Mental Health Act*
Odds and ends	*Drugs*
Off your nut/tits	*High on drugs*
Offy	*Off licence*
Old bill	*The police*
On a Para	*Feeling paranoid*
On top	*Very blatant in criminality potentially risking exposure to the authorities*
Out of Ten	*Purity in numbers as opposed to percentage. i.e two out of ten, 20%*

P1	*Limited Edition Subaru Impreza*
Para	*Paratrooper*
Parade	*Military term for a meeting*
PC brigade	*Politically correct*
Péage	*French word for booth used to pay for the toll road*
Persy	*Personal drugs supply*
Pete Tong	*Wrong*
Pills	*Ecstasy*
Piss, in a	*Not very happy; pissed off*
Pissed up	*Drunk*
Plonk	*Cheap wine*

Plotted/plot up	*To wait or hang around in a designated area*
Pot tin	*A small container used to hold materials and equipment for rolling a joint*
Power output	*Quality or percentage of drugs*
Proper one, the	*Cocaine of a high very purity*
Prossy	*Prostitute*
PTSD	*Post Traumatic Stress Disorder*
Pub Grub	*Low end, cheap coke*
Puff	*Smoke Pot*
Pulled, Get	*Stopped by the police*
Pure	*Pure cocaine 90%+*
Purple One	*500 euro note*

Put one in him, to	*Shoot some one*
Put the kids to bed	*Store the drugs*
Quid	*Pounds/Money/short for a thousand pound*
Rack one up	*To prepare a line of cocaine*
Recall	*Sent back to prison for a breach of licence conditions*
Recardo	*Recardo Seats*
Recce	*Reconnaissance, to have a sneaky look around and gather intelligence*
Reeperbahn	*Red Light District*
Reliable motor	*Consistent supply of coke*
Remedial PT	*Corrective Physical Training*
REMF	*Rear Echelon Mother Fucker/Behind the lines supplies*

Renter	*Hire car*
Replen	*Replenish/To reload*
Repress	*Cocaine that has been adulterated or mixed to reduce purity increase volume*
Rizla	*Cigarette papers*
Runners	*Drug couriers*
Safe house	*Somewhere to store drugs, money or to just stay if it's on top*
Sale or return	*To get drugs on credit*
Score	*Twenty GBP*
Scran	*Food*
Scratcher	*Bed*
Shimfing	*Military term for Moaning*

Shithole — *Rough place*

Shits and Gigs — *Fun and games*

Shopping — *Grassing, informing*

Side burns — *When a joint only burns on one side, potentially spilling its contents.*

Skiddy's — *Dirty pants*

Skin up — *Roll a joint*

Skunk — *Strong herbal Cannabis*

Slug, Army — *Army issue sleeping bag*

Smashed — *Very much under the influence of some kind of substance*

Smashed — *Repressed heavily*

Solids — *Cannabis resin*

SOP	*Standard Operating Procedure*
Sparrows fart	*Early morning*
Speed	*Amphetamine*
Spunk/Spunked	*Spend without care*
Stag	*Shift/Guard Duty*
Stamped on	*Cocaine that has been adulterated or mixed to reduce purity increase volume*
Sticks, The	*The Countryside*
Straight goer	*A person not involved in criminal activity*
Straight phone	*Contract phone/phone not used for illegal activities*
Stuck the nut on	*Headbutted*
T.A.	*Territorial Army*

Tankie	*A soldier that served in The Royal Tank Regiment*
Tenner	*Ten pound note*
The Castle	*Windsor*
Tick	*To obtain drugs on credit. Tick list, list of people that owe money.*
Tracky	*Tracksuit*
Trolley, off of	*Under the influence*
Twat	*British term for a vagina*
Twatted	*Hit/Punched*
U-ey	*U Turn*
Valeted and serviced	*Drugs have been prepared*
Weapon	*Idiot*

Weight   *Large Volumes of Drugs*

Work mode/ Work   *Selling drugs*

Zero in   *Aim for*

RICH JONES
OVERSEAS OPERATIONS